AF753173

BIG BEHAVIORS in ALL containers

105+ Trauma-Informed Play Therapy Interventions for Working with Dysregulated Children and Their Dysregulated Grown-Ups

Paris Goodyear-Brown, LCSW, RPT-S

BIG BEHAVIORS IN ALL CONTAINERS
Copyright © 2026 by Paris Goodyear-Brown

Published by
PESI Publishing, Inc.
3839 White Ave
Eau Claire, WI 54703

Cover and interior by Amy Rubenzer and Emily Dyer
Editing by Jenessa Jackson, PhD

ISBN 9781683738794 (print)
ISBN 9781683738800 (ePUB)
ISBN 9781683738817 (ePDF)

All rights reserved.
Printed in the United States of America.

PESI Publishing
pesipublishing.com

Table of Contents

Acknowledgments

I would first like to thank my husband, Forrest, and my three children, Sam, Madison, and Nicholas, who have taught me more about how to be a Safe Boss, Nurturer, and Storykeeper than anyone else in the world. I would also like to thank all the families who have shared their joys and struggles with me as we have worked to create more connections and deeper understanding between caregivers and their children. To the constellation of caregivers (parents, grandparents raising grandchildren, aunts, uncles, babas, foster and adoptive parents, kinship care providers, and young adult siblings caring for a sibling who is not yet grown), thank you for showing me the many faces of love that caregivers have and the stunning number of ways you show up for the children in your care. To the teachers, childcare workers, occupational therapists, speech therapists, nurse practitioners, psychologists, psychiatrists, nannies, tutors, coaches, and mentors who have worked with me over the years to support traumatized children and their families, your voices and wisdom have also contributed to the way I think about helping.

Lastly, a huge thank you to the growing community of Certified TraumaPlay™ therapists, approved TraumaPlay supervisors, and our core team of TraumaPlay trainers. Your laughter, love, challenging questions, endless creativity, and deep love for people have contributed greatly to the honing of this model. It has been my delight to encourage you and be encouraged as we all stretch our own embodiment of Safe Boss, Nurturer, and Storykeeper for the children, teens, and families we serve.

Special thanks to the following Certified TraumaPlay therapists who contributed to this volume:

Paula Archambault, LMSW, RPT-S

Dora Henderson, LPC-S, MHSP, RPT-S

Dayna Sykes, LPC-S, MHSP, RPT-S

Lindy Swimm, MAE, LCSW

Alyssa Meyer, MSW, LCSW, RPT-S

Introduction

Let me start by saying that I have been delighted at the response to *Big Behaviors in Small Containers: 131 Trauma-Informed Play Therapy Interventions for Disorders of Dysregulation* (Goodyear-Brown, 2022). The global community of mental health professionals who work with traumatized children and their families has found resonance with the belief that big behaviors are simply signals that a child or teen is hurting in one way or another. In fact, the image on the front cover of *Big Behaviors in Small Containers* (depicting a vulnerable, lonely child overshadowed by an angry monster, which is what most adults perceive when a child is acting out or acting in) has become a powerful visual aid in reopening the compassion well of burned-out clinicians and haggard caregivers.

In this follow-up guide, *Big Behaviors in All Containers*, the unspoken truth I hope to amplify is this: Kids have big behaviors, but so do their caregivers. A clinician may have worked very hard to co-regulate with a child client, only for that child to return to a home environment where they are yelled at or called names, their needs are minimized, or attention and affection are withdrawn because the caregiver feels hurt by the child's behavior. Indeed, supervisees frequently lament to me that they have worked really hard with a particular client—equipping them with coping strategies, teaching them self-soothe techniques, and helping them shift their negative self-talk—only for a dysregulated caregiver to undo this valuable therapeutic work. Unfortunately, when grown-ups become escalated themselves, they hurt the situation more than they help it.

I have enormous respect and compassion for the grown-ups who work with dysregulated children day in and day out, who are often not equipped to provide co-regulation for their child. In fact, some of the caregivers my team and I work with do not know how to regulate themselves, which contributes to the escalation of their child's big behaviors in their day-to-day caregiving responses. For this reason, TraumaPlay therapists engage in an extended assessment phase that includes dyadic assessments of the caregiver-child interactions to identify any areas that may benefit from a parental paradigm shift or teaching tweaks. Many of the parents we work with were parented in ways that required them to become adults quickly—they did not get to play as children, and playing with their own child now feels awkward and overwhelming. Many of the teachers we work with had teachers of their own who were punitive or shaming, and they have inadvertently adopted similar styles of interaction. Therefore, sometimes we are working to reparent the parent. Sometimes we are working to retrain the teacher.

After almost 30 years of working with traumatized children and their families, one thing has become abundantly clear: Co-regulation always precedes self-regulation. This foundational TraumaPlay principle informs this volume. Unlike the first volume of *Big Behaviors*—which unpacked the core components of the TraumaPlay model and provided dozens of innovative play therapy interventions for individual children and teens—this volume targets the caregivers of traumatized children, amplifying their critical importance in embodying healing roles for the children in their care. I have reprinted the core set of TraumaPlay components on the next page, in case you don't yet have a copy of *Big Behaviors in Small Containers* (Goodyear-Brown, 2022).

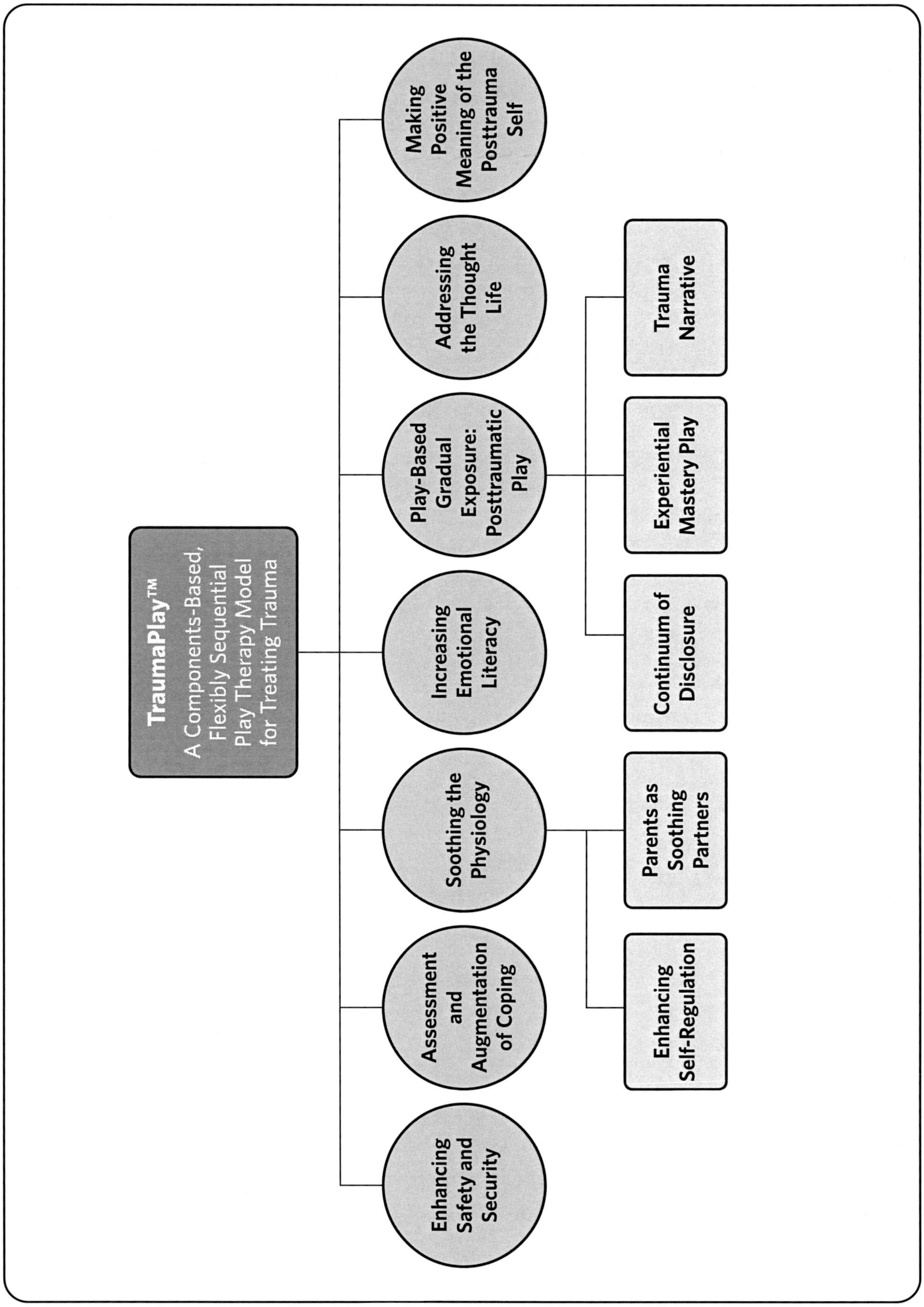
TraumaPlay™
A Components-Based, Flexibly Sequential Play Therapy Model for Treating Trauma
Enhancing Safety and Security
Assessment and Augmentation of Coping
Soothing the Physiology
Increasing Emotional Literacy
Play-Based Gradual Exposure: Posttraumatic Play
Addressing the Thought Life
Making Positive Meaning of the Posttrauma Self
Enhancing Self-Regulation
Parents as Soothing Partners
Continuum of Disclosure
Experiential Mastery Play
Trauma Narrative

In particular, this volume aims to help TraumaPlay therapists approach their work with caregivers in three embodied roles: Safe Boss, Nurturer, and Storykeeper. These three roles are meant to simplify the major tasks of healthy adult attachment figures in good-enough relationships with their children. We use a simplified teaching rubric of the triune brain to help parents understand bottom-up brain development. The triune brain heuristic is mainly a mnemonic device for the order of operations in need meeting, not a hard science, but it can be helpful in shifting parental paradigms. Each part of the triune brain is paired with a guiding question that corresponds with these three roles. Starting from the lowest brain region and moving upward, the reptilian brain stem, which is responsible for regulation, is always asking the question *Am I safe?* The limbic (or feeling) brain, which is responsible for facilitating our connections with each other, is always asking the question *Am I loved?* Only when these two lower-brain region questions are answered with a resounding *YES!* can the neocortex, or the thinking brain, ask the question *What can I learn from this?* These guiding questions and their connection to the expressed needs of each brain region (regulation, connection, and learning) give the caregiver permission to meet their traumatized child's underlying needs by moving in and out of these three roles with intentionality. Clinicians first embody these roles for themselves and then function in these roles for the caregiver so that the caregiver may absorb these roles. We think about the mechanism as putting arms around the adult(s) who is putting arms around the child.

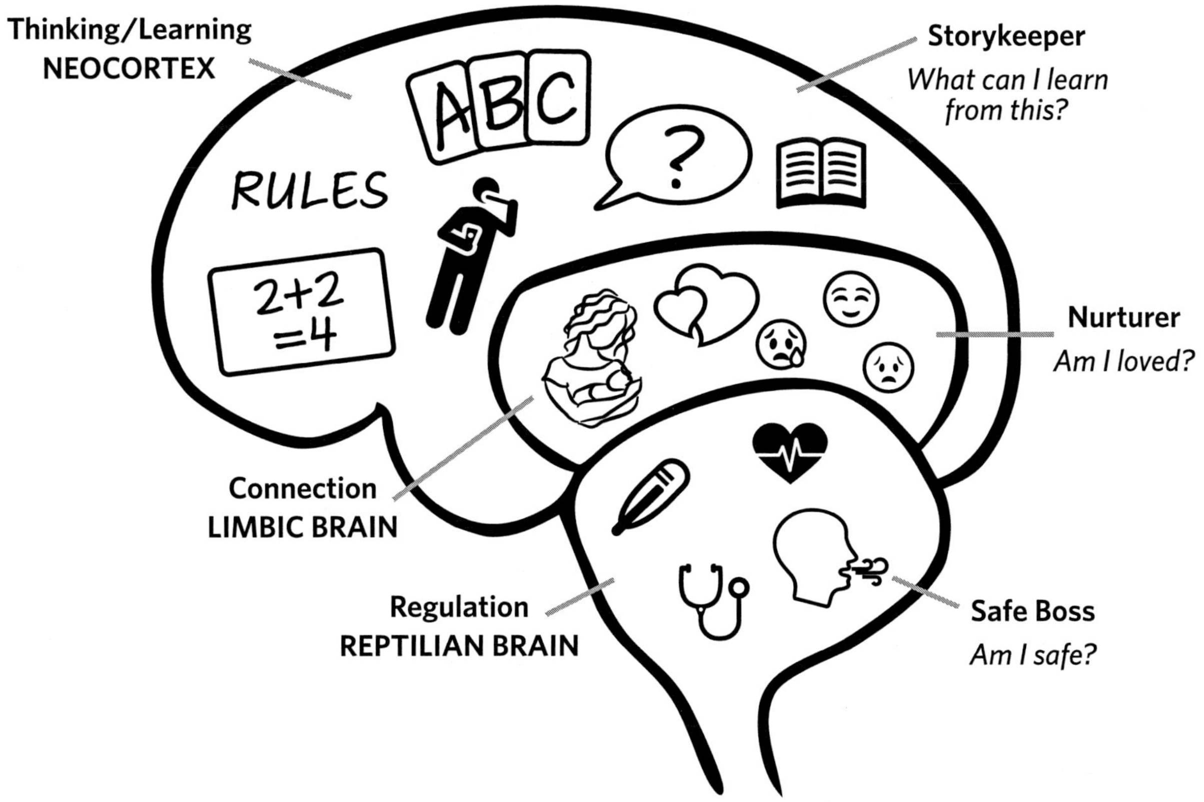

Although many child clinicians report feeling more comfortable working with individual children or teens—rather than with caregiver-child dyads, individual caregivers, or whole family systems—traumatized children have better therapeutic outcomes when their caregivers are engaged in treatment. As caregivers learn to embody the three roles of Safe Boss, Nurturer, and Storykeeper, they can become better allies and sometimes join us in each component of therapeutic work.

Whom This Book Is For

If you are a caregiver working with traumatized children who exhibit big behaviors, this book is for you. If you are a caregiver who sometimes has big behaviors of your own when your child gets dysregulated or upset, this book is for you. *Caregiver* is a word meant to encompass all the grown-ups who provide influence to children and teens. If you help in the feeding, housing, nurturing, teaching, coaching, babysitting, transporting, nursing, or doctoring of children with big behaviors, this book is for you. If, in any of these roles, you sometimes feel triggered, overwhelmed, numb, angry, disgusted, or bewildered with a child in your care, this book is for you. If you have moments when you don't like the child in your care, this book is for you. If you are a helping professional, whether that be a therapist, school counselor, occupational therapist, speech therapist, physical therapist, feeding specialist, psychiatrist, psychologist, case manager, cafeteria worker, or bus driver, this book is for you. My deepest wish is for *all* caregivers who work with dysregulated children (which is all children at one time or another) to understand the influence their own big behaviors can have on the children they serve, as well as the influence they wield to help or harm the lives of these children.

There are better and worse ways to co-regulate with a child who is in a dysregulated state. There are discipline strategies that promote Safe Boss behavior for generations to come and those that are likely to make for Unsafe Bosses. There are nurturing interactions and communications of delight that can solidify the caregiver as a Nurturer for a child who may not feel delightful. There are gentle, developmentally appropriate ways to tell the truth to a child that promotes the role of Storykeeper for the caregiver. In essence, once we know better, we can do better.

In TraumaPlay, we often talk about our "growing edge" as therapists. This phrase is borrowed from Lee Vygotsky's (1978) work and his ideas regarding the *zone of proximal development*. This zone describes the space in which each of us can stretch our understanding of new information by having someone who is a little bit further along in their understanding come alongside us in our learning. TraumaPlay therapists come alongside the caregivers—delighting in parents, teachers, and a multitude of other helpers—as we work to build a community of adults who embody Safe Boss, Nurturer, or Storykeeper. If you have a desire to stretch yourself further in any of these three roles, if you desire to reduce your own big behaviors in response to dysregulated kids, this book is for you.

What Is in This Book

The book is divided into 10 chapters, each covering one area of clinical work with caregivers and children, that support the work depicted in the first volume of *Big Behaviors in Small Containers* (Goodyear-Brown, 2022). All told, over 105 interventions are included, many of which are accompanied by reproducible worksheets or handouts you can immediately use in clinical practice.

Chapter 1 offers interventions to create paradigm shifts when working with caregivers of traumatized children with big behaviors. Clinicians in training may also benefit from the paradigm shifts that support the necessity of working with both children *and* their caregivers to achieve optimal outcomes in trauma recovery work, even if the idea of working with parents and teachers makes us uncomfortable. I share the

TraumaPlay umbrella framework here, complete with the core components for working with traumatized children and their families, as well as the three guiding roles that any and all adult helpers of traumatized children can embody to aid a child in their healing journey.

Chapter 2 offers a short explanation of the assessment phase of TraumaPlay, which extends beyond an initial intake. I also offer a brief introduction to the dyadic assessment we conduct at Nurture House (our local child and family therapy center) to help you understand the systemic nature of TraumaPlay assessment. In addition to the core components of treatment outlined in the umbrella framework itself, I have outlined a set of treatment goals specific to the *parents as partners* work. These additional goals for the caregivers can help clinicians conceptualize cases in a way that provides nuance to what the child needs clinically, but in the context of the psychoeducation, skill building, nurturing support, or reflective attachment work that a parent might also need. Several playful exercises are included in this chapter that invite the caregiver and child to co-create the treatment plan with the therapist.

Chapter 3 focuses on enhancing safety and security as well as increasing coping strategies for the caregiver, child, and dyad as its own system. Attention is paid to helping families understand that coping strategies that might have been adaptive, even genius, during a traumatic experience may not be serving them well now. New adaptive coping strategies can be taught and rehearsed, while caregivers are taught how to avoid reinforcing maladaptive coping strategies for children.

Chapter 4 supports caregivers in becoming Safe Bosses, providing the structure as well as the nurture that the children in their care might need. Notice that the subtitle of this chapter is "Supporting the Dysregulated Child." These interventions remind parents that their primary job as a Safe Boss is to teach and mentor their child, not punish them. This chapter begins by helping parents reflect on their own experiences with authority figures and to define, for themselves, what Safe Boss behavior will look like for them. Since fear-based strategies are those used by Unsafe Bosses and get in the way of learning, offerings such as *The Three Roots of Discipline* (4.5) promote redos, compromises, and limiting with alternatives. Finally, this chapter helps caregivers learn and practice a two-choice procedure. This offers more autonomy to the child, while inviting them to experience the consequences of their choice in a supportive way.

Chapter 5 offers a set of codified co-regulation strategies for adults to employ with dysregulated children. Based on the seminal concept *co-regulation always precedes self-regulation*, the more than a dozen interventions in this chapter help parents and teachers learn how to offer a soft tone of voice and face, organize their child's experiences, offer choices and a way out of stuck behavior, use titrated touch or physical proximity effectively, hear the underlying anxiety when children are engaging in stuck behavior, and use playful ways to end and let go after an escalation.

Chapter 6 focuses on an additional aspect of Safe Boss behavior: increasing trust through need meeting. This chapter offers playful ways for parents to practice visualizing themselves as grounding anchors during a child's behavioral storms. Additional interventions provide connected ways to reinforce a child's positive experiences when they risk vulnerability by asking for what they need from their caregiver, offering repetitions of attuned need meeting in playful or nurturing ways.

Chapter 7 provides a multitude of activities aimed at increasing the caregiver's practice of delighting in the child, which allows the caregiver to embody the role of Nurturer with the children they serve. I provide grown-ups with guidance on how to create safe spaces (called Nurture Nooks) for this attachment-enhancement work, scripts and structures to practice crafting and delivering stories of delight in their children, and interventions aimed at translating these interactions to the home environment.

Chapter 8 discusses how to work with the negative activation of a caregiver. When children have big behaviors, the adults often follow suit. This chapter playfully addresses the *shoulds* that often contribute to a parent's shame when they react negatively to their child's off-putting behaviors. Interventions in this chapter help caregivers explore their own windows of tolerance, including their felt sense of themselves when they are in various states of arousal as well as the felt sense the child might have of the caregiver in each state of arousal. It explores the use of mindful mantras, distancing techniques, and self-care practices to achieve an optimal rhythm of work and family life.

Chapter 9 helps caregivers become curious about the parts of themselves, the parts of their child, and the interactions between these parts. While parents often think about how their own internal parts get triggered by their child's thoughts, feelings, behaviors, or verbalizations, this chapter expands to help the parent reflect on how their own thoughts, feelings, behaviors, or verbalizations may trigger the hurt parts of their child. Interventions in this chapter offer playful gathering places for parents and children to integrate their parts, with the ultimate hope of increasing internal coherence for the parent and child alike.

Finally, **chapter 10** invites caregivers to hone their storykeeping abilities for their child. It begins by defining the Storykeeper role as taking the child's current big behavior and threading the needle backward to the child's earliest experiences. TraumaPlay's philosophy will always be one of telling the truth in developmentally sensitive ways when hard things have happened. To do so, I introduce a variety of interventions to help you bring the trauma content into the room in matter-of-fact ways and offer invitations to use expressive arts mediums that allow you to nonverbally transform somatic context into a coherent narrative. Finally, I offer several interventions that provide play-based ways to name and integrate a variety of somatosensory memories into a child's trauma narrative while supporting the parent in holding these often-painful pieces.

Big behaviors can come in the smallest containers, and the grown-ups who care for these little ones can themselves have the biggest behaviors of all. Every minute you spend with caregivers, helping them understand their own big behaviors and teaching them to co-regulate with their child more effectively, is time well spent. Every minute you spend embodying the roles of Safe Boss, Nurturer, and Storykeeper for the caregiver has a trickle-down effect on the children in their care. This *cascade of care* will lead them to absorb these roles for themselves and enhance the felt sense of safety for the child in their care.

one

Paradigm Shifts in TraumaPlay

There is nothing in the world so powerful as a paradigm shift when it comes to how we view a dysregulated child's big behaviors. After all, the lens through which we view this behavior can either help us calm the storm or make it worse. As caregivers work to remain in the roles of Safe Boss, Nurturer, and Storykeeper, the meaning they assign to a child's behaviors can either support them in embodying these roles or quickly kick them outside of their window of tolerance. When both a child and their caregiver are engaged in big behaviors, a storm is raging with no one to act as an anchor. In these moments, clinicians must become the anchor for the system. When a caregiver is able to move from seeing their child's big behaviors as rejecting, aggressive, or manipulative—and instead see them as indicators of a real and unmet need—clinicians can transfer the anchoring system back to the caregiver.

Paradigm shifts for caregivers begin with paradigm shifts for clinicians. Many trauma protocols encourage clinicians to follow steps in an exact, often procedural, order. Practitioners need help shifting away from these rigid protocols and toward a flexible application of the core components of trauma-informed play therapy. To do so, this chapter offers playful metaphors that give clinicians permission to respond to the needs of each child by flexibly moving in and out of a series of protective treatment goals and play therapy processes. Once clinicians absorb the language of TraumaPlay—and have made the shift from protocol to process—they can move away from providing parents with a set of "answers" or "fixes" and toward packaging big behaviors as expressed needs: a need for safety, security, emotional literacy, and so on. Clinicians can then support caregivers in shifting their own paradigms around a child's big behaviors so that they no longer view these behaviors as manipulative or as a reflection of a child "just trying to get attention." Instead, they can use deeper curiosity to ask: *What is the underlying need that is not being met yet?*

Another paradigm shift for both clinicians and caregivers involves how they see themselves and their roles while in the company of a child with big behaviors. For example, a clinician who is led by behavioral theories may see their role as a provider of positive reinforcement for the child. A parent may see themselves as a policeman or a friend (or even as a doormat if their child acts out frequently, and they feel helpless to interrupt the pattern). A teacher may strictly see themselves as one who provides academic knowledge but is not concerned with the child's social-emotional development. In TraumaPlay, we create a paradigm shift by embracing the roles of Safe Boss, Nurturer, and Storykeeper, depending on a child's moment-to-moment needs. Sometimes, what a child needs most is a Safe Boss, someone who will set the boundaries and enforce safe limits calmly and kindly. Other times, what they need most is a Nurturer, someone who provides care, physical affection, and a felt sense of being delighted in. Still other times, what they need most is a Storykeeper, someone who will help them make more coherent sense of the hard things that have happened, creating and supporting stories that help the child integrate the trauma into a positive sense of themselves.

1.1 THE TRAUMAPLAY UMBRELLA FRAMEWORK

DESCRIPTION:

TraumaPlay is an attachment-based, evidence-informed set of core components for treating traumatized children and their caregivers. The set of core components, normally depicted in flowchart form for ease of understanding, can set the stage for an overly rigid use of the model. Therefore, the TraumaPlay community has employed other metaphors to show the fluid, dynamic nature of the model. As a flexible and sequential play therapy model, certain components of treatment might not be needed in all cases, and certain components may take more time with one family than another. For example, enhancing safety and security may be accomplished between a therapist and a child in just a couple of sessions or may take months (usually when a child with complex trauma has a deeply entrenched distrust of adults). Here, the core components are seen as panels of an umbrella, each providing a certain amount of protection to the child and caregiver from worsening trauma symptoms.

TREATMENT GOALS:

- Educate the caregiver on the components of TraumaPlay treatment
- Provide a metaphor for the protective power of trauma-informed treatment goals
- Create a three-dimensional representation of the core components of TraumaPlay

MATERIALS NEEDED:

- *TraumaPlay Umbrella* handout
- Scissors
- Pipe cleaner
- Glue
- Coloring utensils (e.g., crayons, markers)
- Small drink umbrellas

DIRECTIONS:

1. Prior to meeting with the caregiver, make your own TraumaPlay umbrella and cut it out using the *TraumaPlay Umbrella* handout. Use your clinical judgment in deciding whether to include the child or teen in this explanatory session.
2. Introduce the core components of trauma-informed treatment using the TraumaPlay umbrella. Offer a general explanation of each component to help the family know what to expect in treatment. Use your judgment when deciding whether to invite the caregiver to make their own umbrella while you talk. Like child clients, sometimes caregivers are more comfortable when their hands are engaged with an activity as you talk.
3. Become curious with the caregiver about which components of treatment they believe will be important.
4. Offer a personalized tiny drink umbrella with the first component of treatment you will be pursuing (enhancing safety and security) written on it. This can serve as a

Copyright © 2026 Paris Goodyear-Brown, *Big Behaviors in All Containers*. All rights reserved.

transitional object from the safety of the therapeutic space to the caregiver's home environment, while reminding the caregiver of current treatment goals.

5. Explain that you will send home a new drink umbrella whenever a new treatment component is introduced.
6. Consider offering the gift of a full-size, multicolored umbrella with each component written on the panels as a gift at the end of treatment.

Copyright © 2026 Paris Goodyear-Brown, *Big Behaviors in All Containers*. All rights reserved.

TRAUMAPLAY UMBRELLA HANDOUT

Make your own TraumaPlay umbrella!

- Color with crayons, pencils, or markers
- Cut along the solid lines
- Fold and crease along the dotted lines
- Glue the flaps
- Add a pipe cleaner for a handle

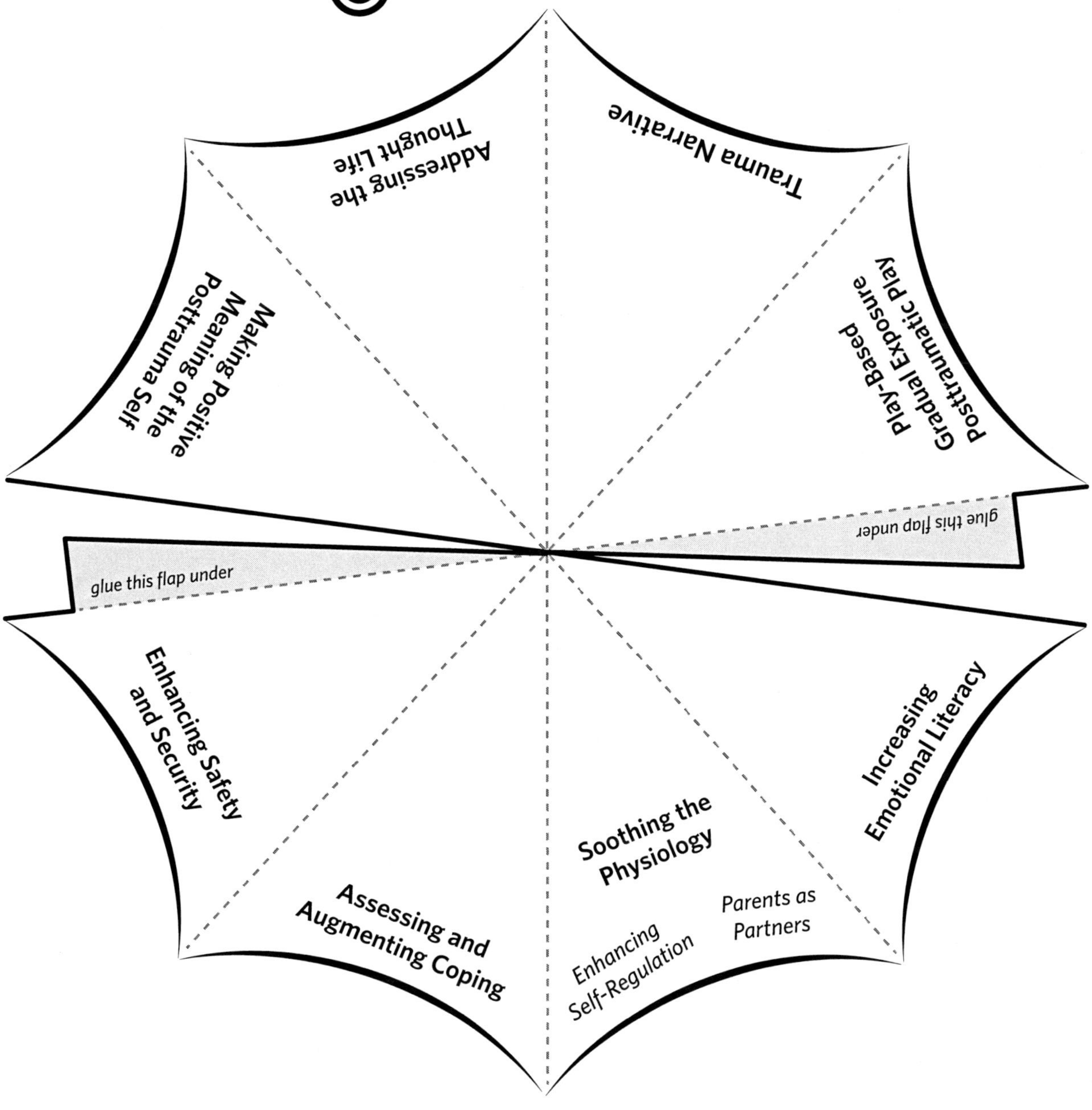

Copyright © 2026 Paris Goodyear-Brown, *Big Behaviors in All Containers*. All rights reserved.

1.2 PROTECTION FROM TRAUMA SYMPTOMS

DESCRIPTION:

This intervention builds on the previous one by offering a visual image of a caregiver and child sheltering together under an umbrella. For many grown-ups, it is a big paradigm shift to move away from the notion that trauma therapy should only involve the child and toward the idea that caregivers are part of the protective team and critically important in treatment as well. Especially in cases where trauma may be intergenerational or the trauma may have been experienced by both the parent and the child, offering this visual imagery of TraumaPlay is important, as it highlights how this modality provides protection for the dyad. It can also serve to help them feel like a team, sticking together through the hard thing.

TREATMENT GOALS:

- Reinforce the idea that the components of TraumaPlay provide protection from trauma symptoms
- Offer a visual reinforcement of the parent and child as a trauma recovery team

MATERIALS NEEDED:

- *Sheltering Under the TraumaPlay Umbrella* handout
- Writing utensil
- Full-size umbrella (if superstition does not make the child or caregiver nervous)

DIRECTIONS:

1. Introduce the completed TraumaPlay umbrella from the previous *TraumaPlay Umbrella Framework* intervention (1.1). Continue to offer a general explanation of each component to help the family know what to expect in treatment. Remember to use your clinical judgment in deciding whether to include the child or teen in this explanatory session.
2. Become curious with the caregiver and/or child about which components of treatment they believe will be important.
3. Offer the dyad a copy of the *Sheltering Under the TraumaPlay Umbrella* handout. Describe how the raindrops above the umbrella represent the various trauma symptoms "raining down" on their child (e.g., aggression, nightmares, withdrawal, depression) and explore the caregiver's understanding of these symptoms. Write each symptom beside a raindrop.
4. Then explain the following:

   "We know a lot now about the kinds of treatment goals needed to heal from trauma, and we see these goals coming together to form an umbrella that protects you and your child from long-term trauma symptoms."

Copyright © 2026 Paris Goodyear-Brown, *Big Behaviors in All Containers*. All rights reserved.

5. Invite the caregiver to open the full-size umbrella and shelter under it with their child.
6. If this seems fun to them, you can augment the activity by inviting the dyad to choose different colored feathers to represent the trauma symptoms they are most concerned about.
7. Stand on a chair, so that you are higher than the umbrella, and let the feathers rain down on the dyad sheltering under the umbrella.
8. Point out the protection the umbrella provides from the feathers and compare this process to the ways in which moving through the TraumaPlay components protects them from exacerbated trauma symptoms.

Copyright © 2026 Paris Goodyear-Brown, *Big Behaviors in All Containers*. All rights reserved.

SHELTERING UNDER THE TRAUMAPLAY UMBRELLA HANDOUT

Label the raindrops with each trauma symptom.

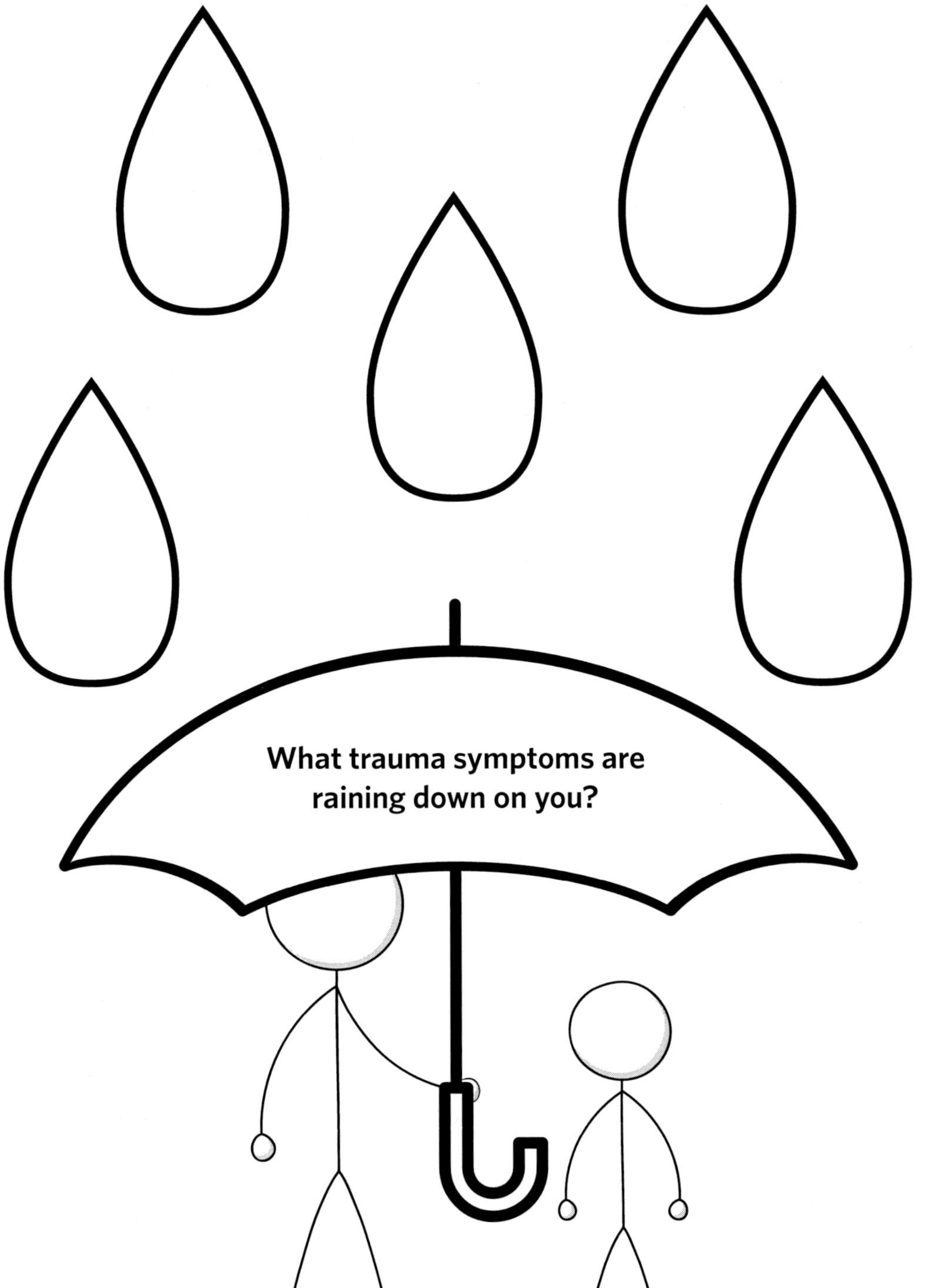

Copyright © 2026 Paris Goodyear-Brown, *Big Behaviors in All Containers*. All rights reserved.

1.3 TRAUMAPLAY PINBALL GAME

DESCRIPTION:

This intervention offers another way to visualize the TraumaPlay framework and gives therapists express permission to move fluidly and dynamically between treatment goals as they follow the child's need in therapy. Since the child's needs at any moment may actually be related to the larger needs of the caregiver-child system, working with the caregiver may be what is most critical to the child's therapeutic success. This intervention also gives caregivers who have been in previous trauma treatment with their child an opportunity to identify which pieces of trauma work they've done already and which treatment goals will need to be the focus of your work together.

TREATMENT GOALS:

- Present the TraumaPlay components in a visual form
- Provide a metaphor for the fluidity of trauma treatment
- Follow the child's needs throughout the continuum of treatment (a core TraumaPlay value)

MATERIALS NEEDED:

- *TraumaPlay Pinball Game* handout
- A real handheld pinball game if possible

DIRECTIONS:

1. Use the following script to describe the fluidity and flexibility of TraumaPlay treatment:

   "You have already been introduced to the core components of TraumaPlay in a flowchart. The thing about flowcharts is that they give the idea that each goal has to be accomplished one by one, to completion, in the same sequence every time. The heart of TraumaPlay could not be further from this idea. Instead, we want to follow the child's need all along the way in treatment.

   "One way to think about this is to imagine a pinball machine, where you and your child are all rolled up into one system. When you pull back the knob, the pinball bounces up to the top of the machine, hitting *enhancing safety and security* first and then ricocheting between *assessing and augmenting coping* and *soothing the physiology*. Eventually, the ball will make its way down to *play-based gradual exposure* of the trauma, and even if you have done everything you can to create safety for your child, facing the trauma content itself may still be overwhelming. In this case, they'll

Copyright © 2026 Paris Goodyear-Brown, *Big Behaviors in All Containers*. All rights reserved.

need to bounce back up to *soothing the physiology* or spend more time on *enhancing safety and security* before revisiting the lower parts of the pinball machine.

"In other cases, you may get all the way down to *addressing the thought life*, but the child seems stuck, and you realize that you have not touched on *parents as partners*, so you intentionally move over there before returning to other treatment components."

2. During your explanation, offer the caregiver the following *TraumaPlay Pinball Game* handout, or an actual handheld pinball game, to reinforce your points.
3. If the family has been in previous trauma treatment, invite the caregiver to reflect on these experiences. Identify the components of trauma work that they've already completed, as well as those to which little attention has been paid. In this way, you and the caregiver can co-create the treatment plan for the current course of therapy.

Copyright © 2026 Paris Goodyear-Brown, *Big Behaviors in All Containers*. All rights reserved.

TRAUMAPLAY PINBALL GAME HANDOUT

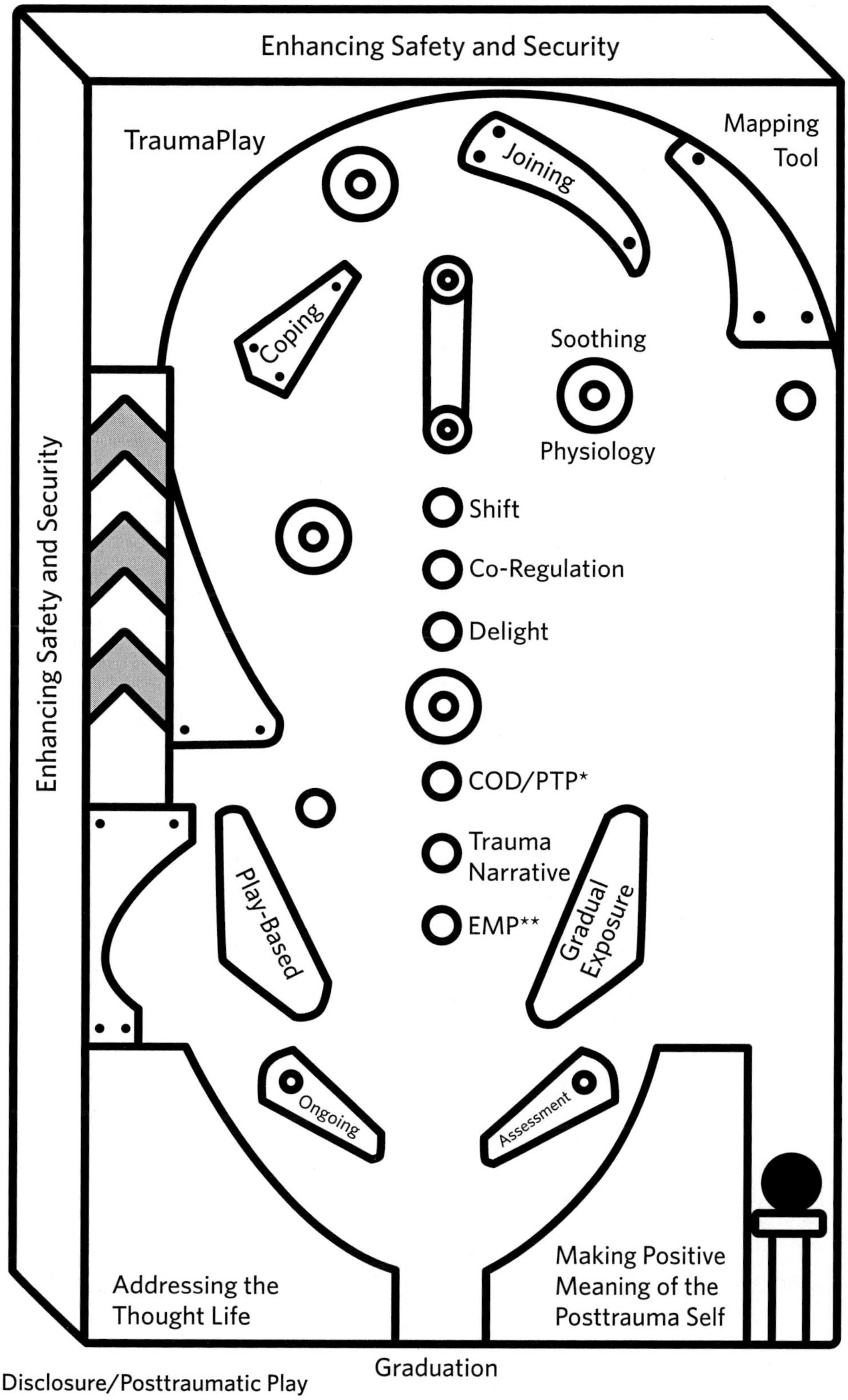

* Continuum of Disclosure/Posttraumatic Play

** Experiential Mastery Play

Copyright © 2026 Paris Goodyear-Brown, *Big Behaviors in All Containers*. All rights reserved.

1.4 THE THREE ROLES OF THE TRAUMAPLAY THERAPIST

DESCRIPTION:

TraumaPlay therapists conceptualize trauma symptoms, including big behaviors, as the result of interruptions in a child's typical development. Attachment trauma in particular robs children of an attuned, responsive caregiver. Therefore, our first goal is to create healthy attachment dynamics between the therapist and child so that these dynamics can eventually transfer to the caregiver involved in treatment. To do so, the therapist must embody three primary roles—Safe Boss, Nurturer, and Storykeeper—known as the *triad of therapist roles*. This exercise will help you, the therapist, categorize attachment behaviors into these three categories and explore healthy attachment behaviors with caregivers.

TREATMENT GOALS:

- Introduce the three roles of healthy attachment figures to the system
- Internalize the triad of therapist roles in TraumaPlay
- Explain these roles to caregivers who are identified as allies in the child's treatment

MATERIALS NEEDED:

- *The Triad of Therapist Roles* handout
- Sand tray and sand tray miniatures

DIRECTIONS:

1. It is important that you are able to embody the three roles of Safe Boss, Nurturer, and Storykeeper before teaching these concepts to caregivers. Therefore, prior to introducing this activity, spend time doing your own person-of-the-therapist exploration of these roles in the sand tray. Use your finger to draw a triangle in the sand. Choose miniatures to represent the way you see yourself in each of the three roles. If possible, complete this exercise with another clinician or in supervision and reflect out loud on how and why you chose the symbols for each role.
2. You can do a second round of person-of-the-therapist work by choosing symbols for the ways you want to embody each goal, especially if there is one role that is harder for you:
    a. For example, if you chose a small child as your symbol to represent how you feel about your ability to be a Safe Boss right now, maybe you choose a larger, wiser figure for the Safe Boss you want to become.
    b. If you chose a small, flimsy fence to represent your ability to set boundaries with clients currently, you might choose a larger brick wall for the kinds of boundaries you want to be able to set in the future.

Copyright © 2026 Paris Goodyear-Brown, *Big Behaviors in All Containers*. All rights reserved.

3. Choosing miniatures allows you to access your right-brain ways of knowing and to work cross-hemispherically. The choice of a symbol also gives concrete form to goals for how you want to grow. This process is the same for your clients and their caregivers.
4. Once you have done your own preparatory work, meet with the caregiver and present them with *The Triad of Therapist Roles* handout. Explain the three roles to the caregiver and discuss how you will be working to become a Safe Boss, Nurturer, and Storykeeper not just for the child but for the caregiver as well. Use the following script:

   "Kids are often asking one of three questions: *Am I safe? Am I loved?* and *What can I learn from this?* Write each question on a point of the triangle. Can you match each of the roles—Safe Boss, Nurturer, Storykeeper—with each question? When you fulfill these roles for your child, you are answering each of these questions with a resounding *yes!*"
5. Draw a triangle in the sand and ask the caregiver to choose a symbol to represent their current sense of self as a Safe Boss. They might choose a scary or punitive-looking person, something that represents a clear and kind boundary, or something that represents a lack of boundaries.
6. After they choose a symbol for the "now," invite them to choose a symbol for how they want to be as they embody the role.
7. Use this same process to explore all three roles with the caregiver. Take a picture of the completed sand tray to refer to in future sessions.

Copyright © 2026 Paris Goodyear-Brown, *Big Behaviors in All Containers*. All rights reserved.

THE TRIAD OF THERAPIST ROLES HANDOUT

SAFE BOSS, NURTURER, STORYKEEPER

We move in and out of these three roles as we follow the need of the child: Safe Boss, Nurturer, and Storykeeper. Label each point of the triangle with one of these roles. Then write the matching underlying question in the space next to each role.

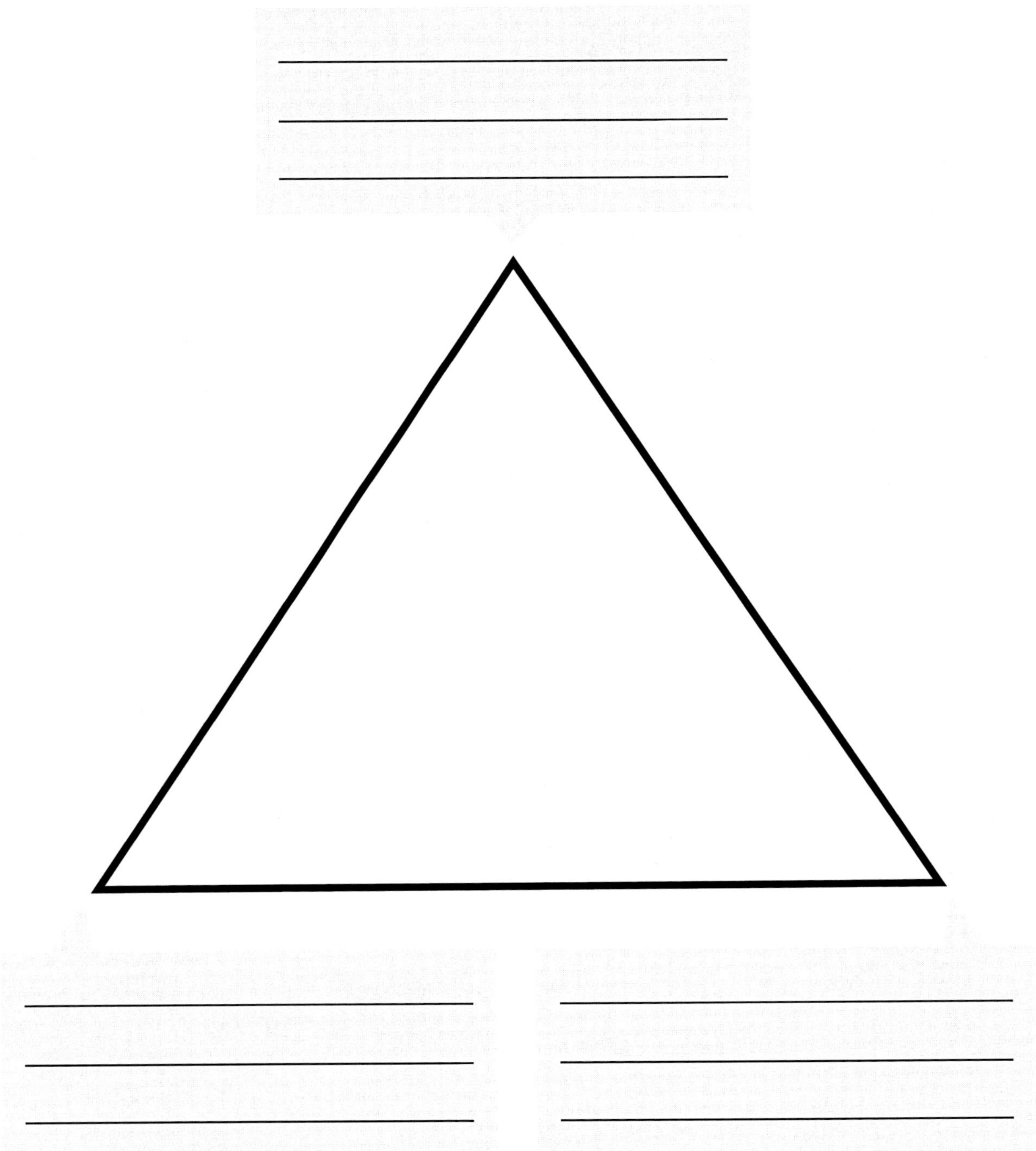

Copyright © 2026 Paris Goodyear-Brown, *Big Behaviors in All Containers*. All rights reserved.

1.5 RACK AND ROLE

DESCRIPTION:

The triad of therapist roles can help us organize the core components of TraumaPlay in much the same way that the rack in billiards organizes the billiard balls. This intervention offers another way for clinicians to conceptualize treatment goals. Moreover, some clients might enjoy tracking their progress with this intervention by putting paper pool balls labeled with the core components inside the rack as each goal is accomplished. This can become another keepsake for the client to take with them while making a meaningful goodbye.

TREATMENT GOALS:

- Organize the core components of TraumaPlay within the triad of therapist roles
- Track progress through components of the model
- Map the client's journey through treatment and offer a completed rack as a graduation gift

MATERIALS NEEDED:

- *Rack and Roles* handout
- A real pool table (this could be as small as a miniature one that sits on a desk or as large as a standard-size table), pool balls, rack, and pool cues
- Scissors
- Glue
- Coloring utensils (e.g., crayons, markers)
- Ziploc bag

DIRECTIONS:

1. Offer the *Rack and Roles* handout to the child and caregiver as a way to explain both the goals of treatment and your roles as a therapist. Explain that these are the same roles you hope to transfer to the caregiver before graduating the client from treatment.
2. Play a game of pool with the client and their caregiver (it's okay to tweak the rules based on the client's developmental age and competency). Have the client rack up the balls and feel them physically confined within the triangle. Remind the caregiver of the three roles while playing.
3. Cut out each of the pool balls inside the *Rack and Roles* handout. Invite the client to color these.
4. Explain that these balls will all be put in a Ziploc bag and glued inside the paper triangle as each treatment goal is completed.
5. Once the client finishes treatment, provide them with the completed *Rack and Roles* handout as a graduation gift.

Copyright © 2026 Paris Goodyear-Brown, *Big Behaviors in All Containers*. All rights reserved.

RACK AND ROLES HANDOUT

The embodiment of these three roles helps us organize the core components as we follow the system's lead.

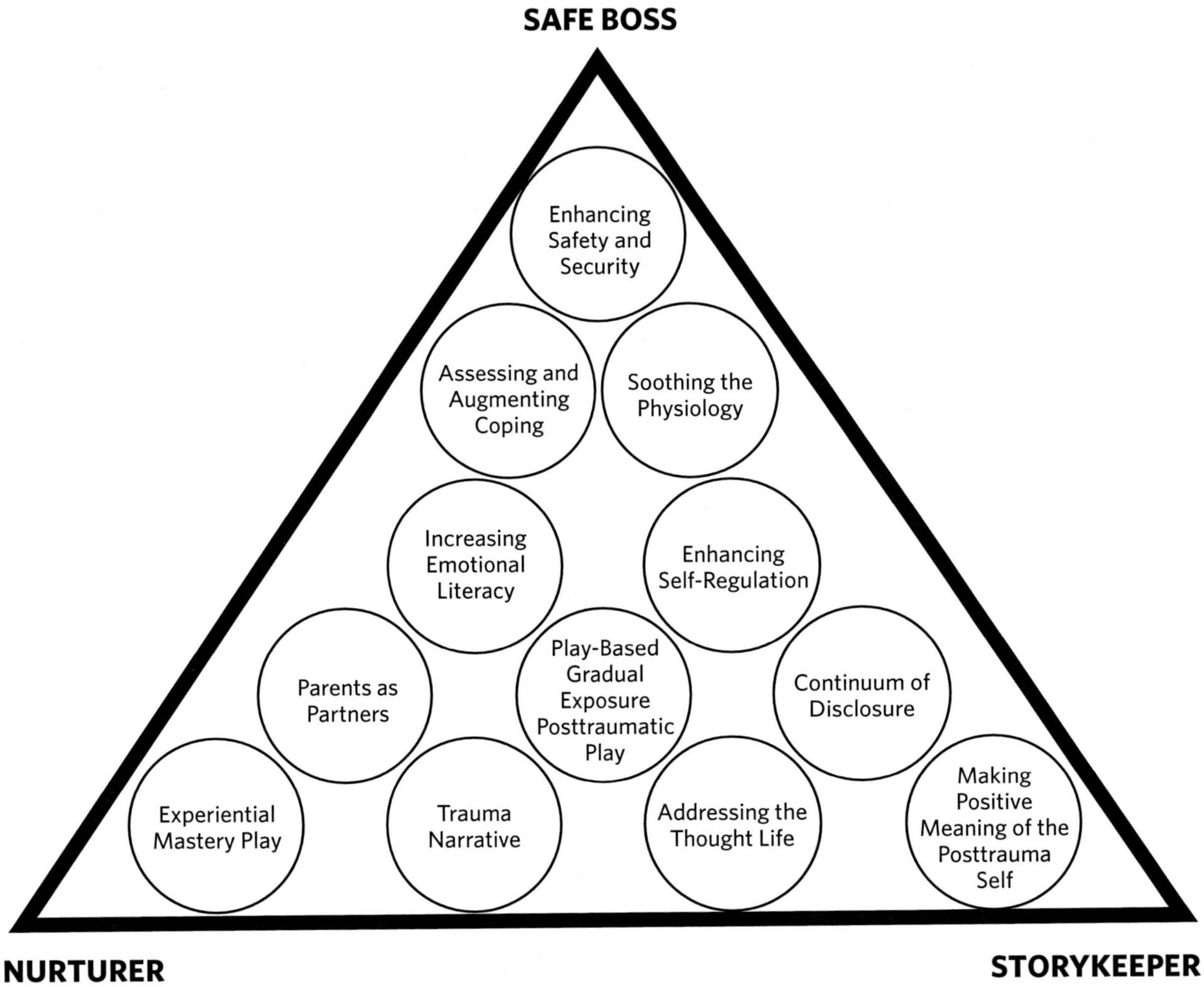

 Copyright © 2026 Paris Goodyear-Brown, *Big Behaviors in All Containers*. All rights reserved.

1.6 THE CASCADE OF CARE

DESCRIPTION:

The cascade of care highlights the process where the TraumaPlay clinician intentionally works to embody the roles of Safe Boss, Nurturer, and Storykeeper with the caregiver in order to grow that caregiver's capacity to embody these roles with their child. We often talk about this as *putting arms around the caregiver who is putting arms around the child.* This begins by having an intake with the caregiver only, with no child or teen present, to hold the caregiver's distress fully. Our goal is to storykeep what it has been like to be a caregiver to this child *before* we storykeep what it is like to be the child of this caregiver. The clinician should provide experiences of Safe Boss when the caregiver is feeling flooded, Nurturer when the caregiver needs attention and care, and Storykeeper in order to remain compassionate to the caregiver's negative thoughts and feelings about their child.

TREATMENT GOALS:

- Introduce the cascade of care as a concept related to caregiver growth
- Help the caregiver reflect on their own needs in an attachment relationship with the therapist
- Offer a visual explanation to accompany the verbal explanation of the cascade of care

MATERIALS NEEDED:

- *The Cascade of Care* handout
- Pitcher of water
- Sponge
- Bowl or cup

DIRECTIONS:

1. Offer *The Cascade of Care* handout while naming the three roles (Safe Boss, Nurturer, Storykeeper) and explore the caregiver's definition of each role.
2. Invite the caregiver to pour water from the pitcher onto the sponge in various amounts as they explore the experiences of people in their own life who have filled this role for them.
3. Once the sponge is full of water, explain that you will be helping them absorb and expand the qualities and skill sets of Safe Boss, Nurturer, and Storykeeper so that they pour into their children more effectively.
4. Invite the caregiver to squeeze the sponge into a bowl or cup, which represents the child.
5. You may find that there is a role that no one is currently filling for the caregiver. For example, the caregiver may be unable to name someone who provides a source of nurture for them. This will signal you to focus on the role of Nurturer in your ongoing interactions with the caregiver.

Copyright © 2026 Paris Goodyear-Brown, *Big Behaviors in All Containers*. All rights reserved.

THE CASCADE OF CARE HANDOUT

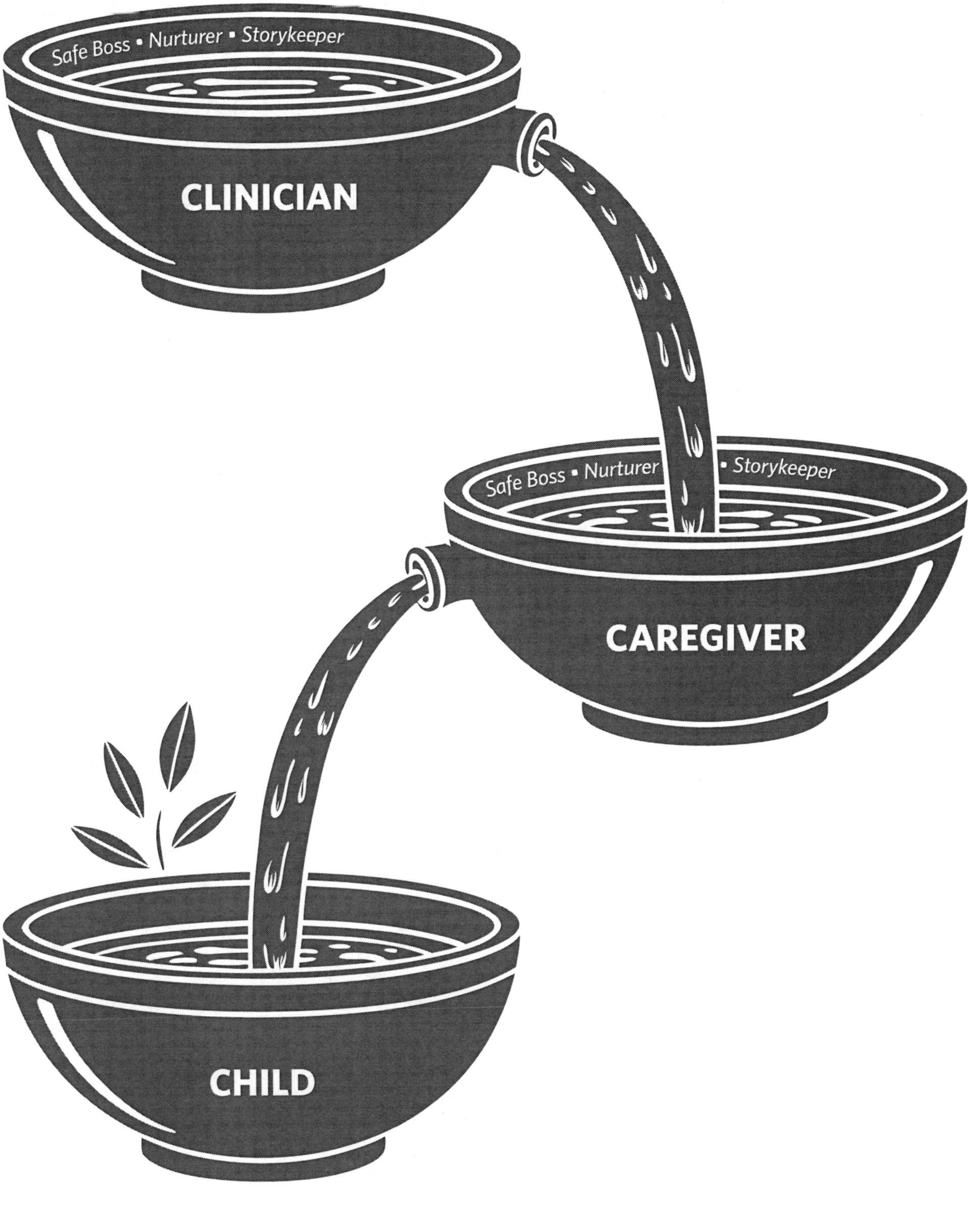

 Copyright © 2026 Paris Goodyear-Brown, *Big Behaviors in All Containers*. All rights reserved.

1.7 TITRATING THE DOSE

DESCRIPTION:

Titration is a concept that has its roots in medicine. When clients begin taking a psychotropic medication, most professionals start at a very low dose and slowly titrate up to higher doses until they find the optimal one. I like to describe this process through the analogy of making the perfect Shirley Temple, which is a children's drink that combines ginger ale and grenadine. If you don't put enough grenadine in it, it still tastes like ginger ale; but if you add too much grenadine, it tastes too sweet. When used in the context of TraumaPlay, the idea is to titrate the amount of change that is "just right" for the client. In addition to the Shirley Temple analogy, I have found that many clients are much more familiar with the drinks at Starbucks, and this process of titration can be explored by examining how much chocolate, caramel, cream, sugar, and so forth they like in their Starbucks drinks.

TREATMENT GOALS:

- Explain the process of titration
- Give the caregiver permission to titrate difficult tasks to stay within the client's just-right zone

MATERIALS NEEDED:

- *Titration and Dosing* handout
- Chemistry bottles, food coloring, and water

DIRECTIONS:

1. Invite the caregiver to talk about their favorite beverage (preferably one that requires titrations of sugar, caffeine, flavoring, and so on) and have them discuss a time when it was not made properly.
2. Explain that each of us has a unique set of titrations needed to stay in our just-right zone. For example, some parents need to get up in advance of their children on school days and drink two cups of coffee before they wake the children. Other parents value sleep over quiet time and caffeine, and the extra 30 minutes of sleep they get by having everyone get up at the same time is just right for them. Another example that parents can relate to may be around exercise. Some parents feel like they are at their most regulated when they exercise three times a week, but for other parents, it may be five days a week in shorter intervals.
3. Invite the caregiver to discuss what "dose" their child needs of things like sleep, food, screen time, homework time, exercise, one-on-one time, and so forth. For example, perhaps their child needs 10 hours of sleep per night and a meal or snack every two to three hours in order to function their best. Perhaps they can only focus on their

Copyright © 2026 Paris Goodyear-Brown, *Big Behaviors in All Containers*. All rights reserved.

homework for 10 minutes at a time before they lose their attention span. Have them color in these areas on the *Titration and Dosing* handout.

4. Explain that when the dose a child needs is very different from what is being asked of them, it is important to titrate up the dose until they can learn how to tolerate the new dose. For example, if a child has only a 10-minute attention span but has a page of math problems that will take half an hour, it will be helpful to chunk the homework into 10-minute intervals separated by play.
5. If you are including the child in the session, give each participant a handout so they can explore titrations together. Children can find it fun to use actual chemistry beakers with water to play with the concept of titration. In these cases, providing food coloring that represents the thing that needs to be titrated can be helpful. You might say, "Let's pretend that this blue food coloring is homework. Each drop you add to the water will equal 15 minutes of homework time. Show me how many drops feel like the just-right amount for you."
6. You might consider giving separate chemistry bottles to the parent and child, as they may offer different titrations. For example, the child may communicate that they can only do "two drops" (30 minutes) of homework at a time, but the parent adds four drops to their bottle, representing their idea that the child should do a full hour of homework. You can lead a process of negotiation and compromise as needed.

 Copyright © 2026 Paris Goodyear-Brown, *Big Behaviors in All Containers*. All rights reserved.

TITRATION AND DOSING HANDOUT

What's the dose your child needs?

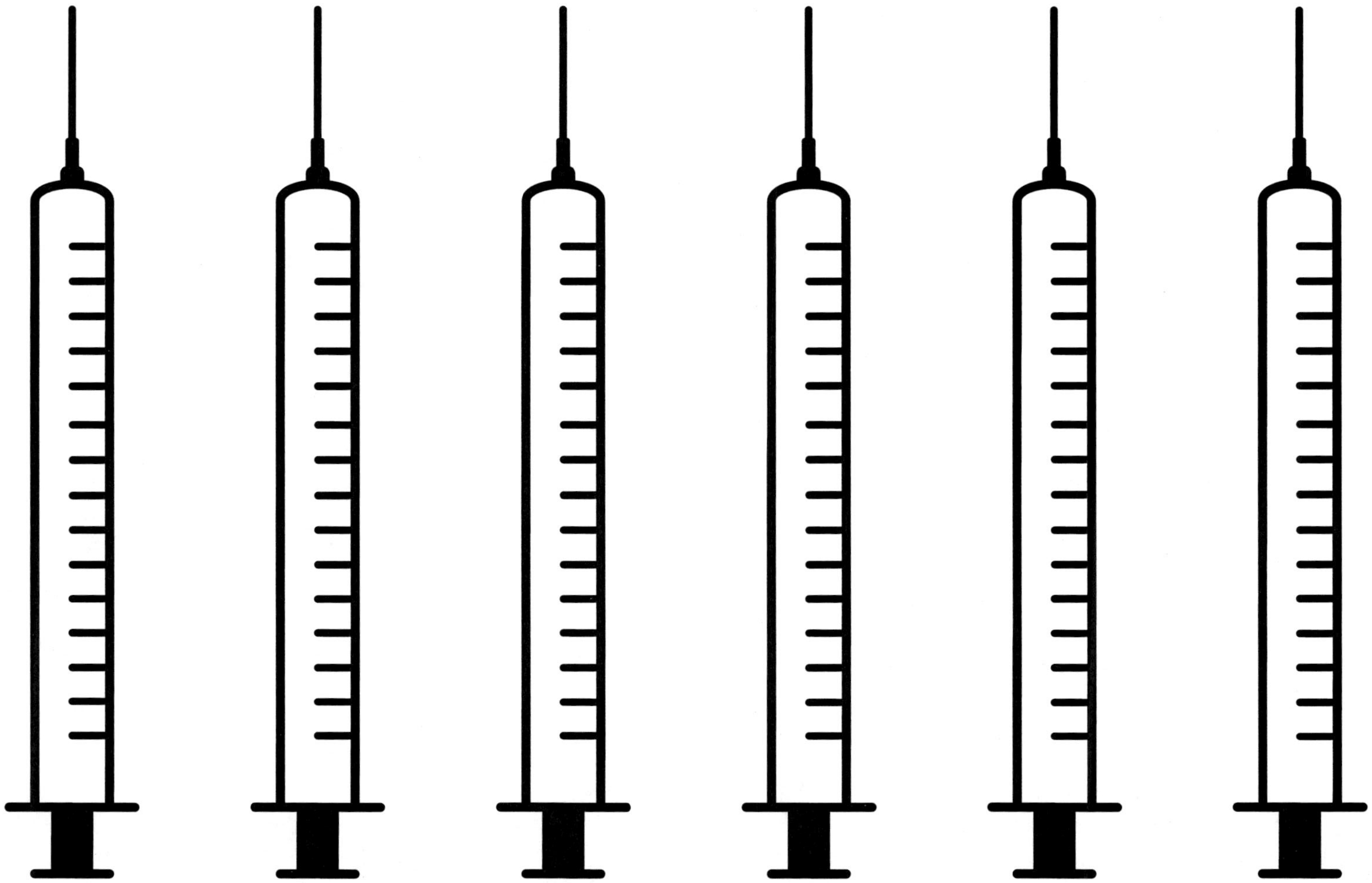

Copyright © 2026 Paris Goodyear-Brown, *Big Behaviors in All Containers*. All rights reserved.

1.8 FRAMING YOUR CLIENT'S WORK

DESCRIPTION:

Many children engage in what TraumaPlay conceives of as a continuum of disclosure (Goodyear-Brown, 2009), meaning they give us glimpses into their trauma through their art, play, or sand tray creations over the course of treatment. In order to titrate doses of posttraumatic play with children, you must carefully match the physical space to each child's exteroception needs. For example, a child who is comfortable using their physical body in big, expressive ways may benefit from a big chalkboard wall that allows them to fill up the whole space with a mural. In contrast, a shy, cautious, and physically constricted client may be overwhelmed by such big space and feel more comfortable creating a drawing in a much smaller, boundaried picture frame. Similarly, you will want to consider how you titrate sensory doses of light, sound, color, temperature, and even verbalizations to your clients. This person-of-the-therapist intervention will help you consider how to best adapt your office to accommodate the needs of various children.

TREATMENT GOALS:

- Assess the versatility of your clinical space to offer titrations of size, light, sound, color, smell, temperature, and so on
- Assess your current ability to match therapeutic use of self-dynamics (e.g., number of words, frequency of touch, proximity to the child) to the needs of your current clients

MATERIALS NEEDED:

- *Framing Your Client's Work* handout

DIRECTIONS:

1. Look at your playroom with curiosity and consider the sensory elements you may need to offer in a variety of doses in this space. This includes elements such as sound, light, color, smell, temperature, texture, and so forth. How can you work with your existing space constraints to make this happen? For example, is there a way you can provide titrations of light for different children? Of smell? Of sound?
2. Using the *Framing Your Client's Work* handout, write down the names of clients who may need smallness of space in the smaller frames and the names of clients who might need a way to use their bodies in more space in the open area on the bottom.
3. Copy off additional handouts and use them to assess your clients' sensory needs in separate categories (e.g., light, sound, verbalizations).
4. Now think creatively about how to tweak your environment to offer those elements in different doses.

Copyright © 2026 Paris Goodyear-Brown, *Big Behaviors in All Containers*. All rights reserved.

5. You may also use the handout to assess how you titrate your use of self, using each frame to identify degrees of verbalization, touch, movement, and so forth that your current clients need from you.
6. While this exercise is designed for clinicians, highly motivated caregivers may also benefit from analyzing the space they have set apart for their child and looking at these same titrations of light, sound, clutter or containment, and so on.

Copyright © 2026 Paris Goodyear-Brown, *Big Behaviors in All Containers*. All rights reserved.

FRAMING YOUR CLIENT'S WORK HANDOUT

TITRATION OF SPACE

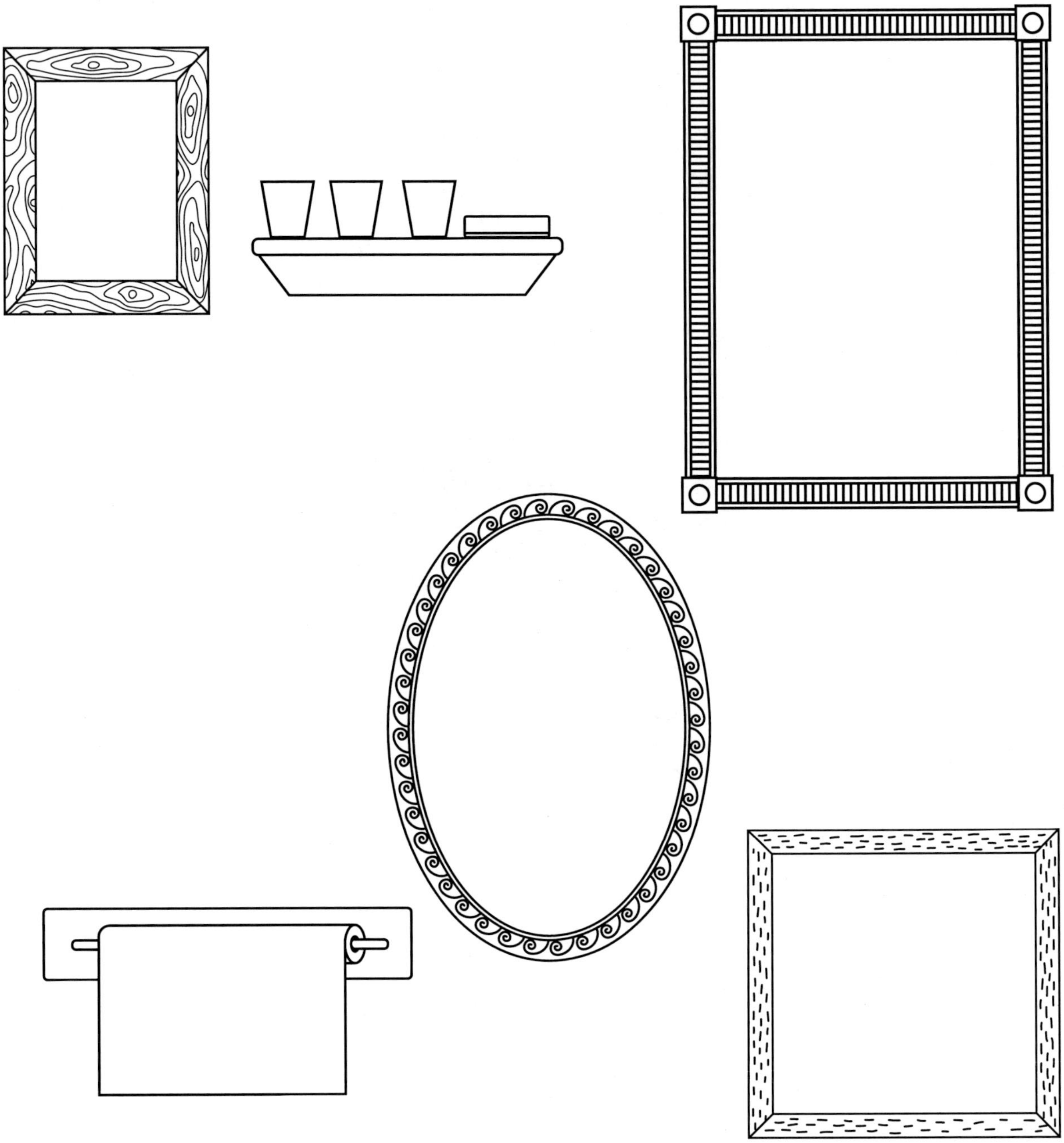

Copyright © 2026 Paris Goodyear-Brown, *Big Behaviors in All Containers*. All rights reserved.

1.9 TENNIS ANYONE?

DESCRIPTION:

Caregivers often need a paradigm shift that amplifies the importance of completing healthy cycles of serve-and-return communication. Healthy attachment relationships develop in an environment where hundreds of thousands of repetitions of completed communication loops occur between a child and caregiver. Newborn babies have no words yet, so good-enough parents work to understand their baby's cries and nonverbal cues. They learn which cry means "I'm hungry," and they feed the baby. They learn which cry means "I'm wet," and they change the baby. They learn which cry means "I'm distressed," and they comfort the baby. This interaction is the beginning of co-regulation. A child who gets their needs met most of the time in this way will begin to believe that the world is a pretty decent place and that their caregivers are trustworthy. This intervention uses the analogy of a tennis game to help caregivers understand the serve-and-return mechanism that wires the brain toward trust and connection.

TREATMENT GOALS:

- Enhance attunement between the caregiver and child by enhancing reciprocity in communications
- Amplify the importance of the caregiver's completion of the serve-and-return communication cycle

MATERIALS NEEDED:

- *Tennis Anyone?* handout
- *Tennis Balls* and *Racquets* templates
- Scissors and writing utensil
- Tabletop tennis, badminton, ping pong, or tetherball game (optional)

DIRECTIONS:

1. Invite the caregiver and child to talk about any serve-and-return games they play. These include any games that involve a two-way interaction between players, like tennis, ping pong, badminton, volleyball, or tetherball.
2. Explain that babies are always trying to communicate their needs, mainly without words. If the caregiver has been with the child since infancy, ask them to describe some cues their child would give them as a baby, as well as the corresponding action the caregiver would make in response. For example, a parent might say, "When you were little, I taught you the baby sign language for 'more please,' which looks like this [*demonstrate baby sign*]. Whenever you wanted more food, you would do the sign with your hands, and then I would give you more."

Copyright © 2026 Paris Goodyear-Brown, *Big Behaviors in All Containers*. All rights reserved.

3. Introduce the *Tennis Anyone?* handout and have the caregiver-child dyad cut out the two racquets and the tennis balls on the accompanying templates. Label each tennis ball with a need, a feeling, or a situation that a child might share with the parent. Examples might include food or drink, a hug, a fear, or a frustrating thing that happened at school.
4. Ask the child to practice communicating the need, feeling, or situation while hitting the ball over the net. Then pause and invite the parent to decide what communication they want to send back and have them hit the ball back over the net while verbally communicating.
5. Continue to practice these "communication loops," where the child and parent both communicate kindly and respectfully to each other. You can also explore how to handle situations in which the other person communicates in a way that is not respectful or kind. Always end with a connecting communication loop.
6. An advanced use of this activity is to practice ways the parent can set a boundary or say no when the child is asking for something that is not possible or would be harmful.
7. An alternative is to do this intervention with a tabletop serve-and-return game. Many miniature sets are available from novelty stores.

Copyright © 2026 Paris Goodyear-Brown, *Big Behaviors in All Containers*. All rights reserved.

TENNIS ANYONE? HANDOUT

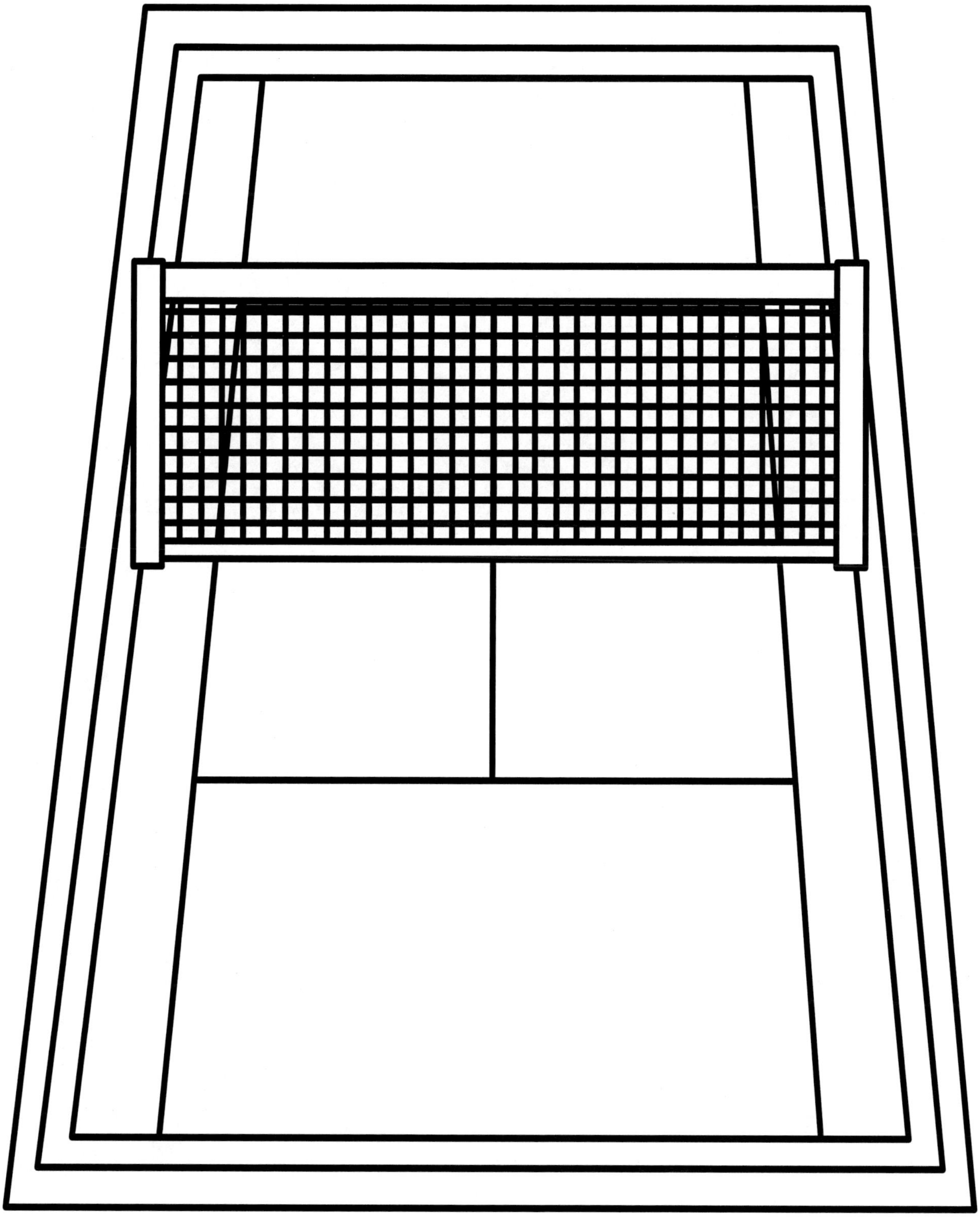

Copyright © 2026 Paris Goodyear-Brown, *Big Behaviors in All Containers*. All rights reserved.

TENNIS BALLS TEMPLATE

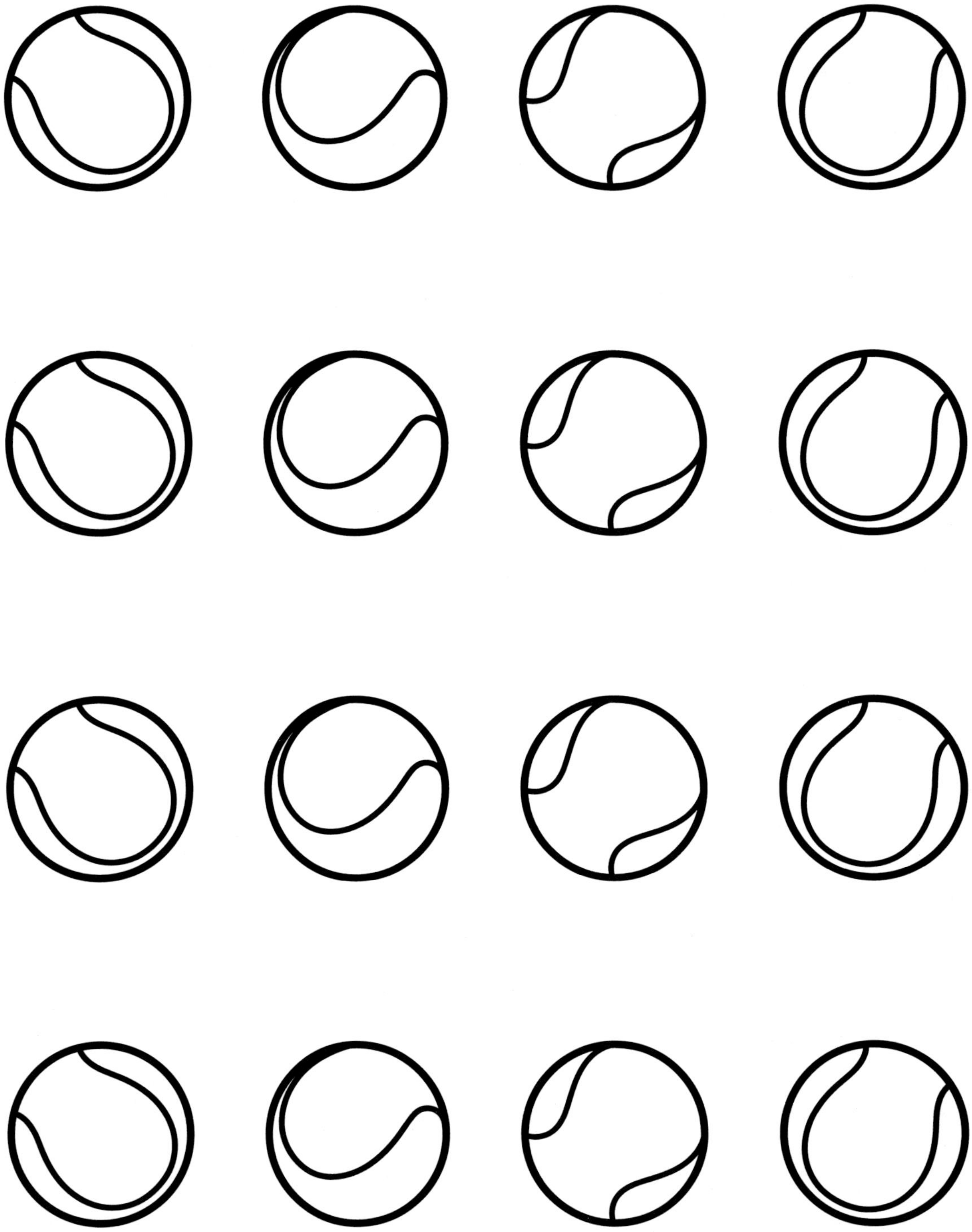

Copyright © 2026 Paris Goodyear-Brown, *Big Behaviors in All Containers*. All rights reserved.

RACQUETS TEMPLATE

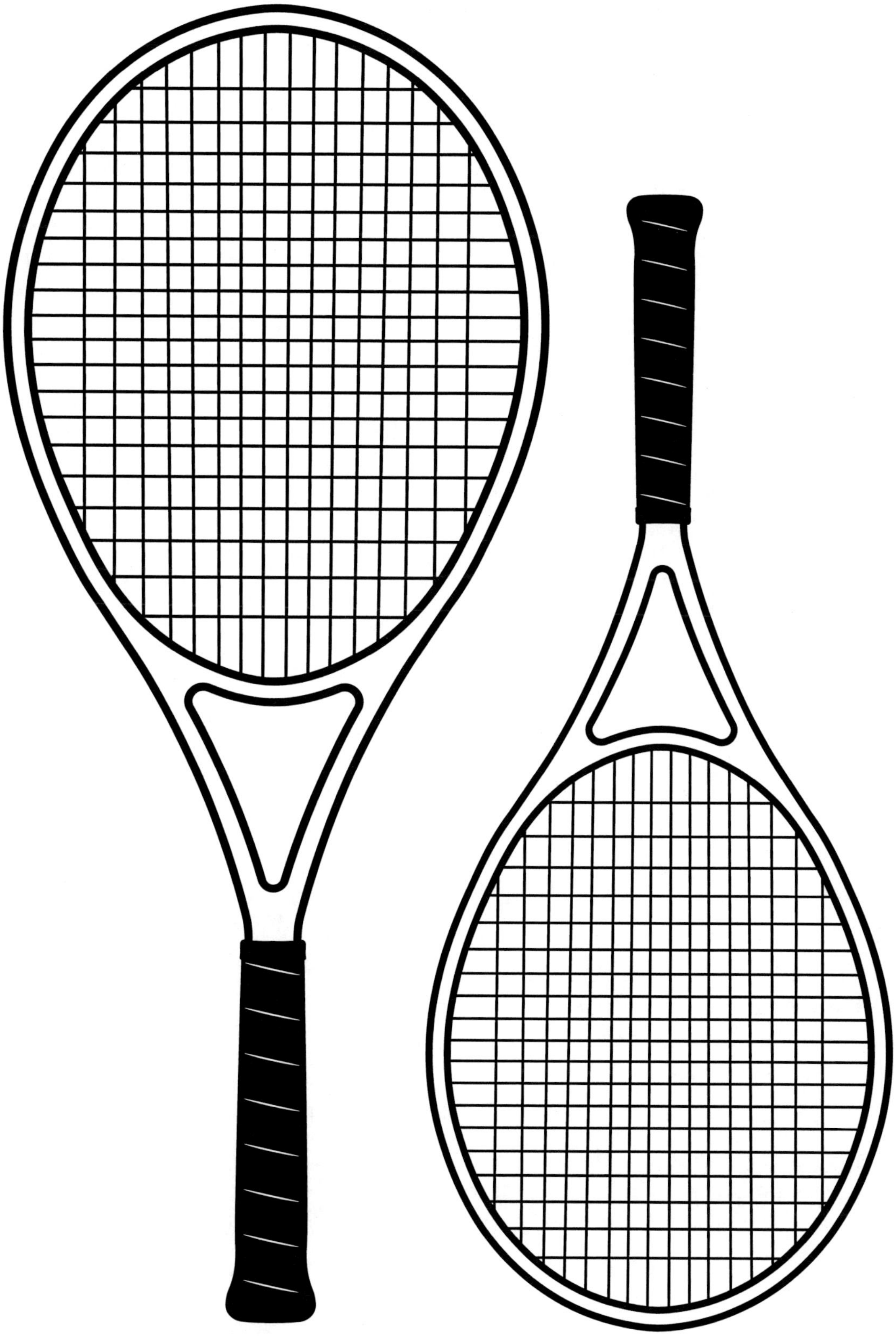

Copyright © 2026 Paris Goodyear-Brown, *Big Behaviors in All Containers*. All rights reserved.

1.10 ARE YOU USING THE RIGHT RACQUET?

DESCRIPTION:

In serve-and-return communications, the caregiver's attuned response is critical for building healthy attachment. However, drug addiction, mental illness, abuse, financial stress, and limited communication skills can all lead to significant miscommunication between caregivers and children. When a caregiver misses a child's cues or responds to these cues in an ineffective manner, it can cause ruptures in the relationship that never get repaired. This exercise is meant to help caregivers examine how they respond to children's bids for attention and assess whether they are actually communicating a response that heightens their Safe Boss status and enhances or hinders the trust and nurture in the relationship.

TREATMENT GOALS:

- Analyze the child's bids for attention and the caregiver's response
- Identify patterns of misread cues or relational ruptures that have arisen from the caregiver's response
- Practice more attuned responses to the child's expressed need

MATERIALS NEEDED:

- *Are You Using the Right Racquet?* handout

DIRECTIONS:

1. Explain to the caregiver that this exercise is geared toward slowing down the back-and-forth interactions that happen between them and their child.
2. Have the caregiver identify a hard moment from the previous week when they did not respond to their child in an attuned manner. Write down the child's action or communication on the corresponding racquet on the *Are You Using the Right Racquet?* handout.
3. Explain that adults can overrespond to their child's behavior (yelling back at their child) or underrespond to it (feeling so overwhelmed that they don't address the behavior at all or withdraw and shut down).
4. Explain that the extra-large racquet on the handout represents the overresponse pattern and that the tiny racquet represents the underresponse.
5. Have the caregiver reenact their interaction from the previous week, choosing the racquet that represents their response in the moment and writing down their behaviors inside the racquet. Work with the caregiver to reflect on how they responded to their child in the moment.

Copyright © 2026 Paris Goodyear-Brown, *Big Behaviors in All Containers*. All rights reserved.

6. Then ask the caregiver to describe any cues the child gave after the caregiver's "return" communication that indicated how the child received the communication. Did they take a deep breath and regulate? Did their face become red, and then they yelled louder? Did they appear to feel misunderstood, rejected, scared, or connected and comforted?
7. Invite the caregiver to write down a more attuned response they could have made on the just-right racquet. You can invite the caregiver to role-play or rehearse these new responses and replay them in slow motion as well.
8. To reinforce the importance of attuned serve-and-return communications, it can be useful to talk about the wise tennis player, who watches the ball come across the net and considers where it is going to land before deciding whether to swing at it. Similarly, caregivers can cut down on power struggles by allowing some of the "volleys" their children throw to go by without returning them.

Copyright © 2026 Paris Goodyear-Brown, *Big Behaviors in All Containers*. All rights reserved.

ARE YOU USING THE RIGHT RACQUET? HANDOUT

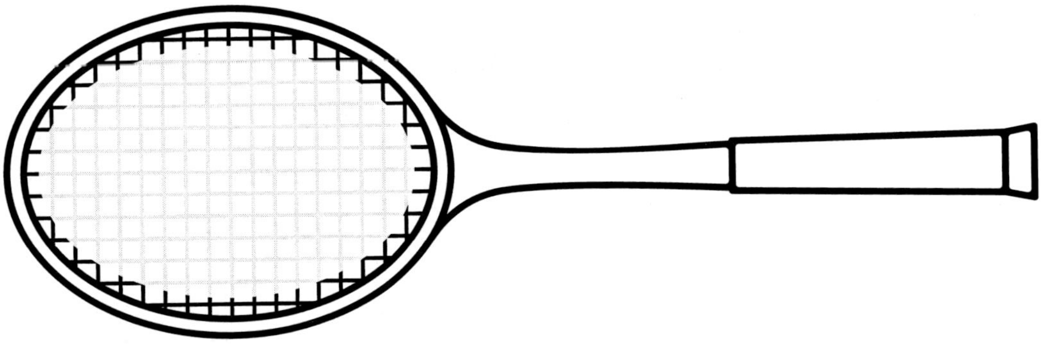

WRITE THE CHILD'S ACTION OR COMMUNICATION IN THE RACQUET ABOVE.

DID YOU OVERRESPOND?

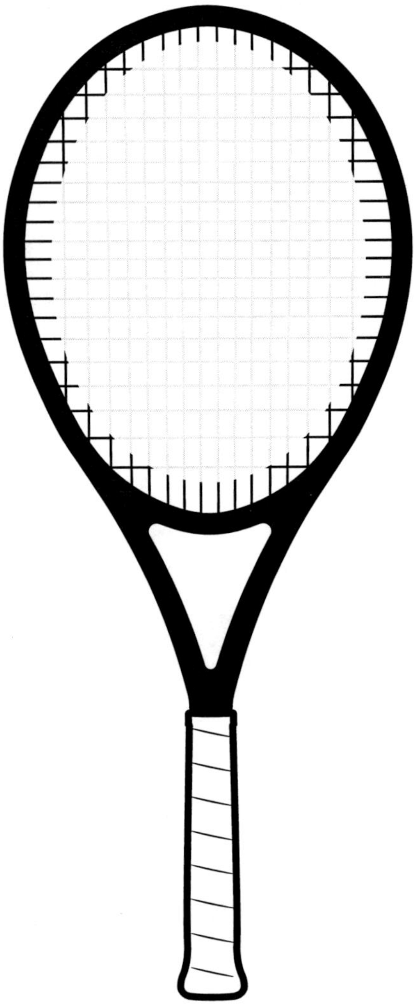

DID YOU UNDERRESPOND?

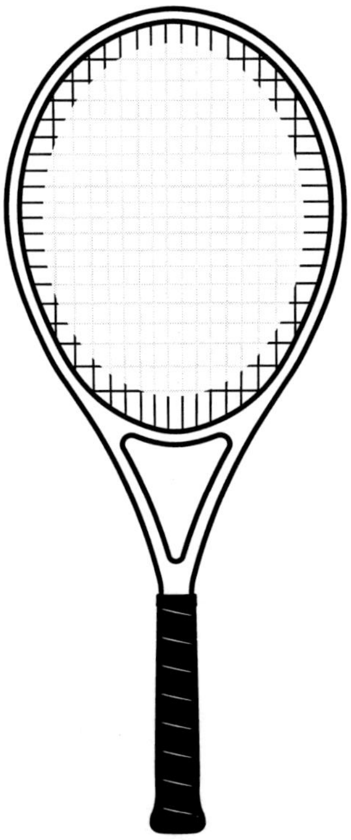

JUST-RIGHT RESPONSE GOES HERE.

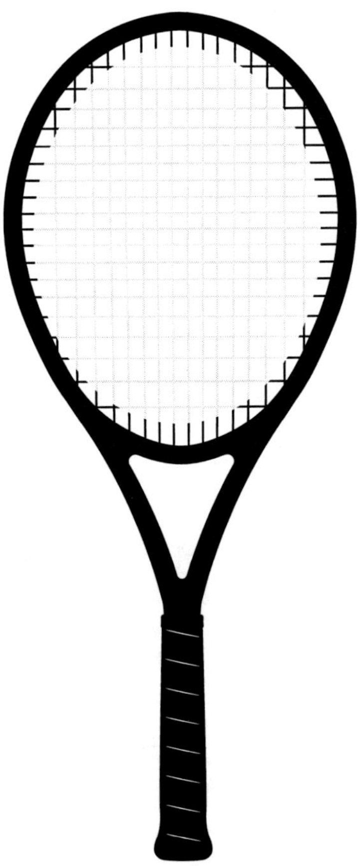

Did your response help co-regulate your child? If not, write a more attuned response you could have used instead in the just-right racquet.

Copyright © 2026 Paris Goodyear-Brown, *Big Behaviors in All Containers*. All rights reserved.

1.11 GRASPING AT STRAWS

DESCRIPTION:

Caregivers are often puzzled by their children's big behaviors. They may believe their child is acting out for attention, to escape responsibility, or simply because they are manipulative. Many times, caregivers come into the intake complaining loudly about a child's big behaviors, but when asked whether they think the behavior is within the child's control, they will exclaim, "I don't know!" This exercise helps caregivers articulate the underlying motivations they ascribe to their child's behaviors. This helps clinicians know which pieces of psychoeducation may be useful in creating needed paradigm shifts in the caregiver's thinking.

TREATMENT GOALS:

- Identify how the caregiver interprets their child's behaviors
- Identify areas of psychoeducation that the caregiver might need based on any faulty interpretations
- Help the caregiver develop more adaptive ways of thinking about their child's behaviors

MATERIALS NEEDED:

- *Grasping at Straws* handout
- Straws
- Colored scraps of paper
- Writing utensil
- Trash can

DIRECTIONS:

1. Explain to the caregiver that this exercise is meant to explore what they think drives their child's problematic behaviors.
2. Hold a group of physical straws in your fist, with each straw representing a different big behavior that the child exhibits. As you name each big behavior, have the caregiver say out loud why they think each behavior happens.
3. Write down each reason next to a straw on the *Grasping at Straws* handout.
4. After the full list of attributions is exhausted, read the first reason out loud while the caregiver writes it on a scrap piece of paper.
5. Provide psychoeducation to help shift the caregiver's thinking and move them away from assigning negative blame to the child. For example, you might ask, "Can you tell me about something that your child does that makes you feel kind of crazy?" The parent might respond by saying, "He refuses to get in the bathtub, he screams and kicks and throws a fit." Once you have investigated, you might identify that this child has a sensory difference related to how he experiences temperature. Explaining this part of the client's

Copyright © 2026 Paris Goodyear-Brown, *Big Behaviors in All Containers*. All rights reserved.

sensory profile may help shift the parent's paradigm. You can then decide on a way to meet the underlying sensory sensitivity while ensuring that the child is clean.

6. When the caregiver makes a shift in their thinking, have them crumple up the paper scrap into a ball.
7. Offer the caregiver one of the straws and invite them to blow the balled-up paper off the table and into a trash can.

Copyright © 2026 Paris Goodyear-Brown, *Big Behaviors in All Containers*. All rights reserved.

GRASPING AT STRAWS HANDOUT

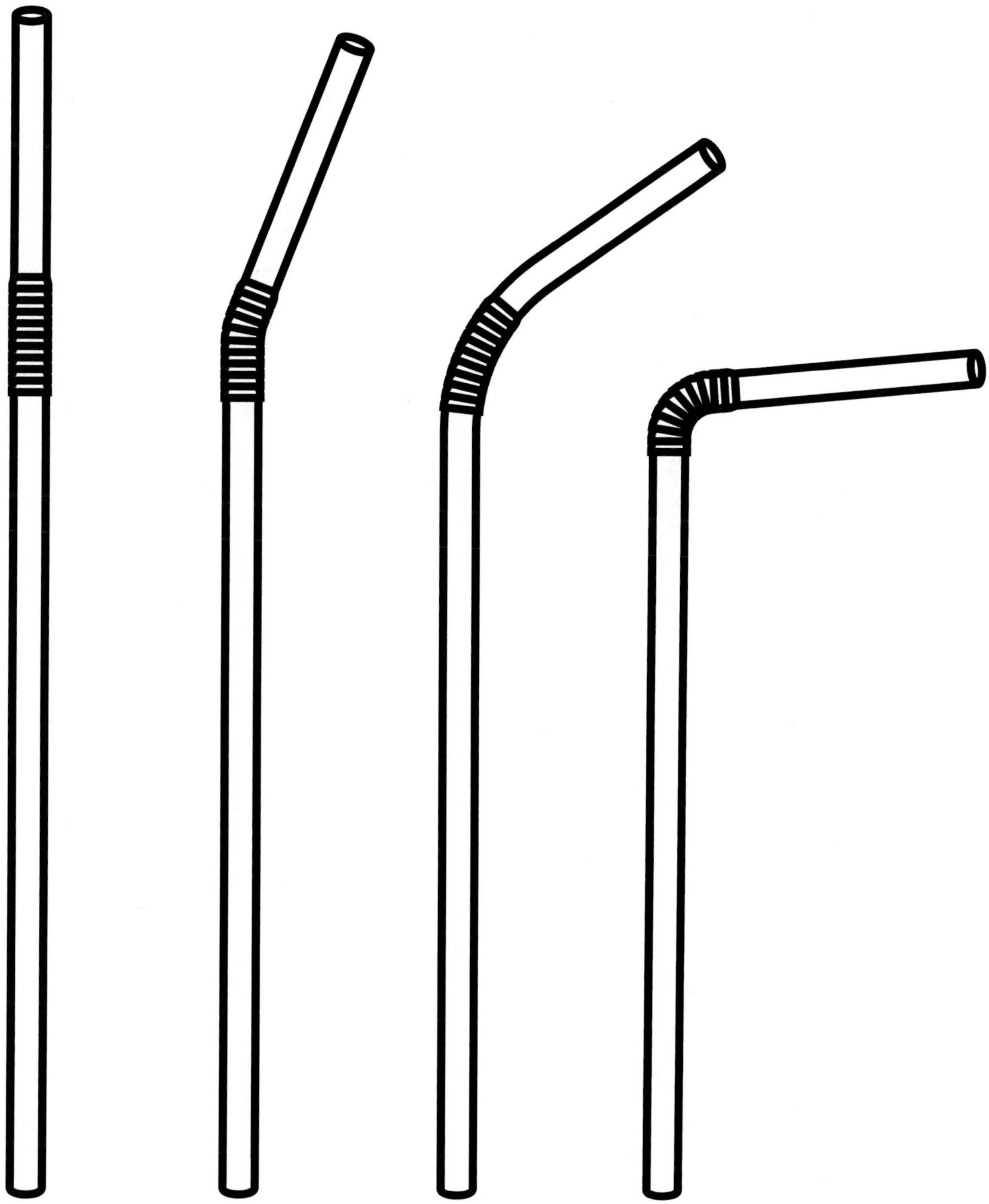

Copyright © 2026 Paris Goodyear-Brown, *Big Behaviors in All Containers*. All rights reserved.

two

Treatment Planning and Goal Setting

TraumaPlay therapists take time to understand the dynamics at play in the family system prior to designing a working treatment plan. Caregivers are seen individually for the intake so the therapist can start becoming a Safe Boss, Nurturer, and Storykeeper for the caregiver. Caregivers may need to express fear, exhaustion, bewilderment, or disgust with some of their child's behaviors. If the child is present and the therapist nods as the caregiver is naming the child's big behaviors, the child (or teen) may perceive the therapist as colluding with the child's "badness." For this reason, the first time the child comes into session is during the dyadic assessment.

During the dyadic assessment, the child has an opportunity to play with their caregiver, which allows us to see how the dyad relates to each other in a variety of interactions. These assessments include time for the child to be in charge of the play, time for the caregiver to be in charge of the play, and at least a couple of minutes when the caregiver is in charge of the clean-up process. Then the dyad switches to tasks pulled from the Marshak Interaction Method (MIM), which is the assessment method offered in Theraplay (Booth & Jernberg, 2009). Some of these tasks pull for structure ("Adult builds a block structure and has the client build one just like it"), while others pull for nurture ("Adult and child feed each other"). TraumaPlay embeds two additional tasks in the assessment, each meant to help the dyad dip their toes into the waters of talking about hard things. The first task reads: "Adult tells the child about a time when the adult made a mistake and then invites the child to tell a story about a time they made a mistake." The second task reads: "Adult tells the child about a hard thing that happened." The therapist is in the room while these interactions are happening so they can function in any of the three roles if the dyad needs support. This whole observation takes about 45 minutes and can give us rich understandings into the dyad's attachment pattern—who leads and who follows, and how they solve problems—while also pointing us to which of the caregiver's skill sets might need to be expanded.

Some caregivers begin treatment with lots of nurture and no structure for their child, while other times the reverse is true. After the dyadic assessments are complete, the therapist has two to three individual sessions with the child. In each session, half the time is spent engaged in child-led play. During this time, the therapist is assessing the play themes and working to enter the child's world. The other half of each session provides a play-based assessment of the child's current emotional life, their current coping repertoire, and the way the child perceives the family dynamics. It might also explore what the child thinks about the presenting problem.

Our treatment planning will always reference the core components of trauma treatment embedded in the TraumaPlay umbrella framework, but nuancing the treatment plan includes identifying treatment goals for the caregiver as well as for the child (Goodyear-Brown, 2021, 2024). To this end, we are always holding two questions in mind as we observe the dyad: *What is it like to be the child of this parent?* and *What is it like to be the parent of this child?* The interventions in this chapter are meant to further nuance the treatment plan for the caregiver, the child, or the dyad in playful ways.

2.1 RULER OF ALL YOU SURVEY

DESCRIPTION:

You can do this intervention with caregiver and child together or separately, or just with the child during the assessment phase of treatment. One of the hallmarks of trauma is that it strips away power and control. In families where intergenerational trauma has occurred, both the caregiver and child may feel that the rules made by those in power were unjust. For example, when a parent and child have been caught in a cycle of intimate partner violence, the rules established by the perpetrating partner were often unjust and only enforced inconsistently. In these cases, it could benefit both the hurt parent and the child to embody the role of a powerful decision-maker, such as a king or queen. Embodying such a role empowers the client and combats their learned helplessness. As you ask the clients to create the laws of the land, the laws they craft often become building blocks for your treatment plan.

TREATMENT GOALS:

- Access the clinically relevant systemic issues to aid in treatment planning
- Help the client create a future template for change and growth
- Provide an empowerment experience that counters previous helplessness

MATERIALS NEEDED:

- *Crown* template
- Scissors
- Construction paper
- Stapler
- Coloring utensils (e.g., crayons, markers)
- Play crown, king's robe, and scepter (optional)

DIRECTIONS:

1. Invite the client (or dyad) to imagine themselves as the Ruler of All They Survey. Explain that they get to be the king, queen, president, or other leader of this world. If both parent and child are present, they each get a crown.
2. Instruct them to write their name(s) in the band of the crown on the provided template.
3. Explain that as this ruler, they get to make the rules or laws for their kingdom.
4. Ask them to create three or four laws for the kingdom and have them write these down in each of the slots offered on the paper crown. Examples of laws might include: "All my subjects must be kind to each other!" "Everyone must share!" "If you hurt anyone, you go directly to jail!" or "No fighting!"

Copyright © 2026 Paris Goodyear-Brown, *Big Behaviors in All Containers*. All rights reserved.

5. When they are finished, cut the crown(s) out so the parent and child can wear them on their head as they playfully embody the role of this ruler. You will need to staple the back of the paper crown on an additional band of construction paper to properly size it to the client's head. You can also invite the client to wear costume items to further enhance the experience.
6. Some children will ask to take their paper crown creations home, and on a case-by-case basis, you may decide that the Safe Bosses at home are supportive of the work happening in the playroom and that the play creation can serve as a therapeutic transitional object.

Copyright © 2026 Paris Goodyear-Brown, *Big Behaviors in All Containers*. All rights reserved.

CROWN TEMPLATE

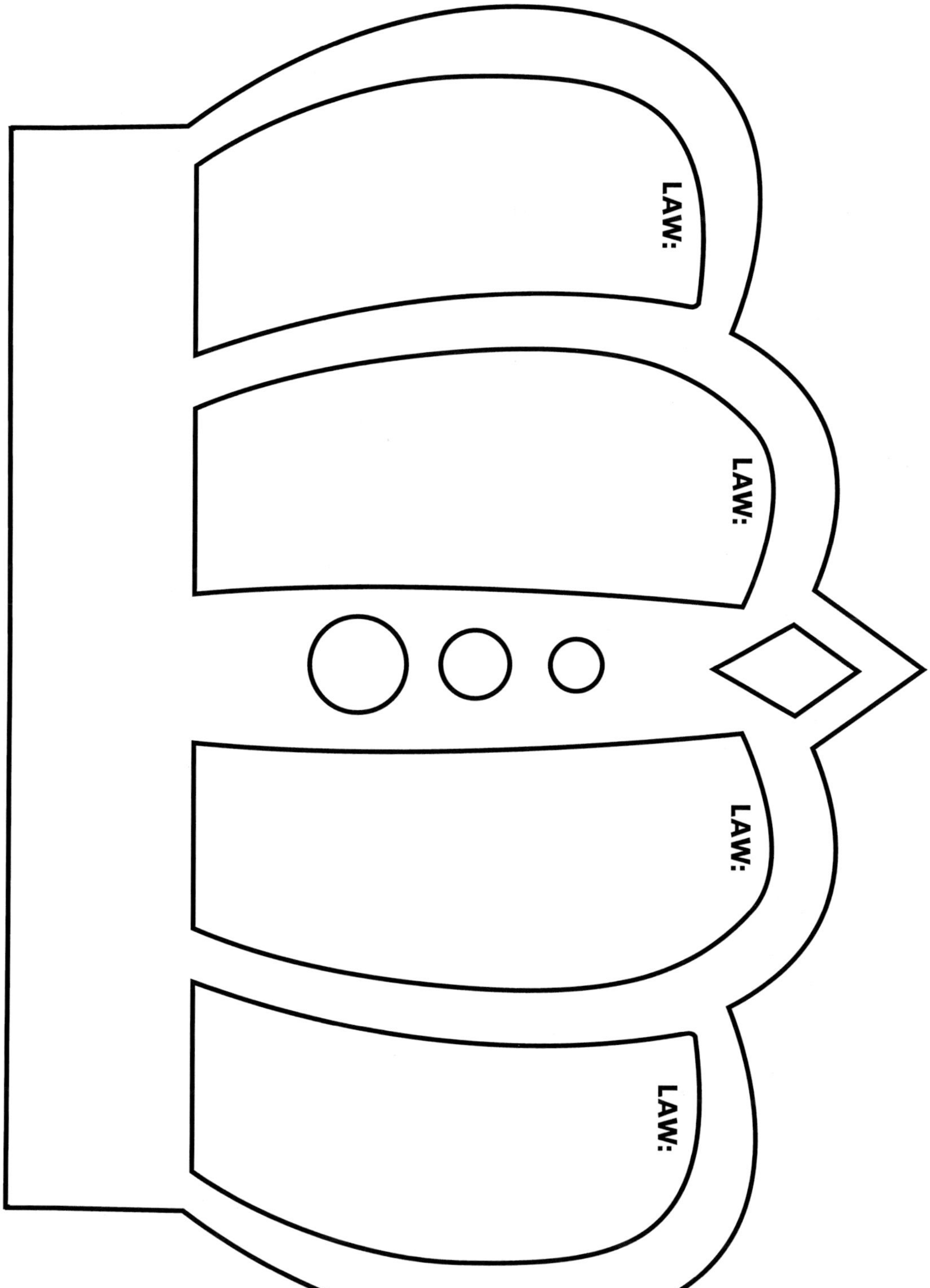

Copyright © 2026 Paris Goodyear-Brown, *Big Behaviors in All Containers*. All rights reserved.

2.2 SEALING THE SCROLL

DESCRIPTION:

The previous intervention, *Ruler of All You Survey* (2.1), offers a tangible, playful representation of the rules the child or dyad would make if they could create the rules. This exercise expands on the previous one by documenting the rules into one scroll that can be agreed on by both the parent and child. This extension of the last exercise invites the dyad to compare rules and then negotiate a set of rules that both parties can agree on. For example, the child may have previously proclaimed, "All children in the land get unlimited candy!" While this proclamation may empower the child, it would not be a sustainable or healthy practice. The therapist helps the dyad reflect on the created rules and then tweak them as necessary before writing them on the scroll. Repeating the rules also allows the dyad to rehearse safe, healthy boundaries that they yearn to have in their own family. This exercise can also be used by teachers as they establish Safe Boss status in their classroom, while also sharing power with their students to co-create the classroom rules.

TREATMENT GOALS:

- Identify overarching goals in the child's life
- Break down these goals into achievable steps
- Provide an empowerment experience that counters previous helplessness

MATERIALS NEEDED:

- *Scroll* template (or long roll of paper)
- Gold and silver permanent markers
- Ribbons of different colors
- Wax
- Alphabet stamps and ink pad

DIRECTIONS:

1. Remind the client of the work you did previously in which they embodied the role of a ruler and created laws for their people.
2. Explain that laws must be recorded and proclaimed to the people being governed in order for everyone to know the rules.
3. Ask whether they can remember the three laws they created while being Ruler of All They Survey. Some children will remember easily, while others may have forgotten the original laws or have had new situations arise that lead them to identify new rules.
4. Write down these laws on the *Scroll* template, including any new ones, as this will allow you to assess themes or patterns regarding safety goals across sessions.

Copyright © 2026 Paris Goodyear-Brown, *Big Behaviors in All Containers*. All rights reserved.

5. Offer the client lengths of ribbon in different colors and invite them to choose one. The client can write their name in fancy gold or silver ink on the ribbon, roll up the scroll, and tie the ribbon around it. Explain that you will keep the scroll safe until next session and then return to child-led play.
6. Alternatively, some children will delight in creating a wax seal on their scroll (my personal favorite). You can buy wax in blocks that look like crayons, the tip of which can be easily melted onto the rolled-up scroll. You or the client can carve the client's initials into the wax before it hardens. Another way to do this is to offer alphabet stamps and ink pads and let the client initial the sealed scroll with these.

Copyright © 2026 Paris Goodyear-Brown, *Big Behaviors in All Containers*. All rights reserved.

SCROLL TEMPLATE

Copyright © 2026 Paris Goodyear-Brown, *Big Behaviors in All Containers*. All rights reserved.

2.3 PROCLAMATION TO THE PEOPLE

DESCRIPTION:

Many traumatized children have endured situations in which they had no voice. This intervention is one way to begin giving a voice to the voiceless. We are learning more every day about the power of the spoken word and the felt sense the client can have in their body as they reclaim their voice by proclaiming things out loud. The following is a playful way to invite a child to experience the reclaiming of voice.

TREATMENT GOALS:

- Verbalize potential treatment goals
- Provide an embodied experience that amplifies the client's voice

MATERIALS NEEDED:

- Sealed scroll from the previous *Sealing the Scroll* activity (2.2)
- *Trumpet* template
- Kazoo
- Crowns, robes, scepters, and gavels for the client to choose from
- A box, step, or raised area within the playroom where the child can address their subjects or people
- Stuffed animals, puppets, or drawing materials

DIRECTIONS:

1. Offer the client the sealed scroll from last session. Explain that you want to make these laws official by gathering the subjects of the kingdom for a reading of the rules.
2. Invite the client to decide who should be the audience for the proclamation. The client might decide to draw pictures of people or choose stuffed animals to be their audience. Arrange these "participants" as the royal audience. If the caregiver is a Safe Boss, this would be an excellent time to invite them into session as part of the royal audience.
3. Invite the child to don a play crown, king's robe, and other costume items if it helps with embodiment.
4. Use a kazoo (or other play instrument) to make a trumpet sound. Alternatively, play trumpet fanfare on your phone or other music device as you introduce the ruler: "Hear ye, hear ye! All subjects of the kingdom, lend your ear as ____ issues a proclamation."
5. Invite the client to stand tall and proud as they break the seal of the scroll and read aloud the laws in a strong voice. Check in with the client about what they are noticing in their body after proclaiming the laws.

Copyright © 2026 Paris Goodyear-Brown, *Big Behaviors in All Containers*. All rights reserved.

6. It may be useful, if permission has been given, to audio or video record the proclamation so you can rehearse and revisit it in future sessions.
7. Using the *Trumpet* template, have the client write down the emotions, sensations, or thoughts they experienced while making their proclamation.

Copyright © 2026 Paris Goodyear-Brown, *Big Behaviors in All Containers*. All rights reserved.

TRUMPET TEMPLATE

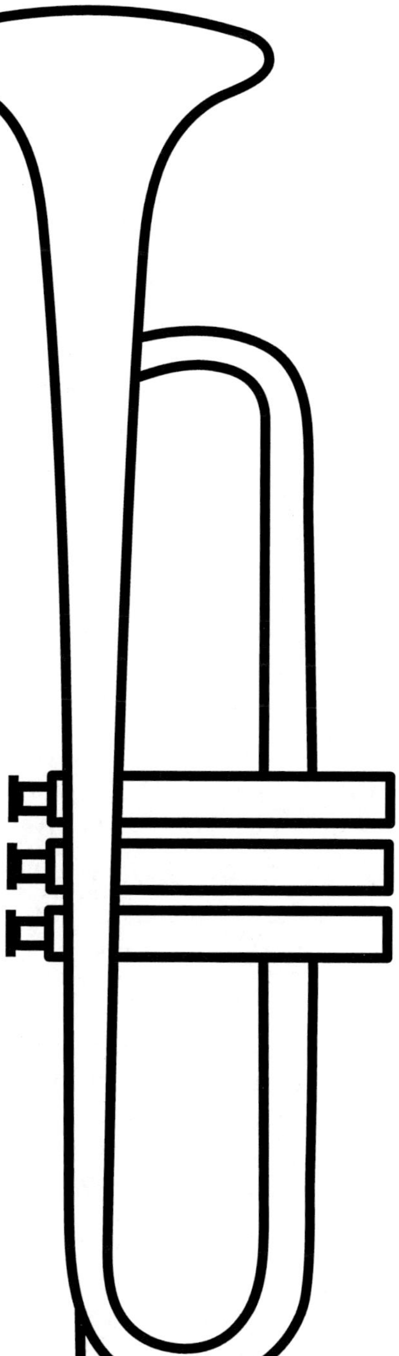

Copyright © 2026 Paris Goodyear-Brown, *Big Behaviors in All Containers*. All rights reserved.

2.4 CHANGE: CAPTURED IN THE COINS

DESCRIPTION:

Most children learn about making change in a monetary context early in elementary school. They learn how to count out four quarters or ten dimes to equal a dollar. Preschoolers will play grocery store and pretend to make change for the groceries that are purchased. In this intervention, coins become a focal point for exploring the kinds of change the child wants to make in other areas of their life, which can then become part of the treatment-planning process.

TREATMENT GOALS:

- Explore areas where the child or caregiver may seek change or growth
- Translate wishes to potential treatment goals
- Support the client's future vision of themselves

MATERIALS NEEDED:

- *Magical Coins* template
- Toy cash register
- Play coins and paper bills
- Real dollar bill (optional)

DIRECTIONS:

1. Offer the toy cash register to the child and their caregiver. Invite them to explore the play money, both the paper bills and the coins, inside the cash register.
2. Invite the child and caregiver to identify the biggest change they would each like to make for themselves or in their relationship with each other. Write these larger goals on dollar bills (either real ones or the ones provided on the *Magical Coins* template).
3. Explain that just like lots of smaller coins can equal a dollar, lots of smaller changes are often needed to achieve a larger goal. Work as a team (therapist, child, and caregiver) to name behaviors, habits, thoughts, or relational interactions they would like to change. For example, if a child with attentional and anger issues names "I want to get in trouble less" as their larger goal, the team might help them brainstorm specific behaviors that result in consequences or angry adult reactions (e.g., hitting, talking back).
4. The client can write these action steps on the coins listed on the *Magical Coins* template, or the caregiver can do so while the child is playing with the cash register. The fun involved in playing with the play money and cash register, as well the novelty of the idea that the coins represent small increments of change, make it likely that the dyad can tolerate this playful treatment planning, even though it requires looking at things about themselves that they don't like.
5. If the child is old enough to understand the monetary values of different coins, you might create a hierarchy of behavior patterns they want to change, translating these to the most important treatment goals for the client.

Copyright © 2026 Paris Goodyear-Brown, *Big Behaviors in All Containers*. All rights reserved.

MAGICAL COINS TEMPLATE

What is the most important change you would like to make in yourself or in your relationship with your caregiver? Write this goal on the dollar bill.

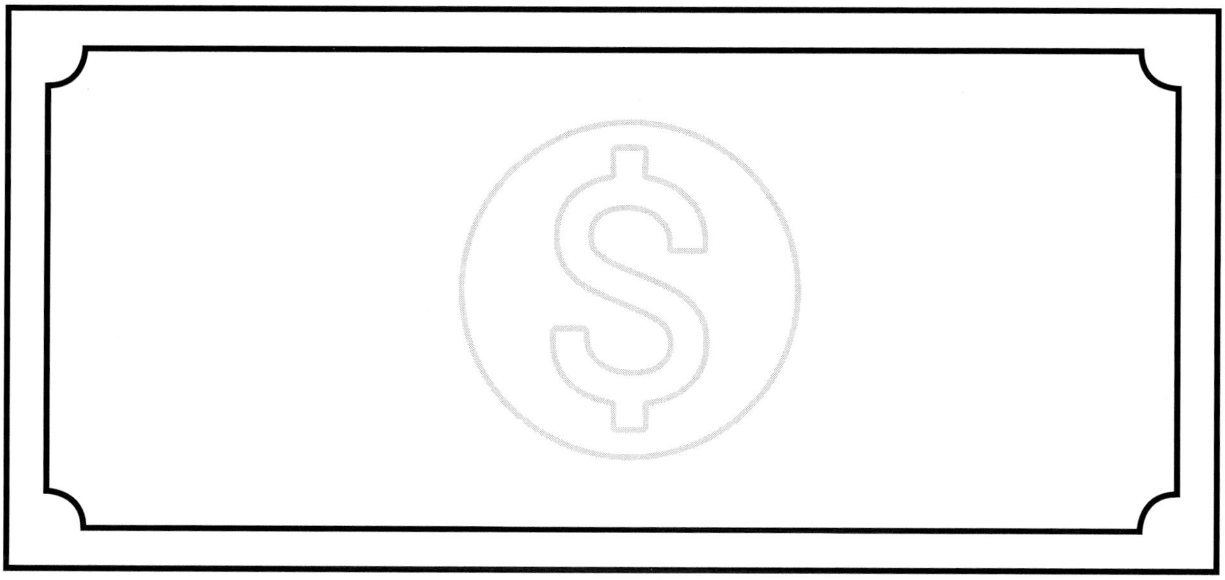

Write one action step you or your caregiver can take toward this goal. You can write big steps on the bigger coins and small steps on the smaller coins.

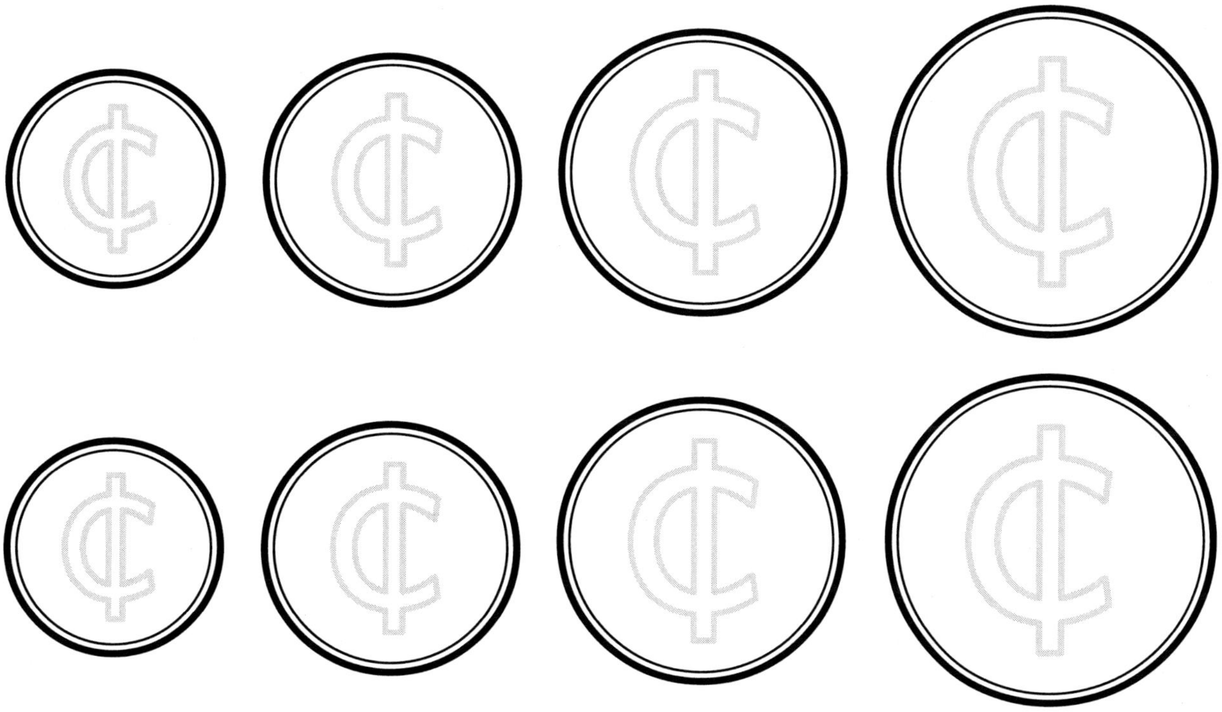

Copyright © 2026 Paris Goodyear-Brown, *Big Behaviors in All Containers*. All rights reserved.

2.5 WISHING WELL

DESCRIPTION:

Traumatized children may be stuck in loops of negative behavior in which they experience a big feeling but have such a small window of tolerance for challenging emotions that they respond by hitting, yelling, and throwing things. The child's caregiver may also be stuck in loops of negative activation because their own window of tolerance for handling the child's distress is small. In both cases, introducing a wish fulfillment activity offers an opportunity for the child and caregiver to imagine how they would like to respond when they have big feelings. These wishes can become part of the treatment-planning process. This intervention can be structured around big feelings or be an open-ended prompt. If you offer a more general prompt, like "What are some things you wish for?" you may get some material things, like "more money" or "a bicycle." If this happens, just make sure you have enough coins to get beyond the material wishes to any psychological wishes. If the child remains focused on physical possessions, you can offer a more specific prompt, like "What are some things you would like to see change in your family?" If the client says, "I don't know," rest assured that the client is probably giving their 100 percent today, and you need to build more safety before wish fulfillment feels safe for them.

TREATMENT GOALS:

- Explore areas where the child or caregiver may seek change or growth
- Translate wishes to potential treatment goals
- Support the client's future vision of themselves

MATERIALS NEEDED:

- *Wishing Well* template
- Completed *Magical Coins* template from previous session (2.4)
- Sand tray
- Three-dimensional miniature wishing well
- Play coins

DIRECTIONS:

1. Invite the caregiver and child to name behaviors or habits they wish they could change.
2. Place a three-dimensional wishing well in the sand tray while showing the client the *Wishing Well* template. Offer them several kinds of play coins in different denominations (many children are fascinated by golden pirate coins) to provide kinesthetic involvement.
3. Bring out the *Magical Coins* template from last session. Invite them to imagine that these coins, when thrown into a magic wishing well, will offer them the behaviors and habits they would like to grow in place of the problematic ones.

Copyright © 2026 Paris Goodyear-Brown, *Big Behaviors in All Containers*. All rights reserved.

4. Invite the caregiver and child to throw one coin into the well while naming their challenging behavior out loud. Have them take a breath, imagine what they would like to see instead, and name it. You can write these new behaviors down on the bricks of the *Wishing Well* template. Together, the coins and the well map the path toward a developmentally sensitive treatment plan.

Copyright © 2026 Paris Goodyear-Brown, *Big Behaviors in All Containers*. All rights reserved.

WISHING WELL TEMPLATE

Copyright © 2026 Paris Goodyear-Brown, *Big Behaviors in All Containers*. All rights reserved.

2.6 DECONSTRUCTION: BRICK BY BRICK

DESCRIPTION:

Once you have completed the *Wishing Well* exercise (2.5), you should have several treatment goals concretized. However, in order for clients to achieve these overarching treatment goals, they often need to deconstruct, or break down, these goals into multiple smaller steps or subgoals. For example, if a caregiver has identified the goal of remaining regulated when their child has a behavioral outburst, they will need to break this goal down into the following steps: (1) be aware enough of what is going on in their body to know that escalation is possible, (2) pause, (3) take a deep breath or repeat a regulating mantra to themselves, (4) sift through possible responses, and (5) choose the best one.

TREATMENT GOALS:

- Deconstruct one treatment goal into manageable subgoals or steps
- Co-create achievable action steps for change with the family system

MATERIALS NEEDED:

- Completed *Wishing Well* template from previous session (2.5)
- *Brick by Brick* template
- Scissors
- Paper
- Coloring utensils (e.g., crayons, markers)
- Tape or glue

DIRECTIONS:

1. Hand the client or dyad the completed *Wishing Well* template and ask them to identify one wish, or treatment goal, they'd like to work with today.
2. Introduce the *Brick by Brick* template and explain that there are multiple steps involved in accomplishing their larger goal.
3. Invite the client to cut out the bricks and color them whatever color they want their completed wall to look like. If you are doing this activity with a caregiver-child dyad, you may decide to split the bricks in half—having the caregiver color the half they will be responsible for and the child color their half in a different color. This can help each person track their follow-through on action steps as the new structure is built.
4. While they are cutting and coloring, help the client name the action steps that will be required to meet their overarching treatment goal. For example, if the global goal for the parent is to be more present for their child, they may break this down into specific bricks that say, "Put my phone away before starting playtime," "Imagine putting the worries of the day in a box in my mind before starting a conversation about my child's day with them," or "Take three deep breaths and refocus my attention when I feel myself thinking again about a work deadline."

Copyright © 2026 Paris Goodyear-Brown, *Big Behaviors in All Containers*. All rights reserved.

5. When they are finished, write one action step on each brick.
6. On a separate piece of paper, invite the client to draw a picture of the problem behavior they want to see disappear. Explain that you will keep their colored bricks, and each time they complete an action step toward their goal, you will glue or tape that brick on top of the picture, tracking the progress of change.

Copyright © 2026 Paris Goodyear-Brown, *Big Behaviors in All Containers*. All rights reserved.

BRICK BY BRICK TEMPLATE

Copyright © 2026 Paris Goodyear-Brown, *Big Behaviors in All Containers*. All rights reserved.

2.7 RECONSTRUCTION: BUILDING BLOCKS OF CHANGE

DESCRIPTION:

After the process of deconstruction (breaking down therapeutic change into bite-sized goals), each of the bricks can be used to rebuild a new structure. The metaphor here is that as we tear down old patterns, we make room for new patterns to emerge. Building something new will also happen brick by brick, and the bricks can function as visual encouragement to the child and their caregiver while also serving as a tracking tool for therapeutic growth in either or both parties. One beautiful use of this tool is to track the client's success in using exposure and response prevention (ERP) techniques to change big behaviors (see Goodyear-Brown, 2010). In this use, each participant externalizes their anxiety or anger into a worried dragon, an angry monster, or some other representation of the troublesome emotion or behavior. Each time the client experiences anxiety or anger (*exposure*) while engaging in more adaptive behaviors (*response prevention*), they glue one brick on top of the troublesome image. It can feel very empowering to watch their new behaviors "brick up" the anger or anxiety. In other uses, the dyad might be better served by constructing a new, welcoming space with the bricks where they can feel safe and soothed together.

TREATMENT GOALS:

- Track titrated doses of new behaviors and habits
- Equip the client with a concrete method for measuring progress
- Practice new skills and celebrate the work

MATERIALS NEEDED:

- Completed bricks from the previous *Brick by Brick* template (2.6)
- Paper
- Coloring utensils (e.g., crayons, markers)
- Glue
- Three-dimensional structure to glue the bricks on (e.g., Pringles can, tissue paper box)

DIRECTIONS:

1. Invite each participant to draw an angry or anxious creature. They can externalize their anger or anxiety in whatever way feels right to them.
2. When they're done, review the individual action steps that were written on the bricks during the last session.
3. Offer each participant additional bricks and explain:

   "Now that we've named the building blocks to handling your anger safely, these new bricks will help us track your practice in using new tools when you are angry. Every

Copyright © 2026 Paris Goodyear-Brown, *Big Behaviors in All Containers*. All rights reserved.

time you become angry and use one of your new skills, you will add another brick on top of your angry creature. Eventually, your angry creature will be all bricked up, and you will have new habits for managing your anger!"

4. Decide together on a way to celebrate their hard work once the creature is bricked up.

VARIATION:

1. Explain to the dyad:

   "Sometimes an angry or anxious part of you takes over because that part doesn't feel safe. Helping that part feel safer may also help you feel better. Why don't we use the bricks to create a safe, enclosed space for your upset parts to rest and feel welcomed?"

2. This variation may require great skill from the therapist, as safety in the new space may need to be negotiated. The caregiver and client may decide that they each need to build separate spaces first with their bricks, and once they have experienced enough change individually, you can circle back and help them create a shared safe space that perhaps documents all the changes they have both made on a clean set of paper bricks.
3. Once they have decided on a structure they want to create (e.g., living room with a fireplace, kitchen with lots of food, a safe room up high in a castle), help them find a three-dimensional object they can use for this purpose. Offer structures like tissue boxes, empty cans, and so on.
4. Each time they practice new behaviors that help them soothe their anxiety or anger, they glue another brick onto the structure.

Copyright © 2026 Paris Goodyear-Brown, *Big Behaviors in All Containers*. All rights reserved.

2.8 EDIBLE WISHING WAND

DESCRIPTION:

This intervention is a fun twist on the *Three Wishes* exercise in *Big Behaviors in Small Containers* (Goodyear-Brown, 2022). Children who have been mistreated or neglected may not have had ready access to food. They may not have had the experience of a healthy attachment system, in which the relationship (the caregiver's attuned response) and the resource (breastmilk, formula, food) are paired. When traumatized children enter therapy and we are working to build trust and a foundational attachment relationship, it can be helpful to integrate food into the treatment process, as it can provide nurture for the child while possibly meeting a previously unmet need. In this intervention, the child will have an opportunity to make a magic wand with real food (so make sure to check for any food allergies ahead of time). If the child's primary caregiver is safe enough to be involved, this is a wonderful way to enhance attachment in the system. It is particularly meaningful when foster and adoptive parents participate.

TREATMENT GOALS:

- Explore potential treatment goals by making wishes
- Harness the child's imagination to help identify areas for therapeutic growth
- Enhance the attachment relationship (with the therapist, caregiver, or both) by providing one form of nurture through food

MATERIALS NEEDED:

- Pretzel rods
- Celery sticks
- Peanut butter or cream cheese
- Bread
- Star-shaped cookie cutters
- Magic wands from your playroom
- *Magic Wand* template

DIRECTIONS:

1. Begin by inviting the client and their caregiver to explore the collection of wands you have available.
2. Explain that the child is going to make their own magic wand today—and they will be able to eat it!
3. Offer the pretzel rods and celery sticks to serve as the bottom of the magic wand.
4. Then give the child two pieces of bread and the cookie cutters so they can cut out two star shapes. Let them decide between filler ingredients like peanut butter, cream cheese, and so on. Put it all together and—voilà!—an edible wishing wand.

Copyright © 2026 Paris Goodyear-Brown, *Big Behaviors in All Containers*. All rights reserved.

5. Invite the child to wave the wand and wish for three things they would like to see change or grow in their own life or in their family. Offer to write these on the *Magic Wand* template so you can remember them together even after the wand is eaten.
6. If the caregiver is present, it can be fun to have each partner feed each other bites of their wand topper.

Copyright © 2026 Paris Goodyear-Brown, *Big Behaviors in All Containers*. All rights reserved.

MAGIC WAND TEMPLATE

Copyright © 2026 Paris Goodyear-Brown, *Big Behaviors in All Containers*. All rights reserved.

2.9 CAN YOU SEE IT?

DESCRIPTION:

This intervention provides another path toward enlisting the dyad in the goal-setting process. It is common knowledge that a client's investment in the treatment process is tied to what they hope to accomplish and what they want to change, but articulating this can be hard to do, especially for children. In adult therapy, we often ask clients, "Imagine yourself in five years. Where would you like to be? What would you like to be doing? Who would you like to have in your life?" Since children do not have this same sense of time, this exercise is meant to enlist the caregiver in detailing what the future can look like. It pairs the novelty of seeing things far away through binoculars with the idea that the completion of a treatment goal may be a long way off, but it can still be identified as the dyad and therapist become curious together.

TREATMENT GOALS:

- Help the client engage in future template work
- Assist the client in developing goals
- Create measurable and specific goals for the treatment plan

MATERIALS NEEDED:

- *Binoculars* template
- Real binoculars
- Sand tray miniatures
- Paper
- Coloring utensils (e.g., crayons, markers)
- Empty toilet paper rolls, string, glue, scissors, and old magazines (optional)

DIRECTIONS:

1. Explain to the dyad that it can be hard to envision life looking or feeling differently than it does right now:

   "It can be difficult to imagine how the changes you make now in yourself and in your relationship can pay off in the long run. This exercise offers a playful way for you two to dream together about what the future can look like as you grow."

2. Offer the binoculars to the dyad. Invite them to take turns finding small objects from your sand tray collection and magnifying them. If you have a window in your office, invite them to find small objects outside the window and then look at them through the binoculars.
3. Invite them to draw a tiny picture that describes one of their goals in treatment. Pin the picture at the far end of the room or even move out into the hallway if allowable. Acknowledge together that it is difficult to see the details right now. Then offer the binoculars again and invite them to magnify the picture this way.

Copyright © 2026 Paris Goodyear-Brown, *Big Behaviors in All Containers*. All rights reserved.

4. Invite the dyad to title the picture or treatment goal and write this goal on the *Binoculars* template. This process can be repeated for multiple treatment goals.
5. Additionally, you can make a personalized set of binoculars by taking two used toilet paper cores and stringing them together. The dyad can write down their treatment goals on the outside of the cores and decorate them in session with old magazine clippings.

Copyright © 2026 Paris Goodyear-Brown, *Big Behaviors in All Containers*. All rights reserved.

BINOCULARS TEMPLATE

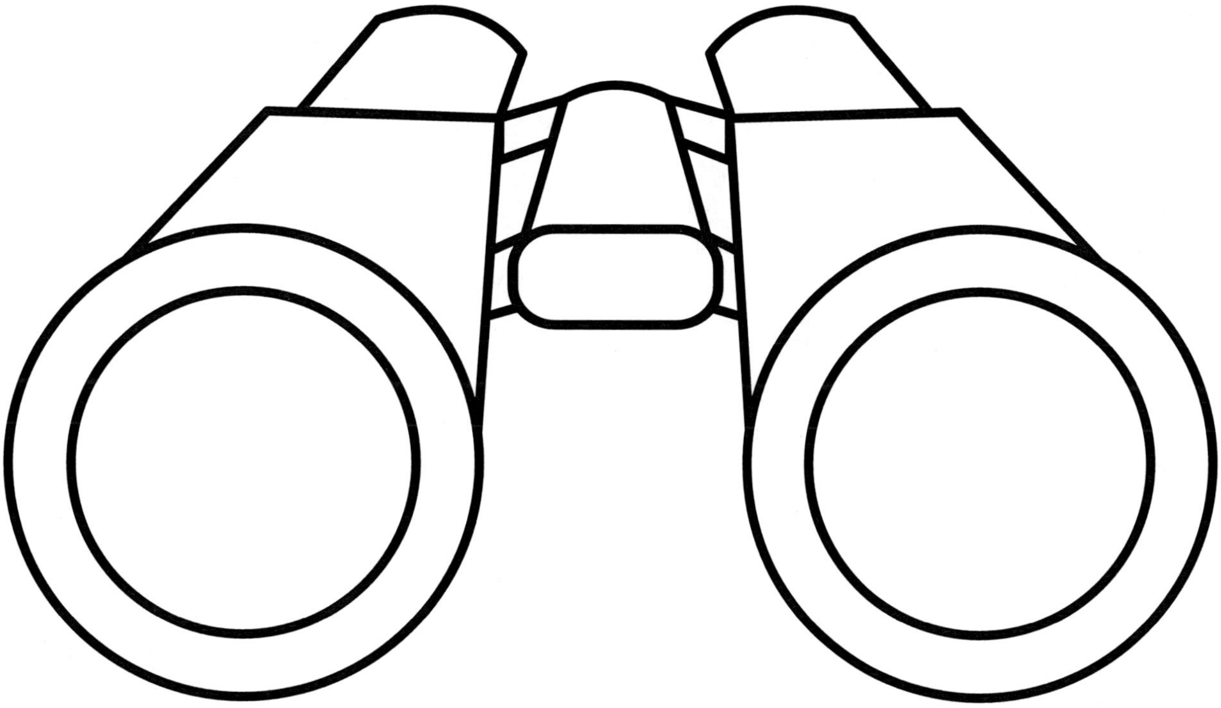

Copyright © 2026 Paris Goodyear-Brown, *Big Behaviors in All Containers*. All rights reserved.

2.10 FAMILY PLAY GENOSTORY

DESCRIPTION:

If you are new to play therapy, you may be unaware of the family play genogram, an elegant information-gathering tool created by Eliana Gil (2014). A pioneer in trauma-informed play therapy, Dr. Gil invites the child to choose miniatures to represent each of their family members. You can gather a wealth of information by this process alone. In this TraumaPlay adaptation, this process of choosing and placing miniatures for each family member is always done within the boundaried space of the sand tray. The child's placement of family members in the sand tray is a powerful way to communicate closeness versus distance, as well as danger versus safety. The child is then asked to make up a story about the characters in the tray, while giving the figures a fictional name, as opposed to saying "Mom" or "Dad." This distancing provides some psychological safety and may help the client create a story that more accurately depicts any thematic issues in the family system.

While many of the interventions in this book involve both the caregiver and child, this intervention is for use with the child individually and the caregiver individually, as choosing symbols to represent each other early on in treatment could feel unsafe to either or both partners. Sometimes, clients choose symbols that might amplify the tensions in a relationship or highlight characteristics of family members that are challenging.

TREATMENT GOALS:

- Assess the child's and parent's perceptions of the family dynamics
- Gather initial impressions of the child's and parent's relationships with each family member
- Access thematic family material that may translate into systemic treatment goals

MATERIALS NEEDED:

- Sand tray
- Miniatures
- Camera
- Paper
- Writing utensil

DIRECTIONS:

1. Introduce the activity to the child or adult. When introducing it to a child, you may use the following script:

   "We are going to create a map of your family in the sand. You can choose anything from the shelves to be 'Mom' and put it in the sand. Then you can choose anything from the shelves to be 'Dad.' And so on. There is no right or wrong way to do this. Let me know when you are done."

Copyright © 2026 Paris Goodyear-Brown, *Big Behaviors in All Containers*. All rights reserved.

2. Older children and adults can be given a more global prompt to represent all the important people in the family.
3. If a child asks whether they can choose more than one miniature to represent each parent, say, "You may do whatever you need to do in here."
4. Younger children may need more structure to this activity and need more specific prompts to find a symbol to represent each family member one by one. You might say, "Choose something to represent your mom and put it in the sand tray." When they have finished this piece of the exercise, ask them to choose the next family member.
5. Once you are confident that they are finished, ask the client to make up a story about the characters in the tray: "Now we are going to make up a story about the tray. Let's name these characters. I'm going to be your secretary—writing down your story as you tell it."
6. Focus your eyes on the paper and write while you say out loud, "Once upon a time there was a . . ."
7. Here is a list of prompts you can give the client that may help jump-start ideas if they get stuck:
    a. When along came . . .
    b. Suddenly they . . .
    c. After some time had passed, they felt . . .
8. Some clients feel self-conscious about telling a story or need some time to come up with one, and it can help for you to focus your attention on the characters in the sand tray, offer the starter prompt, and then wait patiently to see how the client will narrate. Sitting in the silence is a skill that clinicians are often expanding for themselves, and it can be important for this exercise.
9. As the client begins to narrate their story, repeat parts of their story while writing it down on paper or on your computer. Children in particular will want to make sure you write the details down correctly.
10. When the story is complete, you may ask them whether they would like you to read it back out loud to them. This can often serve as a way to close out the exercise, and you might punctuate this by saying "The End" at the end of the story.
11. You may also ask the client for permission to take a picture of the completed sand tray, as it may be useful to revisit later in treatment.

Copyright © 2026 Paris Goodyear-Brown, *Big Behaviors in All Containers*. All rights reserved.

2.11 DARTS AND DEETS

DESCRIPTION:

Caregivers often enter treatment thinking that their child will be able to sit quietly and talk about the clinical issues that need to be addressed, and this intervention offers a paradigm shift by incorporating play into treatment. It is designed to help highly kinetic children pinpoint trauma targets for future work, while using movement and play as mitigators in the approach to hard things. I designed it while working with a newly adopted nine-year-old boy who had experienced myriad traumas. He spent the first few sessions in silence, without making eye contact. His adoptive parent said that he was very athletic and responded to high-challenge activities, so I brought in a dart board. His eyes lit up, and he immediately asked to play. Standing together with joint attention to the dart board was the first step in decreasing his self-consciousness, and every time his arm moved to throw a dart, his mouth opened to share a little. This inspired me to create the following intervention, where children have an opportunity to share about their scary experiences using the rings around the dart board as a guide. Some kids like to go straight to talking about their hardest experiences first (the bull's-eye on the dart board), while others like to start with less scary targets (the outer rings on the dart board).

TREATMENT GOALS:

- Identify potential trauma targets for reprocessing and desensitization
- Determine a hierarchy of trauma targets
- Mitigate the approach to difficult content through kinesthetic involvement

MATERIALS NEEDED:

- *Darts and Deets* template
- Large roll of paper
- Writing utensil
- Real dart board (depending on the age of the child, you may use magnet darts instead of pointed darts)

DIRECTIONS:

1. Invite the child (or dyad) to try out the dart board.
2. While the child is engaged in dart play, draw at least three rings of a dart board on a piece of paper. Bigger butcher paper is sometimes better than standard size for this activity. Alternatively, you can use the *Darts and Deets* template.
3. When you're done, explain to the child, "It can be hard to talk about hard things that have happened, but if we don't look at them, they can continue to make us feel sick inside."

Copyright © 2026 Paris Goodyear-Brown, *Big Behaviors in All Containers*. All rights reserved.

4. Explain that each time they throw a dart that sticks to the board, you'd like them to name one scary thing that has happened to them. Reiterate that you are not going to talk about those scary things today, but you will write the title of that scary thing on the paper dart board.
5. Remind the child that they get to lead this activity:

   "We'll do some work to get ready to look at the details of these scary things, but sometimes once a kid understands that the only way to feel better is to face the scary thing instead of avoiding it, they want to jump straight to the scariest thing. Others want to start with less scary memories. You get to choose. Either way, if you tell me which is scariest as we play, I'll put that target right on the bull's-eye and your other targets in the rings around it."
6. If the child has trouble naming scary things, you can move into the role of Storykeeper by sharing what you know about their trauma (use your clinical judgment in deciding which details to share). If they have trouble giving a title to each experience, ask whether you have permission to come up with a title for now, like *The Death*, *The Abuse*, or *The Tornado*.
7. Feel free to pendulate between this activity and child-led play.

Copyright © 2026 Paris Goodyear-Brown, *Big Behaviors in All Containers*. All rights reserved.

DARTS AND DEETS TEMPLATE

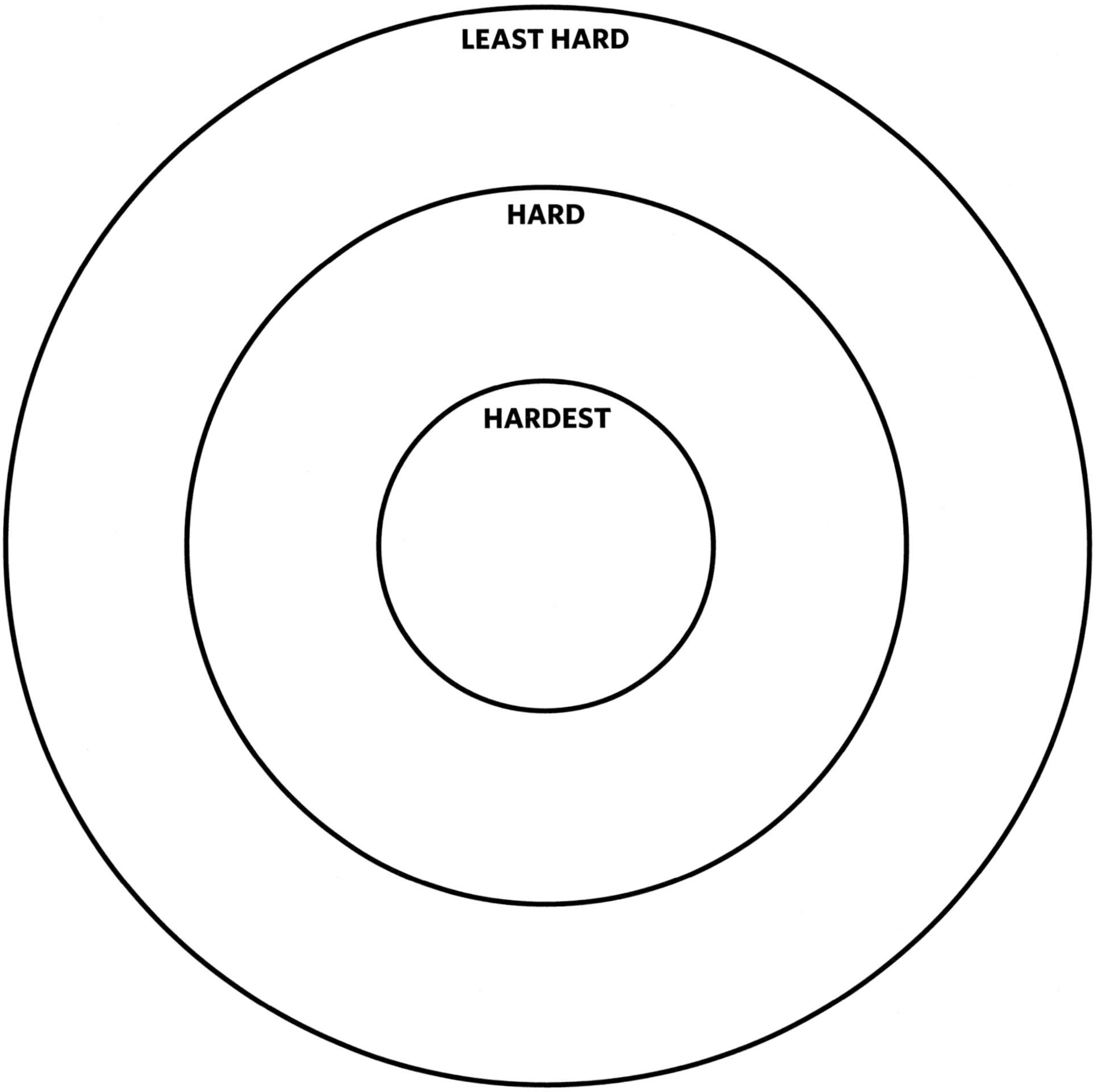

Do you like to start with the hardest stuff and work your way out? Or start with less scary stuff and work your way into the harder stuff?

Copyright © 2026 Paris Goodyear-Brown, *Big Behaviors in All Containers*. All rights reserved.

three

Enhancing Safety and Augmenting Adaptive Coping

This chapter offers playful ways to enhance a child or caregiver's felt sense of safety and augment adaptive coping. For many traumatized children with big behaviors, the big behaviors themselves represent what was once an adaptive coping strategy but has now become problematic. For example, a four-year-old child who was sexually abused by a parent may have coped during their abuse by separating their mind from their body (Goodyear-Brown & Kenney-Noziska, 2024). Even if that child is now in an adoptive home that is physically safe, they may still respond by dissociating whenever they detect danger. To the new caregivers, it may seem like their child is shutting down; punishing them through sullen, withdrawn behavior; or rejecting them. The child's dissociative response to danger was so effective in past years at protecting them from feeling hurt that it is now keeping them from feeling anything or from taking the risk of connecting with their new caregivers.

Stephen Porges, the creator of polyvagal theory, coined the term *neuroception* to speak to the felt sense that each of us has—outside of conscious awareness—that we are safe, in danger, or facing life threat (Porges, 2011). Clinicians are always interpreting this felt sense of safety (or danger or life threat) between the caregiver and child in session and are charged with managing all three autonomic nervous systems in the room: that of the caregiver, the child, and themselves (Porges & Dana, 2018). This is no small task. In *Big Behaviors in Small Containers* (Goodyear-Brown, 2022), I offered playful ways that therapists can teach, explore, and identify stress responses that align with felt senses of safety, danger, or life threat. This chapter is meant to offer additional ways to enlist the caregiver in embodying safety while supporting adaptive coping choices for themselves and the child in their care. When the caregiver's coping clashes with the child's coping, the dyad is at great risk for rupture and disconnection. Therefore, you must seek to understand the adaptive and maladaptive coping responses of the caregiver and the child, work to help them understand each other's coping strategies, and lead them to some mutually agreed-upon coping options.

3.1 DESERT ISLAND SAND TRAY

DESCRIPTION:

TraumaPlay clinicians often ask this question during the assessment phase of treatment: "Imagine that you are stranded on a desert island and can only have one other person with you. Who would you choose and why?" You can ask the child and caregiver this question in separate sessions, as this question can yield rich understanding of who the client perceives as safe, useful, or as a primary attachment figure. For example, if the child chooses their mother, you may decide to harness the felt sense of safety the child experiences when this attachment figure is present to amplify storykeeping narrative work. However, if the child chooses a friend instead of a parent, this information will be systemically useful for you. You might decide that attachment-enhancement work is needed prior to bringing the parent in as a Storykeeper. Similarly, the caregiver's answer to this question may help you identify an adult attachment figure who can function as a supportive person for the caregiver during the process of change.

TREATMENT GOALS:

- Identify at least one meaningful attachment relationship for the child and caregiver
- Explore the elements of a safe place for the child and caregiver
- Invite cooperation between the parent and child as they help create safety together

MATERIALS NEEDED:

- Sand tray with blue bottom
- A wide range of miniatures
- *Desert Island* template

DIRECTIONS:

1. Invite the child or caregiver to imagine a desert island. Begin creating an island by moving most of the sand into the center of the tray, leaving lots of blue bottom exposed to represent that there is no way off the island. For younger children, feel free to tell a story of a shipwreck, inviting the child to choose a boat and act out the shipwreck.
2. Invite the child or caregiver to choose a miniature to represent themselves and place it on the island. Ask them to notice what is going on in their body as they observe themselves on the island. Then invite them to decorate the island however they may wish. Children might get really involved by adding trees to provide shelter, streams for fresh water, wild animals, or poisonous plants. Pay close attention to any additional threats that are added to the island, as the client may be sharing additional communications about the level of danger they experience in the world around them.

Copyright © 2026 Paris Goodyear-Brown, *Big Behaviors in All Containers*. All rights reserved.

3. Ask the following question: "Imagine that you are stranded on this desert island and can only have one other person with you. Who would you choose and why?"
4. If the client names someone, ask them to choose a miniature to represent this person and place that person on the island too. Become curious about their felt sense of safety (or danger or life threat) again. What is happening in their body now that their special person is with them?
5. If the client does not name anyone, or says that they would prefer to remain alone, simply reflect back this decision to them. This might also be an opportunity to normalize a child's core belief that people are dangerous or to wonder out loud whether a child feels like they have to rely on themselves because there is no one else to keep them safe or meet their needs.
6. Invite the client to draw themselves (and possibly another meaningful attachment relationship) on the *Desert Island* template.

Copyright © 2026 Paris Goodyear-Brown, *Big Behaviors in All Containers*. All rights reserved.

DESERT ISLAND TEMPLATE

Copyright © 2026 Paris Goodyear-Brown, *Big Behaviors in All Containers*. All rights reserved.

3.2 FAMILY TREEHOUSE

DESCRIPTION:

The Swiss Family Robinson is a beloved story written by Johan Rudolf Wyss in 1812 that has since been retold in myriad ways. In the story, a family is shipwrecked on a desert island. While waiting for help to arrive, they make a home in a large tree. Over time, they find ingenious uses for some of the things that wash up on shore from the shipwreck and from natural items they find on the island. They create a pulley system to get water up into the treehouse. They create bedrooms and learn how to identify and cook foods from the island. They face an unsafe environment and work to generate more safety in creative ways. The act of taking what you have, even if it feels like wreckage around you, and repurposing it serves as a beautiful metaphor for moving from maladaptive coping to more adaptive coping. In this exercise, the child and their caregiver (or even the whole family) will work together to create their own treehouse, helping each other know the other's cues of safety and enhancing the attachment relationship by jointly working together.

TREATMENT GOALS:

- Identify cues of safety for both the child and caregiver within the home environment
- Find creative ways to take objects and repurpose them
- Increase competency and channel creativity into adaptive coping

MATERIALS NEEDED:

- Toy tree house (if you have one)
- Sand tray
- A wide range of miniatures
- Building blocks
- Coloring utensils (e.g., crayons, markers)
- *Family Treehouse* template
- Craft materials (e.g., felt, yarn, magazine clippings, glue) (optional)

DIRECTIONS:

1. Introduce the activity to the child and caregiver using the following script:

   "Last week, you imagined what it would be like to be stranded on a desert island. You wondered who you might have with you and what you might need to feel safe there. Today, we are inviting your Safe Boss(es) to join us. Do you know the story of the *Swiss Family Robinson*?"

2. If the child is not familiar with the story, describe how the family used items found on the island and repurposed wreckage washed up from the shipwreck to create their home. Explain at least one way that the family had to work together to make things safer and better. For example, they had to haul a big tree limb to help create the treehouse. Explain that it would take at least two people and maybe the whole family working together to move it.

Copyright © 2026 Paris Goodyear-Brown, *Big Behaviors in All Containers*. All rights reserved.

3. Invite the client and caregiver to decide how to create their family treehouse. They can create it in the sand tray, build it with blocks on a table, or draw it on paper using the *Family Treehouse* template. Questions to spark creativity, problem-solving, and compromise are below:
    a. How many rooms will it have?
    b. How high off the ground does it need to be?
    c. How will you comfortably sleep?
    d. How will you stay dry in the rain?
    e. How will you find food?
    f. How will you store food without other animals getting to it?
    g. How will you go to the bathroom?
    h. How will you clean yourselves?
    i. What will you do for fun?
    j. Are there games you can create to play in the treehouse?
    k. How will you be warned of danger?
4. Invite the child and caregiver to think of creative ways to make the family treehouse feel safer or more comfortable—for example, palm fronds to make a bed, shells to create a family crest of their initials, or an animal pelt for a cozy corner. You can also offer drawing tools, magazine clippings, pieces of felt and yarn, or cotton balls to enhance this effect.
5. Once the treehouse is complete (this may take several sessions), invite the dyad or family to reflect on the processes of joint decision-making. Celebrate moments when they were able to flexibly and creatively adapt their design strategies to meet each other's needs and explain that these same skill sets can be applied to the client's current coping needs.
6. If the client used the *Family Treehouse* template, have them write the family surname on top. If they created a three-dimensional version of a treehouse, offer a final exercise in which they create a plaque or sign with their family name on it for the family treehouse. If the client has a different last name from the caregiver, this, too, will require adaptive problem-solving to come up with a name for the shared treehouse that both the child and caregiver can embrace.

Copyright © 2026 Paris Goodyear-Brown, *Big Behaviors in All Containers*. All rights reserved.

FAMILY TREEHOUSE TEMPLATE

Copyright © 2026 Paris Goodyear-Brown, *Big Behaviors in All Containers*. All rights reserved.

3.3 LEARNING TO BEAR IT

DESCRIPTION:

Children and teens with significant trauma histories sometimes come into treatment with self-injurious behaviors or suicidal ideation. Clinicians sometimes have them sign no-harm contracts in which they commit to calling a support person (usually listed in the contract) if they are having thoughts about hurting themselves. I am not a fan of contracts, as clients can white-knuckle their way into upholding the contract for a period of time, only to end up in a crisis that has them slipping back into self-injury. In this case, the client experiences a double whammy—the disappointment and potential self-loathing of returning to the behavior and additional guilt and shame from having broken their contract. Instead of contracts, you can offer the client an autographable bear or other stuffed animal. Older teens can write the names and phone numbers of their support people on the stuffed animal, while younger children may draw pictures of their helping figures instead. The autographed item can then function as a self-care, comfort item while also keeping the client's support people visually represented. If appropriate, you can invite safe-enough caregivers to be a part of this intervention to amplify the child's sense of safety.

TREATMENT GOALS:

- Identify self-injurious behaviors or suicidal ideation
- Amplify the adaptive coping strategy of seeking social support when big feelings are present
- Categorize the support people available to the client in times of distress
- Provide visual reminders of the support people available to the client

MATERIALS NEEDED:

- Autographable fabric bear or other stuffed animal
- Fabric markers
- *Bear* template
- Coloring utensils (e.g., crayons, markers)

DIRECTIONS:

1. Explain that when we have experienced trauma or had hard things happen, our bodies can alert us to the distress through self-harm behaviors. Explain that our minds can also let us know distress is present through thoughts of self-harm.
2. Become curious with the child about when these behaviors show up and who could help them feel better if they are having thoughts of self-harm.
3. Instruct the client to write the names and phone numbers, or draw pictures, of these support people (at least four if possible) on the bear. Caregivers can be an important support in this process.

Copyright © 2026 Paris Goodyear-Brown, *Big Behaviors in All Containers*. All rights reserved.

4. Additionally, you might have the caregiver repeat some of the child's most comforting statements as the child writes these statements on the autographable bear. You might lead the client in a practice of squeezing the bear while saying a positive mantra out loud, like "I have people who will care for me when I feel yucky," "I have people who will help me care for myself when I am feeling low," or "The Safe Bosses are right here to help me when I need them."
5. Invite child and caregiver to come up with a three-part handshake with the bear. Each participant takes one of the paws of the bear and, in synchronous fashion, completes the three-part handshake.
6. You can also replicate the names and phone numbers (or pictures and phone numbers) on the provided *Bear* template so you have a record for future sessions or in case the stuffed bear is lost.

Copyright © 2026 Paris Goodyear-Brown, *Big Behaviors in All Containers*. All rights reserved.

BEAR TEMPLATE

Copyright © 2026 Paris Goodyear-Brown, *Big Behaviors in All Containers*. All rights reserved.

3.4 COPING KITE

DESCRIPTION:

Traumatized children have experienced a lack of safety in their environments. Many of these children will respond to these "out-of-control" feelings by digging in for control over the chaos. These children are often misunderstood and labeled as "oppositional" or "manipulative" when, in fact, there is a river of anxiety running beneath the surface. Although these strategies may be adaptive when they are in their chaotic home environment, they are often problematic in other settings, such as school. This intervention offers the metaphor of a kite, buffeted about by the wild whims of wind, learning to rise above the chaos to be successful.

TREATMENT GOALS:

- Identify chaotic elements in the client's environment
- Reframe "controlling behavior" as an attempt to manage anxiety and chaos
- Brainstorm coping strategies, especially those that can be supported or facilitated by the caregiver

MATERIALS NEEDED:

- Video of a kite being flown
- Coloring utensils (e.g., crayons, markers)
- *Coping Kite* template

DIRECTIONS:

1. Explain to the child and caregiver that they will be making a coping kite with you today.
2. Ask the child whether they have ever flown a kite before. After listening to their answer, offer the following short script:

   "Three main forces control a kite: lift, gravity, and drag. A kite flies because the lifting force of the wind overcomes both the downward pull of gravity and air resistance as you are pulling the kite forward. Finding the right air current for cruising can be tricky, and the kite is often knocked around until it catches the right wind. If you were a kite, your job would be to catch the air current that eases the work you're doing.

   "The hard things that have happened to you may feel like they are pulling you down, but you can learn to cope by rising above, like a kite. Once you've fought your way through the chaotic currents, you can find a current that will actually help you move forward."

3. Show a video of a kite being flown and ask the child to imagine being the kite. Invite the caregiver to imagine being the one who holds the string, providing some grounding for the kite. Be curious with them about how this feels in their body.

Copyright © 2026 Paris Goodyear-Brown, *Big Behaviors in All Containers*. All rights reserved.

4. Help the child and caregiver identify at least four coping strategies that help them rise above in moments of stress, much like the wind. For example, "You can come and sit on Mom's lap and let her rock you," "You and Dad can go on a bike ride to release the excess energy," "You can take a hot bath," and "You and Mom can practice starfish breathing." Write these on the four panels of the *Coping Kite* template.
5. Write positive self-affirmations in the bows of the kite's tail, like "I am a cool kid," "I can ask for what I need," or "I am lovable."
6. You might invite the caregiver to add affirmations for the child, or communications about the dyad, like "When we stick together, we can do hard things."
7. Allow the child to decorate the kite how they wish.

Copyright © 2026 Paris Goodyear-Brown, *Big Behaviors in All Containers*. All rights reserved.

COPING KITE TEMPLATE

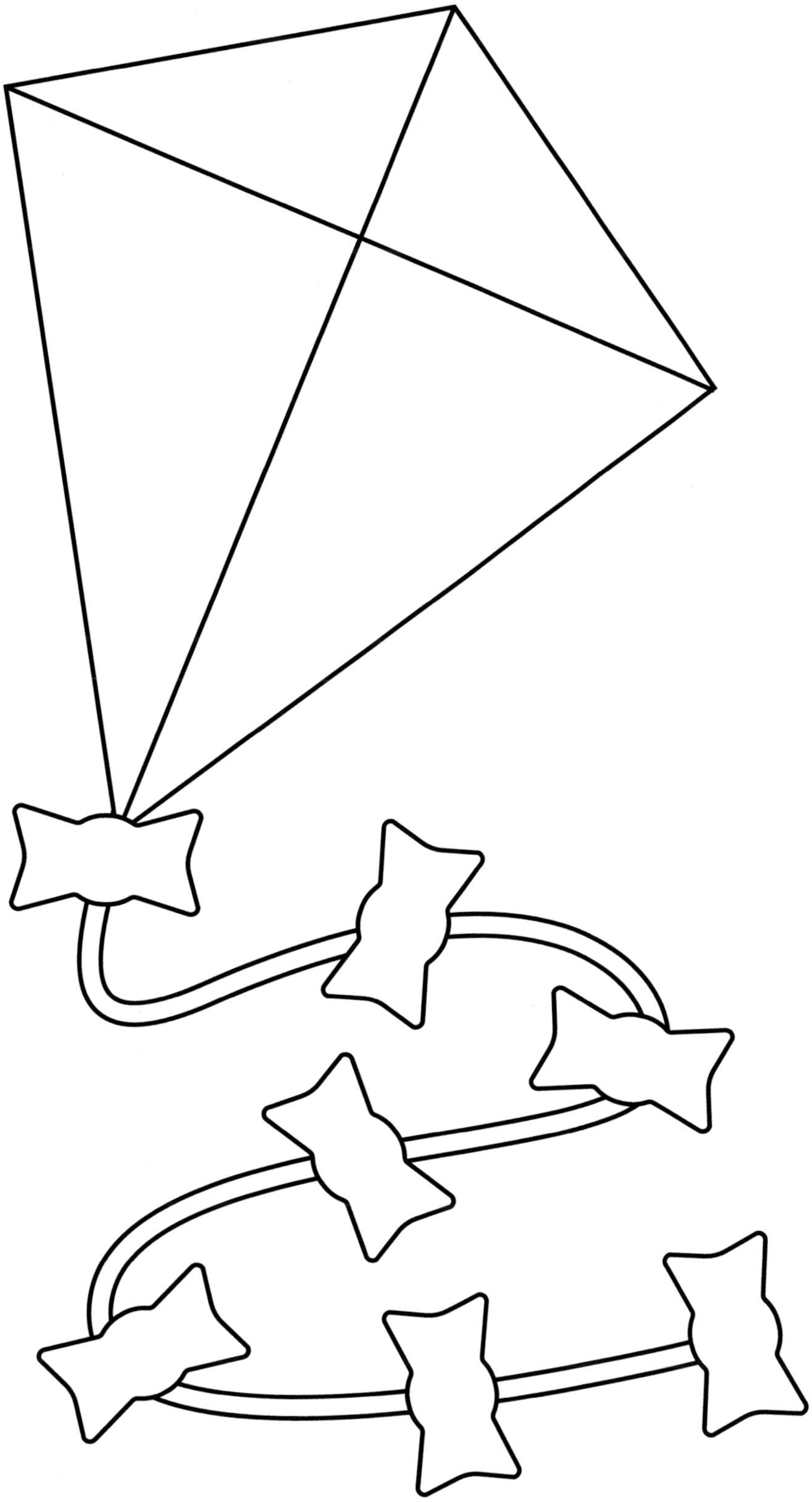

Copyright © 2026 Paris Goodyear-Brown, *Big Behaviors in All Containers*. All rights reserved.

3.5 CATCH THE CURRENT

DESCRIPTION:

Children who have experienced complex trauma have often learned how to disconnect their minds from their bodies in order to feel safe. Through a polyvagal lens, their autonomic nervous systems have moved into a dorsal vagal shutdown state, in which their bodies become numb and they dissociate from the physical environment. In the previous *Coping Kite* exercise (3.4), the child and their caregiver learned about the chaotic winds that kites must endure to get to the air current that will help them move forward. This exercise expands on the previous one by inviting the child to imagine being a kite and to notice what they feel in their body as they get knocked around in the wind and eventually reach smoother air. The caregiver can also imagine what it feels like to hold the string as the kite gets buffeted by the wind. Since both children and their adult attachment figures can have trouble interpreting their bodies' cues, they will need support in honing their interoception abilities. This exercise is one way to help them expand their felt sense of safety.

TREATMENT GOALS:

- Develop the child's sense of interoception
- Use imagery to support the child's sense of felt safety

MATERIALS NEEDED:

- Video of a kite being flown
- *Air Current Body Scan* template
- Coloring utensils (e.g., crayons, markers)

DIRECTIONS:

1. Say to the dyad, "Today we are going to learn about interoception. It sounds fancy, but all it means is that you listen to what your body is telling you from the inside out."
2. Ask the dyad to check in with their bodies. What do they notice? Children in particular will often shrug at this point and say, "I don't know."
3. If so, affirm their response and say:

   "Knowing what your body is saying to you from the inside out can take practice, but it's a sense that you can grow. Lots of people have learned how to ignore their body's cues, especially if they have lived through dangerous situations."

4. Show a video of a kite being flown again, but this time, stop the video during a part in which the kite is being knocked around in the wind. Invite the child to imagine being the kite and the caregiver to imagine being the string. Ask them to describe what they

Copyright © 2026 Paris Goodyear-Brown, *Big Behaviors in All Containers*. All rights reserved.

feel in their bodies when they imagine being caught in these chaotic winds. Write down their responses on the *Air Current Body Scan* template.

5. Restart the video and ask the child to imagine becoming the kite after it has caught the air current and seems to be floating on the wind. Similarly, ask the caregiver to imagine what it feels like to hold the string once the kite has reached smoother air. Ask them to describe what they feel in their body when they imagine the kite floating on an air current. Using a separate color, add these responses to the *Air Current Body Scan* template as well.
6. The goal here is to invite the dyad to identify physiological states that are reactive to their environments, as well as intentional calming practices that work in tandem with their body's needs.
7. If you are trained in eye movement desensitization and reprocessing (EMDR), this would be a good time to further install the felt sense of safety by providing bilateral stimulation as the dyad imagines floating on the wind, feeling the warmth of the sun on their skin, and so on.

Copyright © 2026 Paris Goodyear-Brown, *Big Behaviors in All Containers*. All rights reserved.

AIR CURRENT BODY SCAN TEMPLATE

WHERE DO YOU FEEL IT?

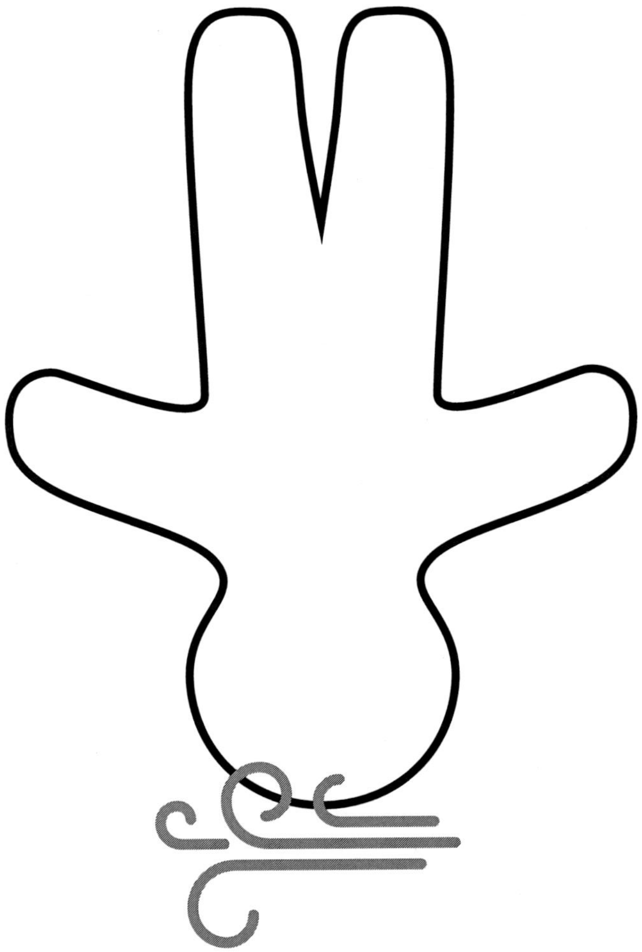

WHERE DO YOU FEEL IT?

Copyright © 2026 Paris Goodyear-Brown, *Big Behaviors in All Containers*. All rights reserved.

3.6 SINGING IN THE RAIN

DESCRIPTION:

TraumaPlay has always embraced the belief that the core components of the model provide protection and relief from trauma symptoms. For this reason, the *T* in the TraumaPlay logo is an umbrella. This umbrella is intended to offer protection from all the behavioral, relational, emotional, physical, and psychological "rain drops," or trauma symptoms, the child may experience. In this exercise, the umbrella becomes a powerful three-dimensional tool to help the client feel embodied protection from the trauma symptoms while they practice their new adaptive coping skills. Importantly, children do not learn new coping strategies by writing them down on a list. They must practice and rehearse these strategies during times of calm so they know how to effectively use them during a storm. By using a physical umbrella in this activity, children and their Safe Bosses have a fun, embodied way to practice these strategies.

TREATMENT GOALS:

- Identify problematic trauma symptoms that tend to surface for the child
- Name coping strategies that are most useful to the child when a trauma symptom is active
- Rehearse adaptive coping responses

MATERIALS NEEDED:

- Multicolored, paneled umbrella
- Colorful feathers
- Small drink umbrellas
- *Singing in the Rain* template

DIRECTIONS:

1. Show the umbrella to the child and explain that umbrellas protect us from getting soaking wet when it is raining outside.
2. Drawing on what you know about the child's trauma history, explore the trauma symptoms that bother them the most. For example, the client might tense up and feel their heart racing when they hear a loud noise that reminds them of their trauma.
3. Identify one adaptive coping strategy the child finds useful during these times (e.g., star breathing) and write it on one of the colored panels of the umbrella. You will only want to identify and practice one coping strategy per session.
4. Rehearse the coping strategy with the client. For example, if star breathing is the child's chosen strategy, you will first practice it with them.
5. Once they feel competent in using the strategy, show the client a handful of colorful feathers.

Copyright © 2026 Paris Goodyear-Brown, *Big Behaviors in All Containers*. All rights reserved.

6. Stand on a chair (so that you are above the client) and have them hold the coping umbrella over their head. Pretend that their identified trauma symptom is present. Continuing with the previous example, you might say:

   "Okay, let's imagine you've heard a loud noise—just like the one you heard in the accident. Your belly is clenching, your teeth are gritting, your heart is racing [*these would all be physical responses the child has identified prior to this session*], and I am going to let the feathers fall. You protect yourself by doing your star breathing."

7. Once the client has rehearsed their adaptive coping strategy and you have let go of the feathers, you can highlight the fact that none of the trauma symptoms could touch them!

8. Write down the adaptive coping strategy you practiced today on a small drink umbrella, which can be used as a transitional object from the safety of the playroom to the child's other environments. It may also serve as a reminder to practice their adaptive coping response at home. You can also write the coping strategy on the *Singing in the Rain* template. Both the template and the actual umbrella can be sent home with the child after they have finished building their adaptive coping repertoire.

Copyright © 2026 Paris Goodyear-Brown, *Big Behaviors in All Containers*. All rights reserved.

SINGING IN THE RAIN TEMPLATE

Copyright © 2026 Paris Goodyear-Brown, *Big Behaviors in All Containers*. All rights reserved.

3.7 CHOICE AMPLIFIES VOICE

DESCRIPTION:

Children who have experienced trauma have, by definition, endured a loss of power and control. One of the processes for healing from trauma involves amplifying a child's sense of agency and autonomy. Offering the child a choice between equally good options is one way to increase their sense of agency, as choice amplifies voice. For example, if you offer the child snacks, make sure to present at least two choices. If you offer play therapy materials such as balloons, modeling clay, or pipe cleaners, be sure to have at least two or three colors available. These continual choices offer the child autonomy, even as they may stretch the child's window of tolerance for choosing. This exercise helps parents and teachers think through various ways that this process of offering choice and amplifying voice can happen in the school and home environment.

TREATMENT GOALS:

- Provide psychoeducation to the caregiver about how offering choices can increase the child's sense of their agency
- Assist the caregiver in cataloging the choices they can offer to their child

MATERIALS NEEDED:

- *Gumball Machine* handout
- Writing utensil

DIRECTIONS:

1. Explain how trauma impacts a child's sense of body autonomy. For example, if the child endured sexual abuse, you might say:

   "Your child was put in a position of powerlessness, where all choice for the use of their body was taken from them. All children should have the right to body autonomy, but your child had that stolen from them. They were also told that if they used their voice to get help, there would be consequences. One of the most corrective experiences we can give your child is to ask them *what they want* in many different categories. Asking whether they want a juice box or a Capri Sun offers one kind of choice. Asking them what shirt they'd like to wear to school can further amplify their voice and sense of agency. There are so many categories of day-to-day decision-making that may amplify the child's voice. You simply have to offer them."

2. Encourage the caregiver to think through their day-to-day activities and, on each gumball in the *Gumball Machine* handout, invite them to write a word for each category of choice they can offer their child. For example, they might write "breakfast options" in one of the gumballs. They might write "TV show" or "board game" in other gumballs.

Copyright © 2026 Paris Goodyear-Brown, *Big Behaviors in All Containers*. All rights reserved.

3. The power of this exercise is in helping caregivers understand the power they have to offer choices that respect the child's decision-making process.
4. Explain how the caregiver enhances their role as a Storykeeper by remembering the preferences of the child in their care. It can go a long way to say to a child, "I'm remembering about you that you really like the pink gumballs." While this one decision may seem inconsequential, think about how special it feels to go into a coffee shop and have the barista already know the way you like your coffee. Recording the child's choices as a Storykeeper may be the fastest way to enhance a child's sense of being deeply known, especially if they are in foster or adoptive care.

Copyright © 2026 Paris Goodyear-Brown, *Big Behaviors in All Containers*. All rights reserved.

GUMBALL MACHINE HANDOUT

Children need to practice choosing. Choosing, whether it is choosing the color of a gumball or choosing how to respond to a stressful situation, helps children develop a sense of agency. When children have big behaviors, it may be because they do not feel powerful. After all, grown-ups decide most things for children. By sharing power, you can enhance your child's personal power and autonomy and decrease their problematic displays of power. In each gumball, write one area in which you can give your child the gift of choice.

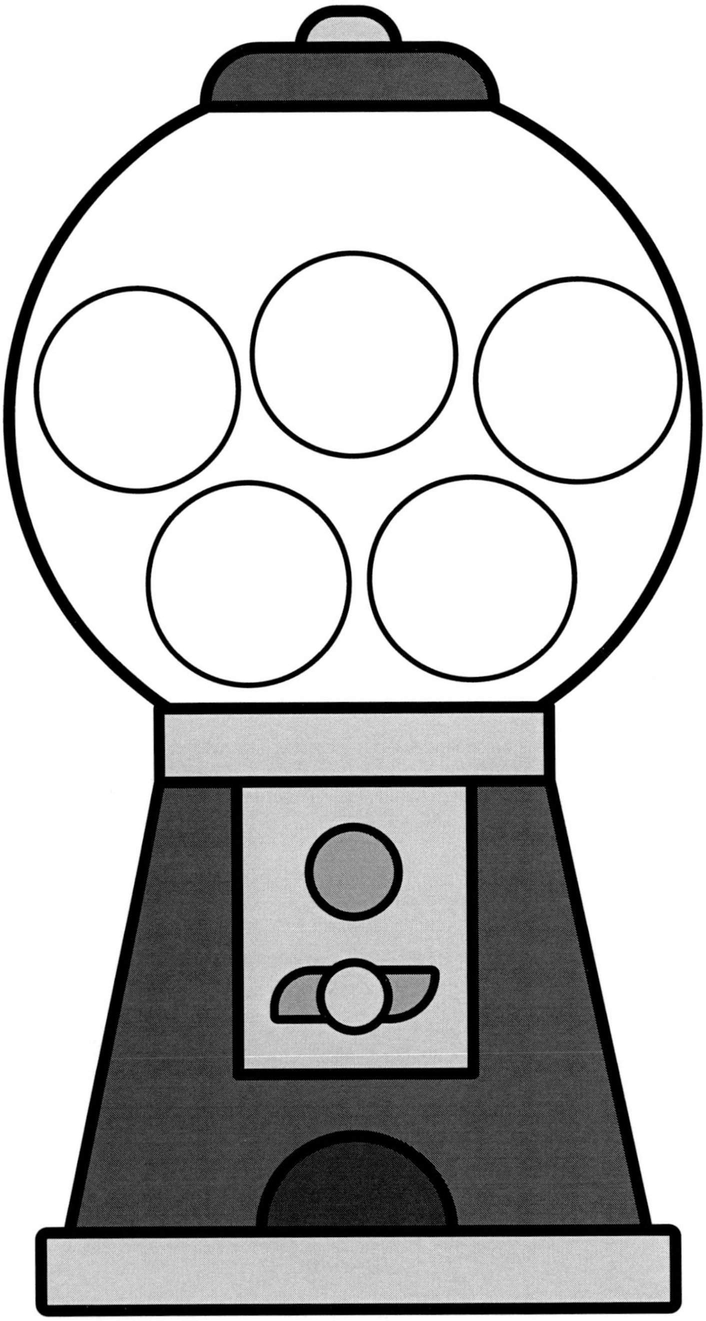

Copyright © 2026 Paris Goodyear-Brown, *Big Behaviors in All Containers*. All rights reserved.

four

Becoming a Safe Boss: Supporting the Dysregulated Child

This chapter explores the foundational importance of Safe Bosses for children who are easily dysregulated. No adult can be a Safe Boss in every single moment, but this chapter begins by exploring with caregivers what Unsafe Bosses look like. If you reflect on this question for yourself, thinking back over all the bosses you have had in your own life, Unsafe Bosses often engage in some sort of big behavior of their own: criticizing you, setting expectations that are too high for you to meet (often without giving you the tools to do what they have asked), being passive-aggressive, withholding attention or praise—the list goes on. In TraumaPlay, we view a child's dysregulated behavior through the lens of bottom-up brain development, and specifically the triune brain. The triune brain consists of three regions: the reptilian brain (which governs basic survival functions like heart rate and breathing), the limbic brain (which governs emotions and the stress response), and the neocortex (which governs higher-order thinking). These three brain regions are always asking the following questions:

- Reptilian brain: *Am I safe?*
- Limbic brain: *Am I loved?*
- Neocortex: *What can I learn from this?*

When a child is dysregulated, their reptilian brain is seeking an answer to the question *Am I safe?* If we believe that a child is asking this question, we can more easily move into the role of Safe Boss by setting limits for the child's safety in a way that supports ongoing attachment. For example, if a dysregulated child is attempting to run out the front door of the house in their distress, the grown-up sets a boundary, perhaps even standing in front of the door and offering to help the child regulate, while holding firmly to the rule that we stick together for safety. Some caregivers are too bossy and controlling in their limits, while others are too permissive. The research is clear that an authoritative parenting style that offers boundaries and choices, but with some freedom and shared power, makes for the most connected caregiver-child relationships while also socializing children to be helpful citizens of the world.

My favorite metaphor for Safe Boss behavior emerged the first time I put on a virtual reality (VR) headset. After strapping it around my head, I saw the room in a static-filled gray scale. The first prompt that came up in the headset was "Set your guardian." I took the haptic sensor I was holding in my hand and drew a circle all the way around myself. The next directive I was given was "Confirm your boundary." Once I had done this, play could commence. In VR, the physical boundary must be defined before you can be immersed in another world, as you can otherwise bang your knee against a coffee table or fall down a flight of stairs. It is equally true in the real world: Nothing else can occur—no exploration, no play, no attachment enhancement, no new learning—until boundaries are set. Therefore, the focus of this chapter is on helping caregivers learn how to set boundaries calmly and kindly, discern the unmet needs under their child's behavior, and determine whether a behavior requires discipline or soothing.

4.1 BET YOU'VE HAD A BOSS WHO . . .

DESCRIPTION:

Adult caregivers, whether they are parents, teachers, nannies, coaches, or doctors, are all meant to be a Safe Boss within the TraumaPlay framework. However, most adults have lived long enough to have had experiences with bosses who were unsafe in one or more ways. In fact, I have never had an adult client who couldn't identify someone in their life who had hurt them in some way due to a power differential in the relationship. This exercise is meant to help caregivers reflect on any abuses of power they have experienced in order to help them show up differently in their role as a Safe Boss to their child. The goal is to help them learn how to parent in a way that supports healthy attachment and development for the children in their care.

TREATMENT GOALS:

- Identify controlling or dictatorial adults in the caregiver's own early life
- Explore relational consequences of Unsafe Boss behavior
- Reopen the caregiver's ability to extend compassion to their own child

MATERIALS NEEDED:

- *Unsafe Boss* handout
- Writing utensil

DIRECTIONS:

1. Explain to the caregiver that this exercise is meant to identify characteristics of Unsafe Bosses.
2. Ask them to float backward in their memories and find a teacher, parent, older sibling, coach, tutor, babysitter, or extended family member who was given power or control over them in a way that hurt the client.
3. Ask the caregiver to circle characteristics from the *Unsafe Boss* handout that describe their experiences with this person.
4. Invite the caregiver to add their own adjectives to describe their experience of an Unsafe Boss.
5. If the caregiver is willing, invite them to process some of the specific experiences of injustice that they experienced.
6. As you move into the role of Storykeeper for the caregiver, you have an opportunity to provide a corrective emotional experience for the injustice done to them and the helplessness they felt as a result. This may reopen the caregiver's compassion well for the child currently in their care.

Copyright © 2026 Paris Goodyear-Brown, *Big Behaviors in All Containers*. All rights reserved.

UNSAFE BOSS HANDOUT

Are controlling

Minimize your concerns

Give you authority but no power

Are mean

Give commands

Are dismissive

Promote themselves

Don't listen

Laugh at you

Are critical

Are impatient

Don't allow feedback

Blame you for their mistakes

Copyright © 2026 Paris Goodyear-Brown, *Big Behaviors in All Containers*. All rights reserved.

4.2 SAFE BOSS CREED

DESCRIPTION:

Now that you have encouraged the caregiver to remember the Unsafe Bosses in their own life and examined the relational fallout and self-doubt caused by the Unsafe Bosses' behaviors, this intervention is focused on painting a picture of what a Safe Boss looks like. Some of the caregivers we work with, especially those who have experienced multiple adverse childhood experiences themselves, will not have had an adult who functioned in a Safe Boss role. This is why we introduce the Safe Boss creed, to serve as a set of qualities for the caregiver to embody while also offering some behavioral standards that engender felt safety in those they lead. You can return to this tool throughout treatment to celebrate parenting behaviors that fit these criteria.

TREATMENT GOALS:

- Highlight the importance of setting safe boundaries and expectations to support healthy development
- Identify characteristics of a Safe Boss

MATERIALS NEEDED:

- *Safe Boss Creed* handout
- Two different colored highlighters
- Sand tray miniatures (optional)

DIRECTIONS:

1. Reinforce the caregiver's learning from the previous session and connect this with what it means to be a Safe Boss: "Each of us has had experiences of Unsafe Bosses, those who use their power in a way that is hurtful to those they lead. So what is a Safe Boss then?"
2. Offer the caregiver the *Safe Boss Creed* handout and invite them to talk about any Safe Bosses they have experienced. If they are able to identify a Safe Boss in their own lives, ask them to identify any of the statements listed on the creed that they feel were true of that boss.
3. Read each statement out loud and process, as needed, examples of each kind of behavior.
4. Invite the caregiver to choose one color highlighter to highlight the characteristics of a Safe Boss that they already embody. Then invite them to use a different color highlighter to highlight the Safe Boss characteristics that they want to work toward.

Copyright © 2026 Paris Goodyear-Brown, *Big Behaviors in All Containers*. All rights reserved.

5. Explain that you will share a set of strategies for co-regulating their child as a Safe Boss as therapy progresses (e.g., the *Two-Choice Procedure* [4.10]).
6. After taking the caregiver through the Safe Boss creed, invite them to say out loud, "I am a Safe Boss."
7. Then invite them to make a gesture or take an embodied pose that represents an Unsafe Boss (for example, they might get in your personal space and point their finger at you while having an angry look on their face).
8. Next, invite them to make a gesture or take an embodied pose that represents a Safe Boss. This posture is likely to be more open and softened, opening their arms lovingly while having a curious or calm expression on their face. You can also use sand tray miniatures to represent each kind of boss, which can serve as visual icons for embodied states as therapy progresses.

Copyright © 2026 Paris Goodyear-Brown, *Big Behaviors in All Containers*. All rights reserved.

SAFE BOSS CREED HANDOUT

Highlight in one color all of the Safe Boss statements that you already think are true of you. Highlight in another color all of the Safe Boss statements that you are still stretching to become.

Safe Bosses function both in authority and under authority.

Safe Bosses delight in those they lead.

Safe Bosses assign good intentions to those they lead.

Safe Bosses set clear limits when needed.

Safe Bosses share power when possible.

Safe Bosses use their power to protect those they lead.

Safe Bosses can hold all the big feelings of those they lead.

Safe Bosses can hold the hard stories of those they lead.

Safe Bosses provide instruction when needed.

Safe Bosses help those under their authority practice new skills.

Safe Bosses earn the right to speak into the lives of those they lead.

Safe Bosses see the gifts in those they lead and know how to call them out.

Safe Bosses give the people they lead a clearly defined path for communicating problems, distress, or confusion.

Safe Bosses know what the people in their care are capable of and how to encourage them at their growing edges.

Copyright © 2026 Paris Goodyear-Brown, *Big Behaviors in All Containers*. All rights reserved.

4.3 SAFE BOSSES SET THE BOUNDARIES*

DESCRIPTION:

When TraumaPlay clinicians spend time observing caregiver-child dyads, it often becomes clear that some caregivers need help becoming more nurturing, while others need help providing more structure. This intervention helps caregivers understand the foundational role that the Safe Boss plays in setting limits and structuring a child's experiences in a way that supports ongoing attachment. For caregivers who need encouragement to provide additional structure in their caregiving, you can use a VR headset metaphor to shift their paradigm to *safety first*. Just like a VR game can't start until the "guardian boundary" is set, healthy play and connection between parents and children require clear boundaries to create a safe and enjoyable experience. This intervention uses the process of setting up a VR headset as a metaphor for defining personal and relational boundaries. Parents and children will work together to establish what they need to feel comfortable, safe, and engaged in shared play, ultimately strengthening communication and mutual respect.

TREATMENT GOALS:

- Assist the parent in defining the boundaries they need to set with their child prior to play or exploration
- Assist the child in defining the boundaries they need prior to play or exploration
- Facilitate conversation between the parent and child regarding what they both need to feel safe to engage in play together

MATERIALS NEEDED:

- VR headset (Meta Quest or similar)
- Open play space free of obstacles
- Paper and writing utensils for note-taking
- *Safe Bosses Set the Boundaries* handout

DIRECTIONS:

1. Remind the caregiver of the three roles you are working to embody with them (and that you hope they will eventually embody themselves): Safe Boss, Nurturer, and Storykeeper.
2. Of these three, emphasize that the Safe Boss is the most foundational. Even when a child is screaming at us and telling us, "You're not the boss of me, you can't tell me what to do!" there is a part of them desperately seeking someone who will provide structure and limits to help them grow and develop safely. Healthy development is really about titrated exploration of the world. For a child to feel free to explore, they need clear boundaries first.

* Created with Alyssa Meyer, MSW, LCSW, RPT-S.

Copyright © 2026 Paris Goodyear-Brown, *Big Behaviors in All Containers*. All rights reserved.

3. Use the VR metaphor introduced at the start of this chapter to further emphasize the importance of setting healthy limits. Use the following script:

   "Have you ever played a VR game? Once you put the headset on, the first thing it prompts you to do is to set your boundaries so you don't run into furniture or fall downstairs while you are immersed in the virtual world. It will often do so by saying something like 'Confirm your guardian.' You have to know where the boundaries are before you can begin to play. No play in the virtual world can begin until these boundaries are clearly set. This is true in our relationships with each other as well. Knowing where your boundaries need to be set to feel safe sets the stage for playful interaction."

4. Explore what boundaries they'd like to set in physical space first by helping answer questions, like "Where do you want your play area to be?" "What would feel like too much space or too little?" and "If this were an actual VR game, how would we make sure we don't bump into each other?"
5. Let the caregiver and the child take turns in the headset, using the haptic sensors to draw the circle around themselves that defines their virtual play space.
6. Offer each participant the *Safe Bosses Set the Boundaries* handout and invite them to write down the boundaries they need to feel safe to play or explore with each other.

Copyright © 2026 Paris Goodyear-Brown, *Big Behaviors in All Containers*. All rights reserved.

SAFE BOSSES SET THE BOUNDARIES HANDOUT

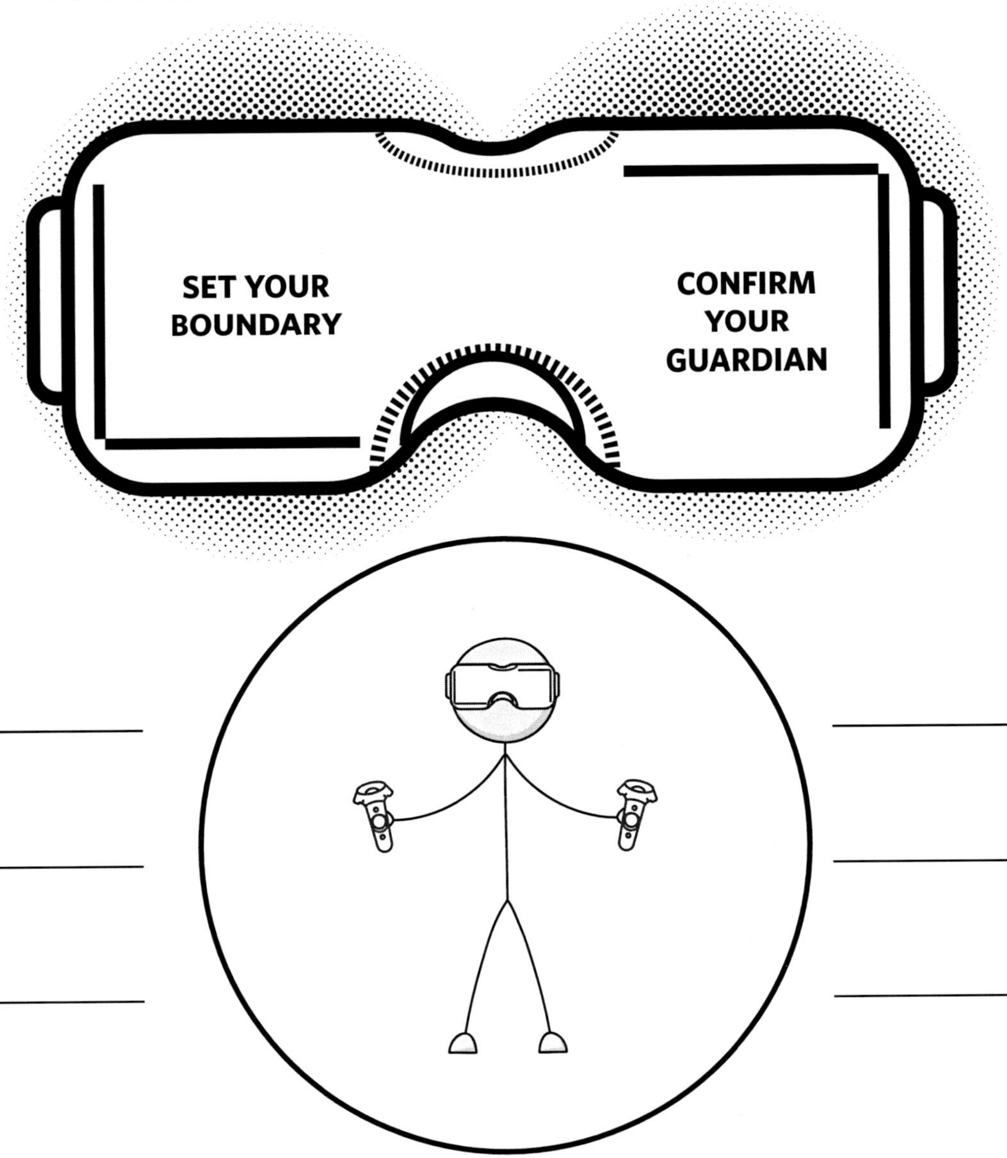

Copyright © 2026 Paris Goodyear-Brown, *Big Behaviors in All Containers*. All rights reserved.

4.4 BOUNDARIES FOR BOTH

DESCRIPTION:

Boundaries are a necessary part of caregiver-child relationships, but they can become blurred in all sorts of ways. For example, the boundaries that a grown-up sets might be overly rigid. Their caregiving mantra might be *It's my way or the highway*. The children in these caregiving systems may have very little voice, with no ability to even ask clarifying questions or negotiate getting their needs met. In other cases, a caregiver may treat their child more like a friend, giving too much adult content and asking for the child to meet the caregiver's needs. In still other cases, a child may be offered no privacy or boundaries of their own. Healthy caregiving systems negotiate a balance between independence and interdependence. This exercise allows you to begin exploring boundaries within the caregiver-child dyad.

TREATMENT GOALS:

- Identify the boundaries the caregiver sets in relation to the child
- Identify the boundaries the child is allowed or encouraged to have in the system
- Provide psychoeducation about the importance of interdependence and independence

MATERIALS NEEDED:

- *Door Hanger* handout
- Foam door hangers
- Craft materials (e.g., sequins, glitter, pom-poms, permanent markers)

DIRECTIONS:

1. Introduce the topic of boundaries to the caregiver and the child:

   "A boundary is something that separates one thing from another. Some families have lots and lots of boundaries, while other families have very few. For example, some kids tell their parents everything that happens to them, while others keep to themselves. Some kids have lots of toys they share with their siblings but have a few that stay in their own space, and family members have to ask permission before playing with them. Some teenagers can go into their parents' closet and borrow clothes anytime, while others have to ask to borrow a piece of clothing. Some kids have their own rooms, while others share with a sibling. In some families, kids can come into their parents' bedroom whenever they like, while in others, parents or kids lock their doors for privacy."

2. Explain that boundaries aren't right or wrong and that today you hope to learn more about the boundaries between family members.
3. Offer each person a foam door hanger. Ask them to each write down the three most important boundaries that are currently enforced in the family. Allow them to decorate this side of the door hanger with whatever craft materials they'd like. On the other side,

Copyright © 2026 Paris Goodyear-Brown, *Big Behaviors in All Containers*. All rights reserved.

invite them to list three (or more) boundaries they wish they could enforce in their family.

4. If you do not have foam door hangers on-site, feel free to use the attached *Door Hanger* handout instead.
5. As you process their door hangers, normalize the idea that while family members share lots of things, there may be areas they want to keep private. For example, is the teen allowed to have a diary that is kept private? Does this same rule of privacy apply to social media? This exercise leads to rich discussion and can become a jumping-off point for further exploration of interdependence and independence.

Copyright © 2026 Paris Goodyear-Brown, *Big Behaviors in All Containers*. All rights reserved.

DOOR HANGER HANDOUT

Write the boundaries that are most important to you.

1. ______________________________
____
____

2. ______________________________
____
____

3. ______________________________
____
____

Copyright © 2026 Paris Goodyear-Brown, *Big Behaviors in All Containers*. All rights reserved.

4.5 THE THREE ROOTS OF DISCIPLINE

DESCRIPTION:

Caregivers can feel overwhelmed by the number of discipline strategies they can use when children are having a big behavior. They may have competing voices in their heads, some of whom are saying, *You need to put that child in time out!* and others who are saying, *You need to show that child who's boss!* Still other voices might tell them to take things away from the child as a consequence or to ignore the child's behavior altogether. Just as TraumaPlay therapists follow the child's need in working through the components of trauma treatment, we also follow the child's need in moments when discipline of some kind is required. We have narrowed down discipline to three simple strategies, which are the focus of this intervention. Deciding which strategy to use is based on the root need.

TREATMENT GOALS:

- Provide three discipline strategies to the caregiver
- Assess which discipline strategy is attached to each root need

MATERIALS NEEDED:

- *Three Roots of Discipline* handout
- *What Is the Root?* handout

DIRECTIONS:

1. Acknowledge that when a child is engaging in a big behavior, deciding on a discipline strategy can be overwhelming. Explain to the caregiver that today they are going to learn three separate strategies, each of which traces back to an underlying need called *the root of discipline*. Let them know that you will take a deeper dive into each strategy in future sessions, but for today you'd like to introduce them to each strategy and its corresponding root.
2. Provide the caregiver with the *Three Roots of Discipline* handout as you explain the three different discipline strategies:

   "When the child's underlying need is safety—whether it's keeping the child safe, yourself safe, or the playroom safe—your strategy is to set limits and offer alternative uses for dangerous objects or alternative ways for getting underlying needs met.

   "The second strategy is to offer a redo. You offer a redo when the child's underlying need is to practice an adaptive behavior more or learn something new.

   "The third strategy is to ask for a compromise, in which the child gets some of what they want and you get some of what you want. You offer this strategy when a child's

Copyright © 2026 Paris Goodyear-Brown, *Big Behaviors in All Containers*. All rights reserved.

underlying need involves learning how to negotiate and express their needs. This strategy is critically important for children who were maltreated and neglected."

3. Help the caregiver reflect on their own child's behaviors. If you have any examples of the child's big behaviors that you can trace back to any of these root needs, offer these to the caregiver.
4. Give the caregiver the *What Is the Root?* handout.
5. Instruct them to use one tree per day whenever their child experiences a big behavior. Their homework assignment is to ask themselves, *What happened?* and then act like a detective by working backward to uncover the root need of discipline in this moment and the corresponding discipline strategy.

Copyright © 2026 Paris Goodyear-Brown, *Big Behaviors in All Containers*. All rights reserved.

THREE ROOTS OF DISCIPLINE HANDOUT

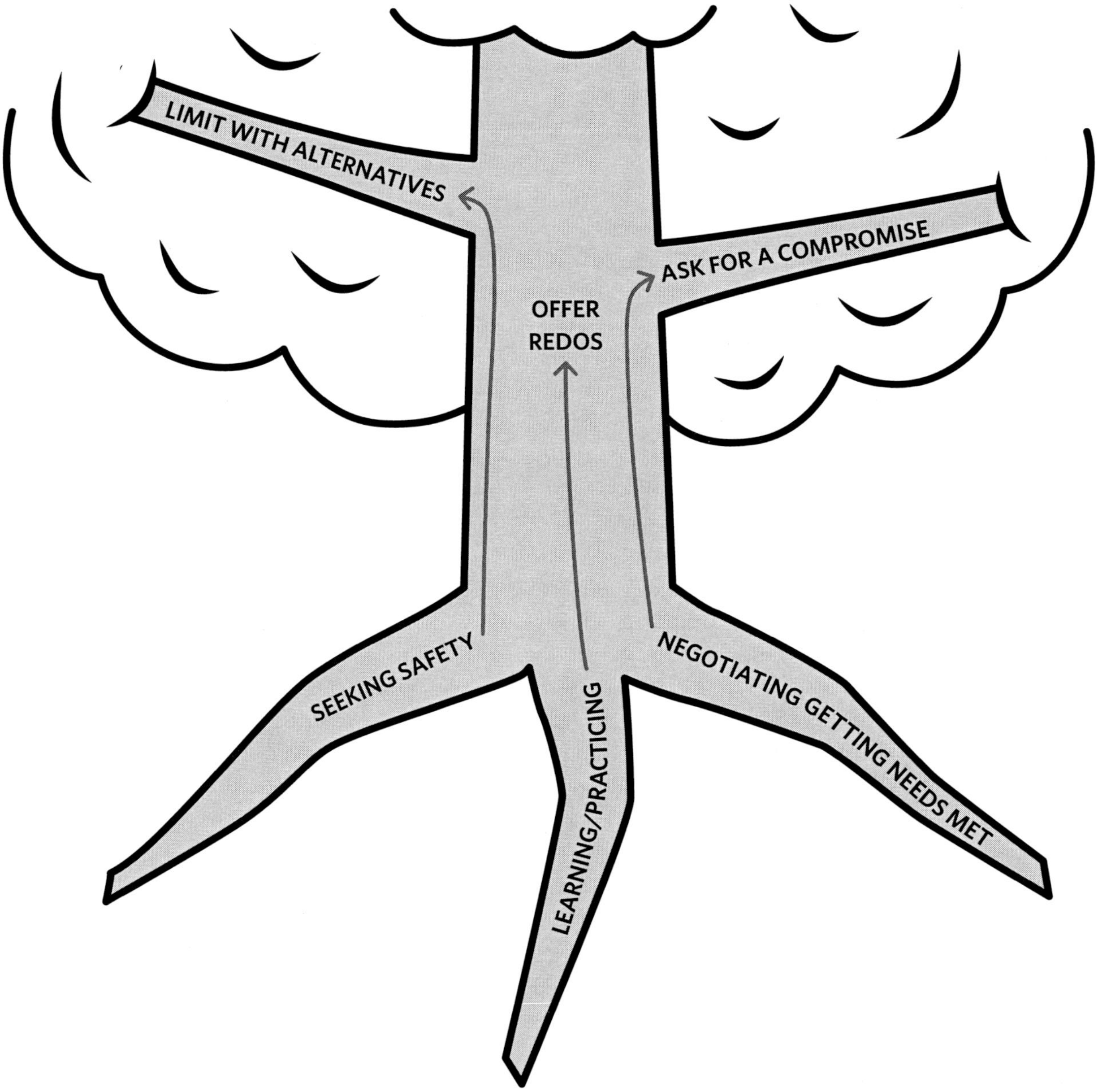

 Copyright © 2026 Paris Goodyear-Brown, *Big Behaviors in All Containers*. All rights reserved.

WHAT IS THE ROOT? HANDOUT

Write down the big behavior to the left of *The Three Roots of Discipline* tree. Then circle your guess for the root need underlying the attached discipline strategy.

What happened?

____

____

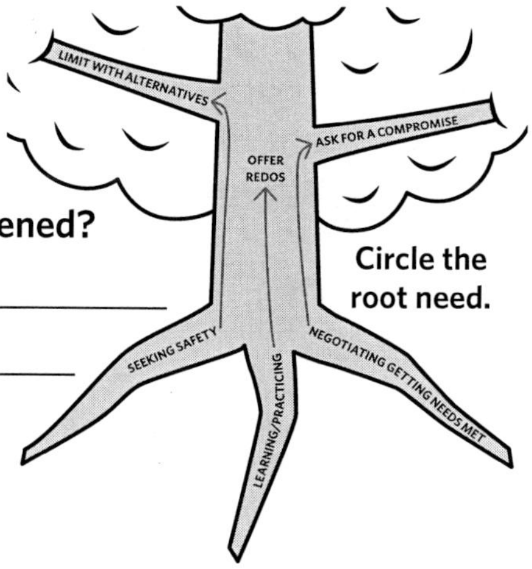

What happened?

____

____

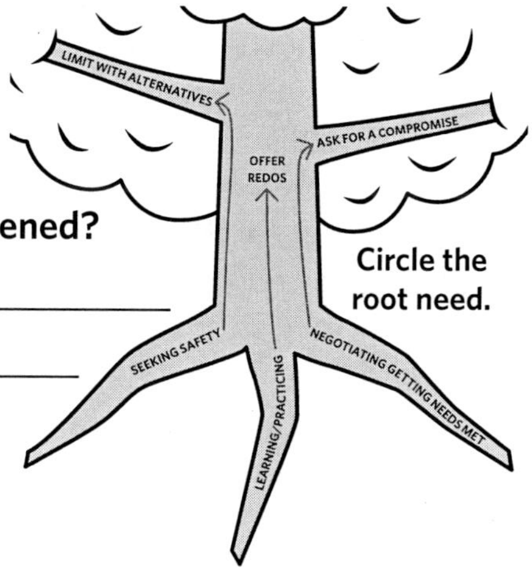

What happened?

____

____

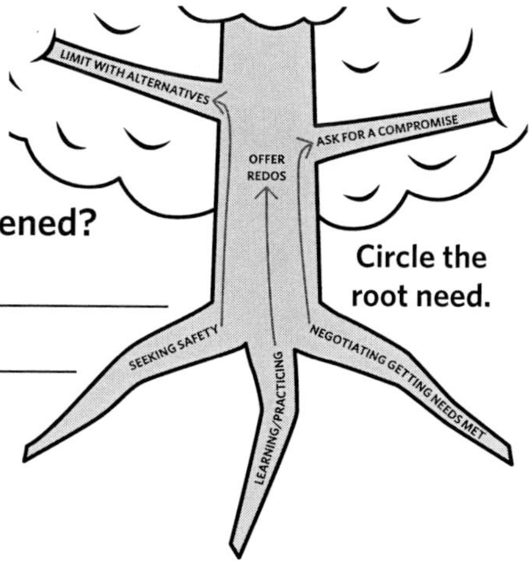

What happened?

____

____

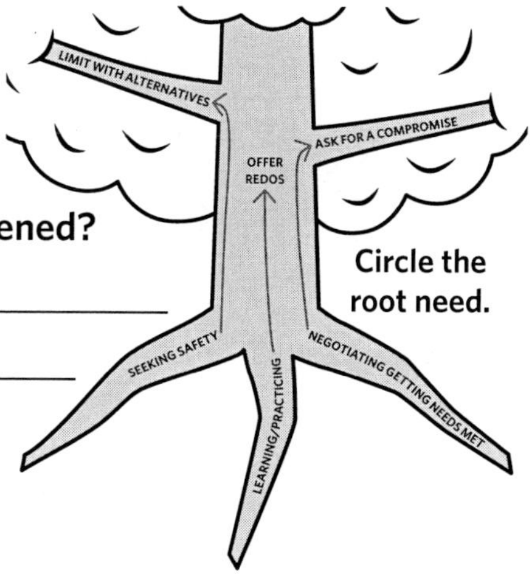

What happened?

____

____

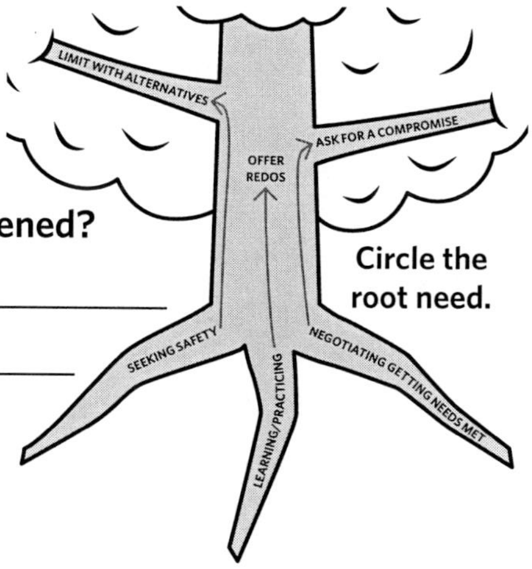

What happened?

____

____

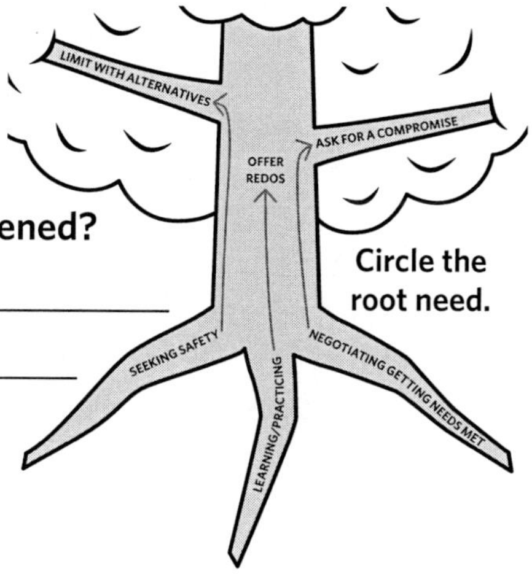

Copyright © 2026 Paris Goodyear-Brown, *Big Behaviors in All Containers*. All rights reserved.

4.6 OBJECTS AND OFFERS

DESCRIPTION:

This intervention offers a deeper dive into the correction strategy caregivers can use when the root of discipline is safety. In TraumaPlay, therapists train parents to shift the focus away from controlling the child and instead toward limiting the use of a specific object when there is a safety limit that needs to be enforced. For example, if the child is about to throw a handful of sand from the sand tray at the caregiver, the therapist coaches the parent to say, "The sand is not for throwing at me," as opposed to "You cannot throw sand on me" or "Stop it!" When children are corrected directly ("Johnny, put that down. Johnny, stop banging on that!"), it further arms the child's stress response and can actually escalate their behavior. If you instead say, "That sword is not for swinging at me. You may swing at the bop bag or the pillow," the child is protected from feeling like the target of the correction. You are simply talking about the uses and the prohibited uses of objects.

TREATMENT GOALS:

- Demonstrate ways to limit the use of an object (or action) instead of directing the correction at the child
- Provide examples of safe alternatives to problematic behavior

MATERIALS NEEDED:

- *Objects and Offers* handout

DIRECTIONS:

1. Use the following script to explain to the caregiver that many traumatized children have a control foundation instead of a trust foundation:

   "A trust foundation is developed after a child has expressed their needs and had them met over and over again across the first few years of life. For example, the baby is hungry, and the parent feeds the baby. These attuned caretaking behaviors build a belief in the child that the world is a pretty safe place and that the caregiver can be trusted. But when attachment trauma has led to many repetitions of the child expressing a need and not having it met by a caregiver, the child builds a belief that their caregivers cannot be trusted. In this case, what develops instead of a trust foundation is a control foundation. This child's core belief may be *I must control everything at all costs, or I'll die*. If we confront these children directly when they are acting out, demanding that they do something different from what they are doing, they may become even more dug into the behavior we are trying to change."

2. Offer two examples to illustrate this point:

   "For example, if Johnny is jumping on the couch, many caregivers would say, 'Johnny, stop jumping on the couch.' This statement shines a spotlight on the *child*, and

Copyright © 2026 Paris Goodyear-Brown, *Big Behaviors in All Containers*. All rights reserved.

children who need to feel powerful may dig in for control and even do the opposite of what is being asked. Using a child's name at the beginning of a correction can also increase their defensiveness and decrease their ability to shift gears into a new behavior. Instead of correcting the child directly, you limit the *use* of the object: 'The couch is not for jumping on.' Instead of Johnny being in trouble for jumping on the couch, information about the use of the couch is conveyed. You then offer alternatives for other ways the child can accomplish the same goal (in this case jumping): 'You can jump from tile to tile on the kitchen floor, or you can jump on the trampoline in the back yard.'

"Another example could involve a sibling. For example, when Johnny hits his sister, you might become quickly upset and yell, 'Johnny! You must not hit your sister!' This response may escalate the situation and doesn't offer any alternatives. Instead, you could say, 'Your sister is not for hitting. If you need to hit something, you can go hammer on your tool table or punch your pillow.' If the underlying need is to release anger that is stored in Johnny's body, you might say, 'Your sister is not for taking your anger out on. If you need to get your anger out of your body, you can stomp around the yard or punch the boxing bag.'"

3. Review the *What Is the Root?* handout from the previous session (*The Three Roots of Discipline* [4.5]) and identify a moment from the previous week when their child's use of an object (or their actions) became unsafe.
4. Brainstorm ways the caregiver can correct the child's behavior by limiting the use of objects and offering alternatives.
5. Introduce the *Objects and Offers* handout. Help the caregiver identify the object or action that needs to be limited. The top of the handout shows a circle with a line slashed through it, a universal communication that the symbol within it is off-limits. Invite the caregiver to draw a symbol for that object or action within this circle.
6. Explain that when we limit the use of an object or action, this can disconnect us emotionally from the child momentarily. None of us likes to be told no in any form. But when we offer an alternative, we are figuratively extending our hands to the child in an attempt to reconnect. We work to offer an acceptable way to meet the need underlying their original use of the object or action.
7. Support the caregiver in generating two alternatives for the use of the limited object or action and write one in the palm of each hand.

Copyright © 2026 Paris Goodyear-Brown, *Big Behaviors in All Containers*. All rights reserved.

OBJECTS AND OFFERS HANDOUT

Draw the limited object in here.

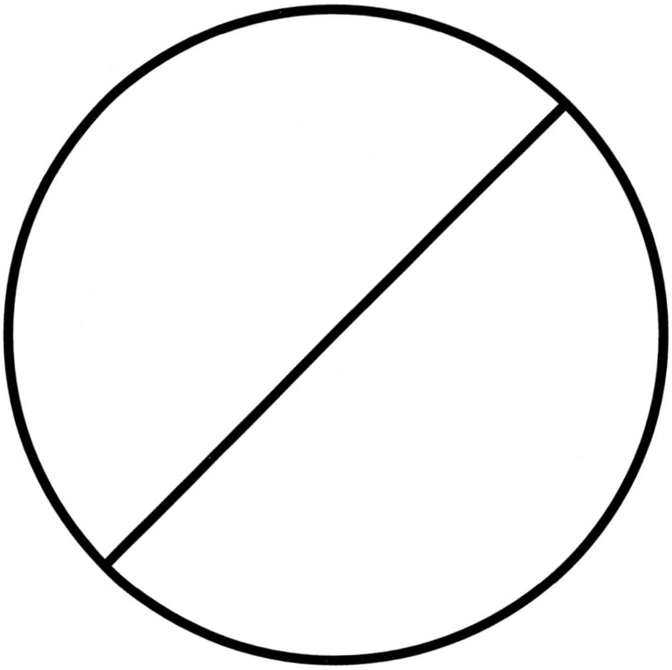

Write one alternative way to use the object, or one alternative action that can be taken, in each hand.

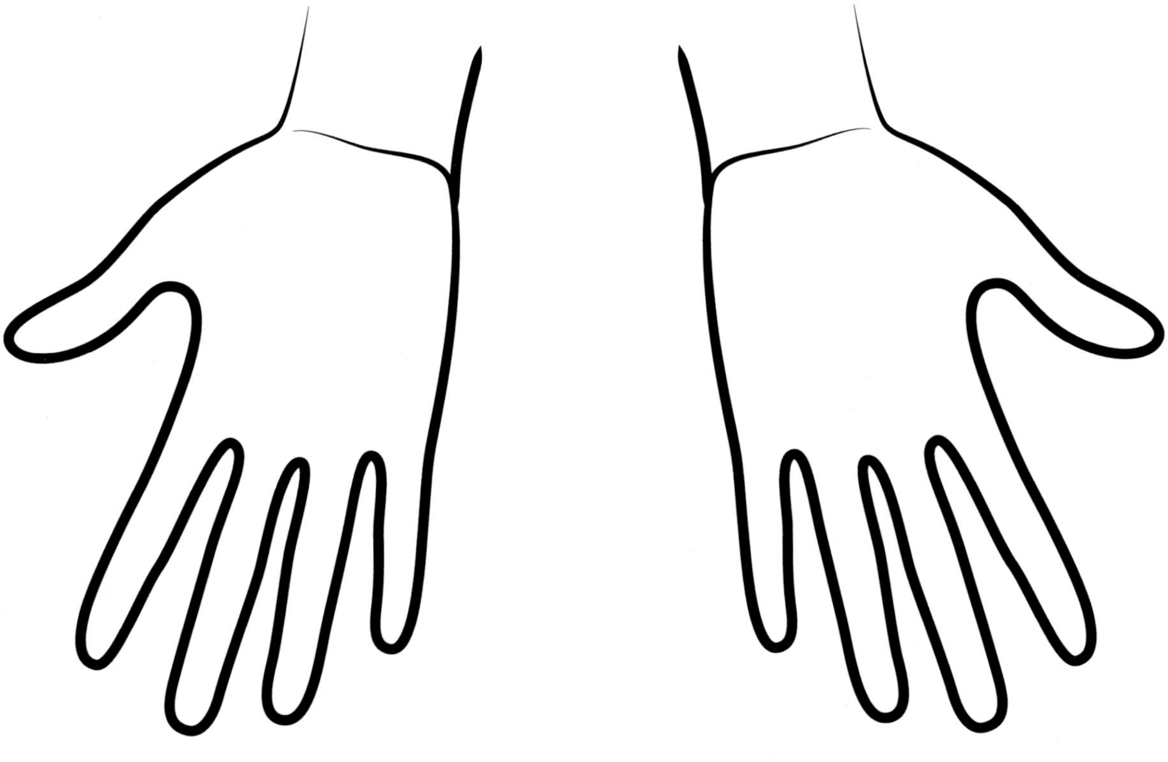

Copyright © 2026 Paris Goodyear-Brown, *Big Behaviors in All Containers*. All rights reserved.

4.7 RUTS AND REDOS

DESCRIPTION:

This intervention helps caregivers practice completing redos with their children when the root of discipline is learning something new or practicing something more. In TraumaPlay, we are not just trying to interrupt difficult behaviors; we are laying down new neural pathways that help kids build healthy relational habits. This process is akin to forming a rut in a dirt road. You form a rut in the road by driving over the same dirt path, again and again. In fact, once a rut forms, you may unconsciously drive over that same path time and time again, as it offers the path of least resistance. Similarly, you can mold a child's behaviors by having them repeat and rehearse these prosocial interactions over and over again, deepening adaptive neural pathways with practice. Laying down alternative pathways requires lots of practice, and one way to achieve this is by offering a redo, in which the child is given an opportunity to replace their big behavior with more adaptative behavior. This intervention is a concrete way to support the practice of redos, a technique outlined in Trust-Based Relational Intervention (TBRI; Purvis et al., 2013).

TREATMENT GOALS:

- Educate the caregiver about neural pathways and how new behaviors become habits
- Demonstrate the redo with behaviors that need correction
- Create specific redos for the caregiver to use with the child client

MATERIALS NEEDED:

- Sand tray with kinetic sand
- Sand tray miniatures, including wheeled vehicles and supplies for making pathways (e.g., stones, wood pieces, train tracks)
- Digging and molding tools

DIRECTIONS:

1. Explain to the caregiver that the *redo* is a strategy they can use when their child is having a big behavior and their underlying need is to practice or learn a more adaptive behavior. Offer an example to illustrate the redo:

    "Let's say two children are playing with toy cars together. Sally is playing with the golden Hummer car, which both children think is the coolest toy car. Johnny reaches out and grabs it from Sally. Some adults might say, 'Johnny, you can't grab toys from other children. Go to time out.' The thing is, time out can be wasted time for some children. They are sitting apart from the group, and there is no way to know whether they are actually thinking about their mistake or thinking about what they will eat for lunch. They are certainly not learning anything new or practicing anything more

Copyright © 2026 Paris Goodyear-Brown, *Big Behaviors in All Containers*. All rights reserved.

during that time. What if, instead of time out or other consequences, the adult simply offered a redo?"

2. Explain that a redo requires an adult to help a child practice a new behavior that can replace or extinguish the old behavior. Continue with the previous example to illustrate how this might look:

   "In the example above, the adult might say, 'Johnny, let's have a redo. It looks like you want a turn with the Hummer, so let's practice asking for it with your asking words.' The adult then has Johnny give the toy back to Sally and supports Johnny in asking for a turn: 'Okay, Johnny, can you ask her for the Hummer?' Johnny asks for the Hummer, and in the best-case scenario, Sally gives it to him right away. Sally may say no, and then she may need a redo that supports her practice of sharing. Perhaps Sally is coached to say, 'I'll take one more loop around the road, and then I'll give it to you.' Then Johnny might need to be supported in waiting patiently for his turn."

3. Explain that many grown-ups make the mistake of thinking that children should be able to just "work things out between them," but they often need help learning how to get their needs met before they can engage in this new pattern independently.

4. Explain that redos may need to be played out in full-body scenarios supported by the adult. In other words, the two children may need supported practice with the adult helping each child rehearse their part of the redo. For example, if Johnny grabs a toy out of Sally's hand (and in turn, Sally screams and hits him), the parent could put the toy back in Sally's hand, have Johnny ask to play with it appropriately (and wait for the answer), and then coach Sally on giving it to him or stating that she will play with it for one more minute and then give it to him. The children are supported all the way through the redo, and their positive practice is celebrated.

5. Create pathways in the kinetic sand as the caregiver articulates specific situations that may require redos with their own child. Explain that as the child continues to replace old behaviors with more adaptive behaviors, the pathways (or ruts) in the sand will get deeper over time until these new behaviors become habits.

6. Have the caregiver create deep pathways in the sand to represent the healthy relational habits the child already has laid down (things like "He always says please and thank you" or "She asks for what she needs now instead of demanding it") and more shallow pathways to represent those behaviors the child is still working to deepen (things like "He often puts his sister down when she is trying to share something with him" or "She often says negative things about herself when she misses a homework problem").

Copyright © 2026 Paris Goodyear-Brown, *Big Behaviors in All Containers*. All rights reserved.

4.8 TAKE TWO

DESCRIPTION:

This intervention offers caregivers another playful way to engage in redos with a child who is practicing a new skill or behavior. It uses the analogy of a movie, in which a director asks to "take two" when they want to try filming a scene a different way. This type of playful practice is always easier for children, and it increases the likelihood that they will identify their own behavioral missteps and practice the behavior they wish they had chosen instead.

TREATMENT GOALS:

- Practice turning new adaptive behaviors into habits
- Demonstrate "taking two" with behaviors that need correction
- Role-play doing a take two with puppets

MATERIALS NEEDED:

- *Take Two* handout (several blank copies)
- Two real clapboards
- A variety of puppets

DIRECTIONS:

1. Offer the caregiver and the child each a physical clapboard while explaining the following:

   "Do you have times when you said something you wish you hadn't or did something you wish you could do again differently? Well, that's what take twos are for. In the movies, they try a scene one way, then yell cut, write the new take on the clapboard, clap the board, and do the scene again. In here we will practice getting to do just that."

2. Offer each person a *Take Two* handout. Invite them to think of a relational situation from the last few weeks that they wish they could have handled differently. Invite them to label this scene on their clapboard. They might title it *The Night I Yelled at You* or *When I Sent You to Your Room*. Any title that makes sense to the client is fine.
3. Have them describe the scene as it happened, in writing or verbally. Make sure that each section of the clapboard is filled in. For example, if the child demanded milk, you might fill in the clapboard this way:
   a. Scene: *Johnny Demanded Milk*
   b. My need: For Johnny to respect me.

Copyright © 2026 Paris Goodyear-Brown, *Big Behaviors in All Containers*. All rights reserved.

c. My action: I yelled at him, "I'm not your servant!"

d. Their response: He screamed and stomped off.

4. If the dyad is open to it, invite conversation about how it felt to be on either side of the interaction that occurred.
5. Invite them to write down the way they wished they had handled the interaction instead. Invite them to give this second take a title just like they titled the original interaction.
   a. Scene: *Johnny Demanded Milk* (Take Two)
   b. My need: For Johnny to ask me instead of giving me commands.
   c. My action: I offer the words, "May I have some milk please?"
   d. Their response: He repeats my words, gets practice in asking for what he needs, and I stay in my Safe Boss self.
6. Invite them to use the real clapboards to say out loud the name of the second take while clapping the board (this part can be very satisfying for clients) and ask them to act out the scenarios using puppets.
7. If the child is old enough to engage in therapeutic homework, give the dyad extra blank copies of the *Take Two* handout and explain that this week, they each get to use the take two. If either one of them engages in a behavior they wish they could redo, they can just say, "Can I take two please?" and try again in a more regulated way.
8. Invite them to bring their homework back next week for processing.

Copyright © 2026 Paris Goodyear-Brown, *Big Behaviors in All Containers*. All rights reserved.

TAKE TWO HANDOUT

Scene: Name the event.

My need: Write down a short phrase to describe what you needed from the interaction.

My action: Write down the way you want to communicate that in words and deeds.

Their response: How did the other person respond? How did that feel to you?

Copyright © 2026 Paris Goodyear-Brown, *Big Behaviors in All Containers*. All rights reserved.

4.9 THE CHOOSING MIND

DESCRIPTION:

When a child is exhibiting big behaviors, they are often so dysregulated that they are unable to access their neocortex to weigh in on their choices. In other words, they are not in their *choosing mind*. Helping the child come back to regulation needs to be our first goal in times like this. When a child is not in their choosing mind, they may appear as if they are making an intentional choice to misbehave, when the truth is that their autonomic nervous system has been taken over. In these moments, the role of the caregiver as Storykeeper becomes important. The caregiver often needs to narrate what has happened to throw the child outside of their window of tolerance, as having their experience verbally organized to them by a trusted caregiver can help them come back into their choosing mind. This intervention provides psychoeducation to the caregiver to help them understand times in which they must step in as a Storykeeper to help their child co-regulate more effectively.

TREATMENT GOALS:

- Educate the caregiver about regulation and dysregulation
- Describe when to offer choices to the child with big behaviors versus when to co-regulate with the child
- Shift thinking around big behaviors with the question *Is the child in their choosing mind?*

MATERIALS NEEDED:

- *The Guiding Question* handout

DIRECTIONS:

1. Provide *The Guiding Question* handout to the caregiver. Explain that deciding on which discipline strategy to use with their child can be confusing. Sometimes, children will benefit from being given choices, while other times they are in need of co-regulation. Traumatized children may need both methods in the same day, or even within the same hour. When deciding on which discipline strategy to use, grown-ups should always ask themselves this question whenever they are confronted with a child's big behavior: *Is the child in their choosing mind?*
2. Provide the caregiver with an example to illustrate what it means to be in a choosing mind:

   "Let's say it is 9 a.m., and three-year-old Sally has had a good night's sleep and a good breakfast, and she is making up puppet plays with her mother in the playroom. Mom says, 'Please put on your shoes. It's time to go to the store, and then we will go to the park.' Sally says no and runs away. If Mom asks herself, *Is Sally in her choosing mind?* the answer will likely be yes because Sally is regulated. She is rested and fed,

Copyright © 2026 Paris Goodyear-Brown, *Big Behaviors in All Containers*. All rights reserved.

and her thinking brain is on board. She simply doesn't want to stop playing. Mom can say, 'You have two choices. You can choose to put your shoes on quickly, and we will have time to go to the park after the store. Or you can choose to take longer to put them on, in which case we won't have time to go to the park.'

"Here, Mom sets up the behavior she wants to see as one choice and the natural consequence of not doing that behavior as the other choice. Hopefully, Sally chooses to put her shoes on quickly, and they get to go to the park. But even if she doesn't, it will still be good learning for her because her thinking brain was engaged at the time she made the choice."

3. Provide the caregiver with an example to illustrate what it means to *not* be in a choosing mind:

   "Let's say it's 9 p.m., and Sally and her mom have been out running errands all day. Sally did not get a good nap and had fast food for dinner. Sally and her mom are both exhausted. Mom tells Sally to put her pajamas on, and Sally yells, 'I'm not gonna!' She is clearly overtired and outside her normal window of tolerance for distress. At this point, if the mom offers choices (e.g., telling Sally she can put on her pajamas quickly or lose her book privileges at bedtime), she will be setting Sally up for failure because Sally has outlasted her ability to regulate herself. She needs her mother to come in closer and co-regulate her instead."

4. Explain what it means to co-regulate in this situation. Practically speaking, this often means treating the child as if they are a couple of years younger than their chronological age. That's because stress decreases our connection to our neocortex and can be seen as providing an almost developmental delay. In Sally's example, the mom might become Storykeeper for Sally by saying, "I'm remembering that you didn't get a nap today and are so tired! Here, I'll hold your pajamas and help you get your legs in. One leg in . . . good job! Other leg in . . . good job." Then Mom can carry Sally to the bed, give her a big squeeze, and tuck her in. As with Sally's example, emphasize to the caregiver that there will be times when their child is in a choosing mind and will benefit from consequences (even if they don't feel good), and other times when they will not be able to choose and will need the caregiver to co-regulate them through a hard moment.

5. Explain that you will be equipping the caregiver with two strategies they can use depending on whether their child is in their choosing mind: *Two-Choice Procedure* (4.10) and *SOOTHE Strategies* (5.1).

Copyright © 2026 Paris Goodyear-Brown, *Big Behaviors in All Containers*. All rights reserved.

THE GUIDING QUESTION HANDOUT

THE GUIDING QUESTION:

Is the child in their choosing mind?

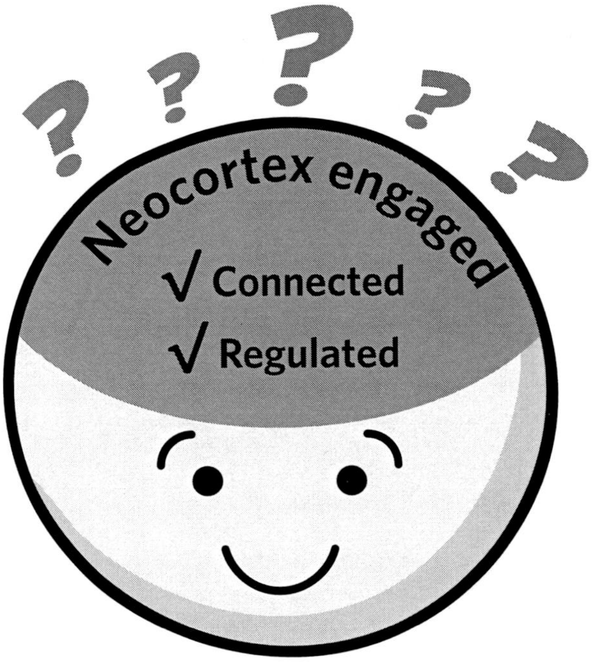

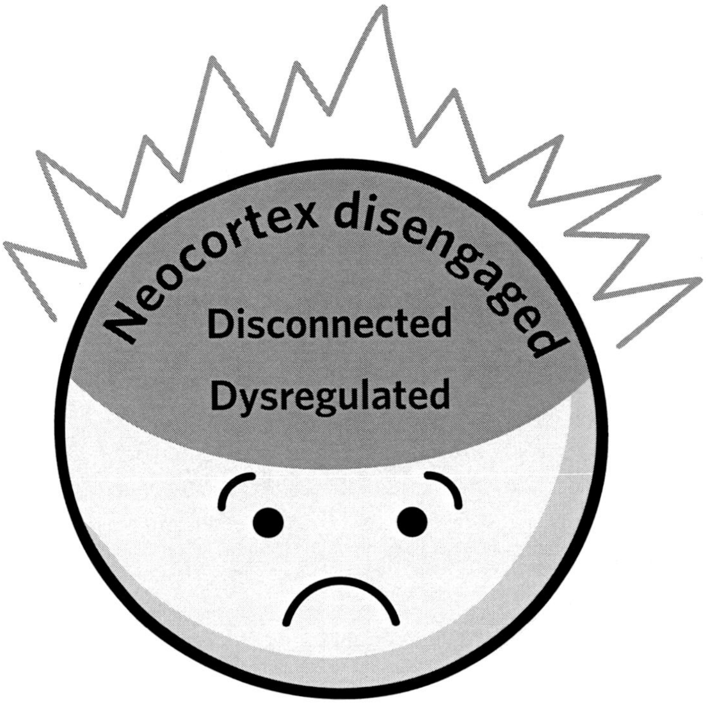

Copyright © 2026 Paris Goodyear-Brown, *Big Behaviors in All Containers*. All rights reserved.

4.10 TWO-CHOICE PROCEDURE

DESCRIPTION:

This intervention offers a very practical strategy caregivers can use to provide more structure for a child who needs it. Two different pathways for offering choices are provided, with each tracking backward to the need that underlies the two choices offered. Some children are in their choosing mind (e.g., regulated, connected to their caregiver). When choices are offered to these children, the goal is to help them experience the consequence, positive or negative, of their choice in order to help them learn to choose good things for themselves. Other children, particularly those with complex trauma, have not had a Safe Boss historically. In fact, they have often had only hurtful or dangerous grown-ups in charge. These children may be asking a core question: *Is there anyone I can trust to care for me?* The goal is to help these children learn that their caregiver is available to help.

TREATMENT GOALS:

- Educate the caregiver about the two-choice procedure
- Help the caregiver discern which choices to offer based on the availability of the child's choosing mind

MATERIALS NEEDED:

- *Two Choices* handout (several blank copies)

DIRECTIONS:

1. Explain to the caregiver that when a child is in their choosing mind, the focus of discipline is on helping them choose good outcomes. For example, they can tell the child: "You have two choices: You can choose to put your shoes on quickly and we will have time to go to the park, but if you choose to take longer than [*insert time frame here*] to put your shoes on, we won't have time to go to the park."
2. Role-play several choosing mind scenarios. For example, if their child often struggles with getting out of bed in the morning, you might role-play how to offer two choices: "You can choose to get out of bed on time to put your clothes on and have breakfast, or I will put your school clothes and your breakfast bar in the car. You can choose to change on the way to school or change at school."
3. Discuss with the caregiver that there are also times when a child is not in their choosing mind. This includes times when the child didn't get to sleep until two o'clock in the morning. In this case, the Storykeeper might say, "I'm remembering about you that you didn't get to sleep for long. You can choose to put your clothes on yourself, or I can help you put your school clothes on." This example of two choices is most important when a child is clearly outside of their window of tolerance or doesn't have a trust-based relationship yet with their caregiver. Those children who were hurt by Unsafe Bosses

Copyright © 2026 Paris Goodyear-Brown, *Big Behaviors in All Containers*. All rights reserved.

early in life don't have the core belief that their caregiver can be trusted to help them. When these children act out, the focus is to enhance attachment and build trust.

4. Role-play several scenarios in which the caregiver can offer support in each of these ways.
5. Offer the caregivers extra blank copies of the *Two Choices* handout and instruct them to practice offering their child two choices once daily for the next week, depending on the child's needs in that moment. Explain that they will bring this back and review it with you at the next session.

Copyright © 2026 Paris Goodyear-Brown, *Big Behaviors in All Containers*. All rights reserved.

TWO CHOICES HANDOUT

TWO CHOICES:
When focus is enhancing attachment and building trust

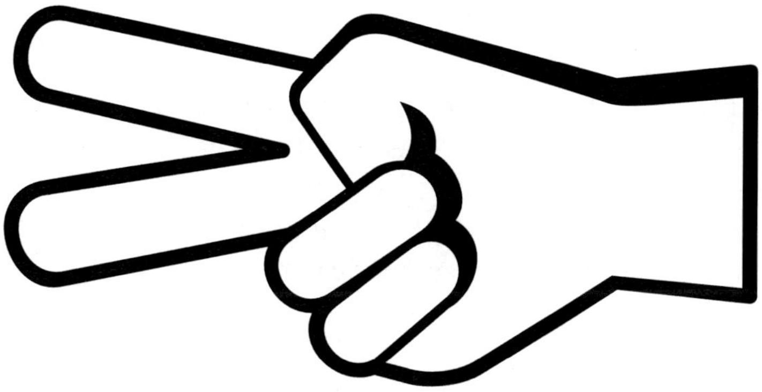

You can choose to ____________,
or I can help you do it.

The first choice is doing the thing you asked. The other choice is doing it with your support in some way.

TWO CHOICES:
When focus is learning to choose good outcomes

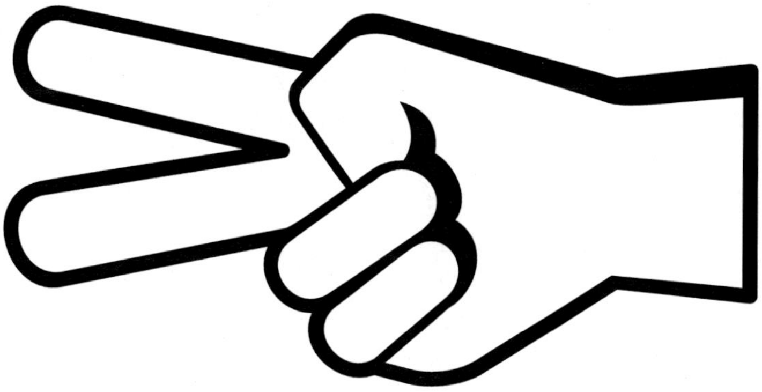

You can choose to ____________
or ____________.

The first choice is doing the thing you asked. The other choice is a natural consequence of not doing it.

Copyright © 2026 Paris Goodyear-Brown, *Big Behaviors in All Containers*. All rights reserved.

4.11 KEEPING YOUR COMPASSION WELL OPEN

DESCRIPTION:

Caregivers of children with big behaviors often show up to treatment exhausted by their interactions with their child. They may even feel disgusted by the time they seek help—disgusted with the child and with themselves. This disgust is a human response to the helplessness they feel to change their child's behavior. Most caregivers, especially those who are foster or adoptive parents, begin in a place of compassion for a child's big behaviors. However, the daily grind of co-regulating and correcting the angry or anxious child (especially while keeping other children in the family safe from the tantrums and escalations) can drain the well. In some cases, parents or teachers have such compassion fatigue that they have trouble remaining connected to their child. This exercise can be helpful to do just after the *Threading the Needle* exercise (10.1), as examining the child's history can reopen the compassion well of parents who are so immersed in the day-to-day tensions with their child that they have forgotten the unmet needs underlying the big behaviors.

TREATMENT GOALS:

- Provide psychoeducation around compassion fatigue to caregivers
- Help the caregiver identify self-care strategies, mindful mantras, and reminders of the child's early history that help their compassion well remain open and filled

MATERIALS NEEDED:

- *Compassion Well* handout (several blank copies)
- Sand tray and miniatures

DIRECTIONS:

1. Explain the concept of a compassion well to the caregiver using the following script:

   "You have been caring for this child with big behaviors day in and day out for a long time. Most caregivers start out with a heart full of compassion and lots of hope for change. But co-regulating your child through tantrums day after day, losing sleep because of the big behaviors, learning to dread the daily (weekly?) calls from the school, and worrying about how these behaviors are affecting your other children or your relationship all take a toll on your compassion. Some parents report feeling numb or disconnected, but your compassion is still in there. We think about it as a well of compassion. That well can get drained from all the hard things, but we've found two things that help refill the well: (1) reminders of the vulnerable, hurt child within the big behaviors and (2) self-care strategies that help you replenish your mind, body, and emotions."

Copyright © 2026 Paris Goodyear-Brown, *Big Behaviors in All Containers*. All rights reserved.

2. Referencing the *Threading the Needle* exercise (10.1), ask the caregiver for a piece of developmental information about the child that sparks their compassion. For example, their child may have been abandoned by a river, had painful medical procedures, or been born addicted to methamphetamine.
3. Introduce the *Compassion Well* handout and ask the caregiver to write down any reminders about the child's history that spark their compassion on the roof slats of the well.
4. On the stones around the well, ask them to identify what behaviors, rituals, or routines they use to take care of themselves. Examples might include exercise, a night out with friends, or a spiritual practice.
5. Finally, explain that rehearsing positive mantras can also help keep their compassion wells open. Help them identify or create two or three statements they can say to themselves that will spark compassion, like *I am bigger, stronger, wiser, and kind;*[*] *This is happening around me, not to me*; or *I have lots of love to give*. There are no right or wrong mantras; the only criterion is that they make it easier for the caregiver to connect with the child in their care. Ask them to write these statements around the well.

---

* Adapted from Coyne et al. (2019).

Copyright © 2026 Paris Goodyear-Brown, *Big Behaviors in All Containers*. All rights reserved.

COMPASSION WELL HANDOUT

Write the statements, mantras, and truths about you and your child that keep your compassion well full.

YOUR COMPASSION WELL

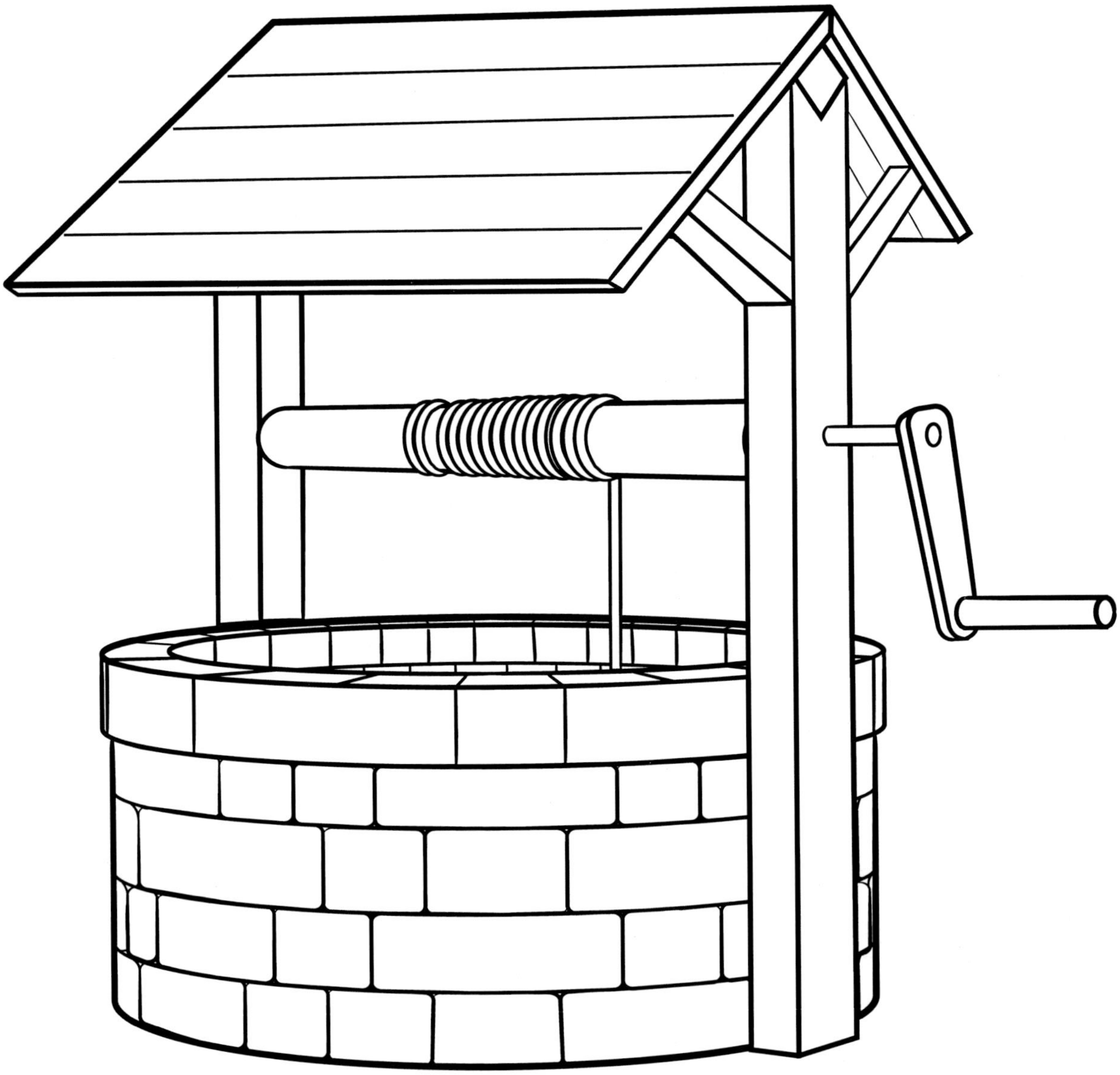

Copyright © 2026 Paris Goodyear-Brown, *Big Behaviors in All Containers*. All rights reserved.

five

Co-Regulation for Caregivers

Co-regulation always precedes self-regulation (Goodyear-Brown, 2021). From the moment a baby is born, the good-enough caregiver begins to co-regulate with them, as babies are born with very few ways to regulate themselves. They are protected from dangers by their Safe Bosses, they are breastfed or bottle-fed by their Nurturers, and their caregivers learn to become Storykeepers by discerning which cry means "I'm hungry," "I'm cold," "I'm scared," "I'm tired," or "I'm lonely." Each time the child expresses a need and the caregiver meets this need, it reflects a moment of co-regulation.

Children require thousands of repetitions of first being soothed by *others* before they can internalize this soothing and do it for themselves. Consider an infant who wakes up from sleep in a panic—they are wet, hungry, and crying at the top of their lungs. In turn, the parent picks the baby up, holds them close, and says, "Shhhh, shhhh, I've got you. I'm here." The baby feels the parent's warmth, hears the parent's soothing tone, and begins to relax, molding their body to their parent's. This co-regulation is satisfying for the parent and the child alike.

This cycle happens thousands of times in the first year of life: The infant wakes suddenly from napping, the infant cries for their parent, and their parent comes and co-regulates them. As the baby grows older, they begin to anticipate that the soothing is coming. For example, when the baby is eight months old, they wake up from a nap crying, hear the parent's footsteps on the stairs, and stop crying, as they anticipate the soothing that is almost there. They can manage themselves and exert self-control for the few seconds it takes for the parent to arrive. This process of anticipating the soothing that is to come signals the start of the child's ability to soothe themselves. The older children get, the more they can engage in self-soothing strategies that allow them to comfort themselves until they can return to the comforting presence of their caregiver.

The previous chapter offers a variety of discipline strategies that caregivers can use depending on whether a child is in their choosing mind. In this chapter, I unpack several co-regulation strategies caregivers can use when a child is *not* in their choosing mind. These strategies are codified in the acronym SOOTHE: Soft tone of voice and face, Organize, Offer, Touch/physical proximity, Hear the underlying anxiety, and End and let go.

5.1 SOOTHE STRATEGIES

DESCRIPTION:

This exercise introduces the caregiver to a set of co-regulation strategies they can use when a child is not in their choosing mind. While each strategy will be broken down and more thoroughly explained in subsequent exercises, an initial introduction is offered here first. Caregivers often need to hear things several times before a paradigm shift occurs. They will also need to practice each strategy multiple times before they will feel competent in implementing it in their day-to-day caregiving.

TREATMENT GOALS:

- Reinforce the idea that co-regulation by the caregiver always precedes self-regulation
- Introduce a set of co-regulation strategies to the caregiver

MATERIALS NEEDED:

- *SOOTHE* handout
- *SOOTHE Tracking Tool* handout

DIRECTIONS:

1. Remind the caregiver of the example you gave regarding three-year-old Sally in *The Choosing Mind* exercise (4.9). You can use the following script:

    "Remember the example I gave of three-year-old Sally being told to put her pajamas on late at night? It became clear that Sally was not in her choosing mind. She had outlasted her ability to regulate herself, and she needed her caregiver to come closer and co-regulate her more overtly. When a child is not in their choosing mind, the co-regulation strategies named in the acronym SOOTHE offer a treasure trove of powerful tools that help you stay connected to your child while being their Safe Boss, Nurturer, and Storykeeper. I will explain what each letter stands for in this session, and we will spend time unpacking each strategy in future sessions."

2. Offer the caregiver a copy of the *SOOTHE* handout and explain what each part of the acronym represents:

    "The *S* in SOOTHE stands for *soft tone of voice and face*. This has to do with enhancing your self-awareness around how the stress, tension, anger, and so forth in your face (or the harsh tone in your voice) may cue your child's threat response to activate.

    "The first *O* stands for *organize*. This has to do with organizing your child's daily schedule and routines and setting expectations for how their time away from you will be organized.

Copyright © 2026 Paris Goodyear-Brown, *Big Behaviors in All Containers*. All rights reserved.

"The second *O* stands for *offer*. This has to do with how you offer parameters of choice to dysregulated children and how you offer a way out when a child is dug into a big behavior.

"The *T* stands for *touch*. Offering nurturing touch is a powerful way to soothe a child in distress. You can also use the power of physical proximity when touch is not an option, which we'll talk about later.

"The *H* stands for *hearing the anxiety* that often underlies your child's NO and responding in a way that storykeeps their anxiety.

"Finally, the *E* stands for *end and let go*, which has to do with helping your child return all the way back to baseline in behavior so that you are not putting out fires all day and night and letting go of the tension and frustration you may have felt while weathering your child's behavioral storm."

3. Explain that you will unpack each strategy more deeply with the caregiver.
4. Offer the *SOOTHE Tracking Tool* handout to the caregiver. Explain that their homework over the next week will be to use a SOOTHE strategy whenever their child is engaged in a big behavior. Remind them that figuring out what a child needs in these moments can be challenging. Some trials may end well, while other times the caregiver may feel like they have failed. Remind them that you are helping them lay down new competencies and encourage them to be patient with themselves.

Copyright © 2026 Paris Goodyear-Brown, *Big Behaviors in All Containers*. All rights reserved.

SOOTHE HANDOUT

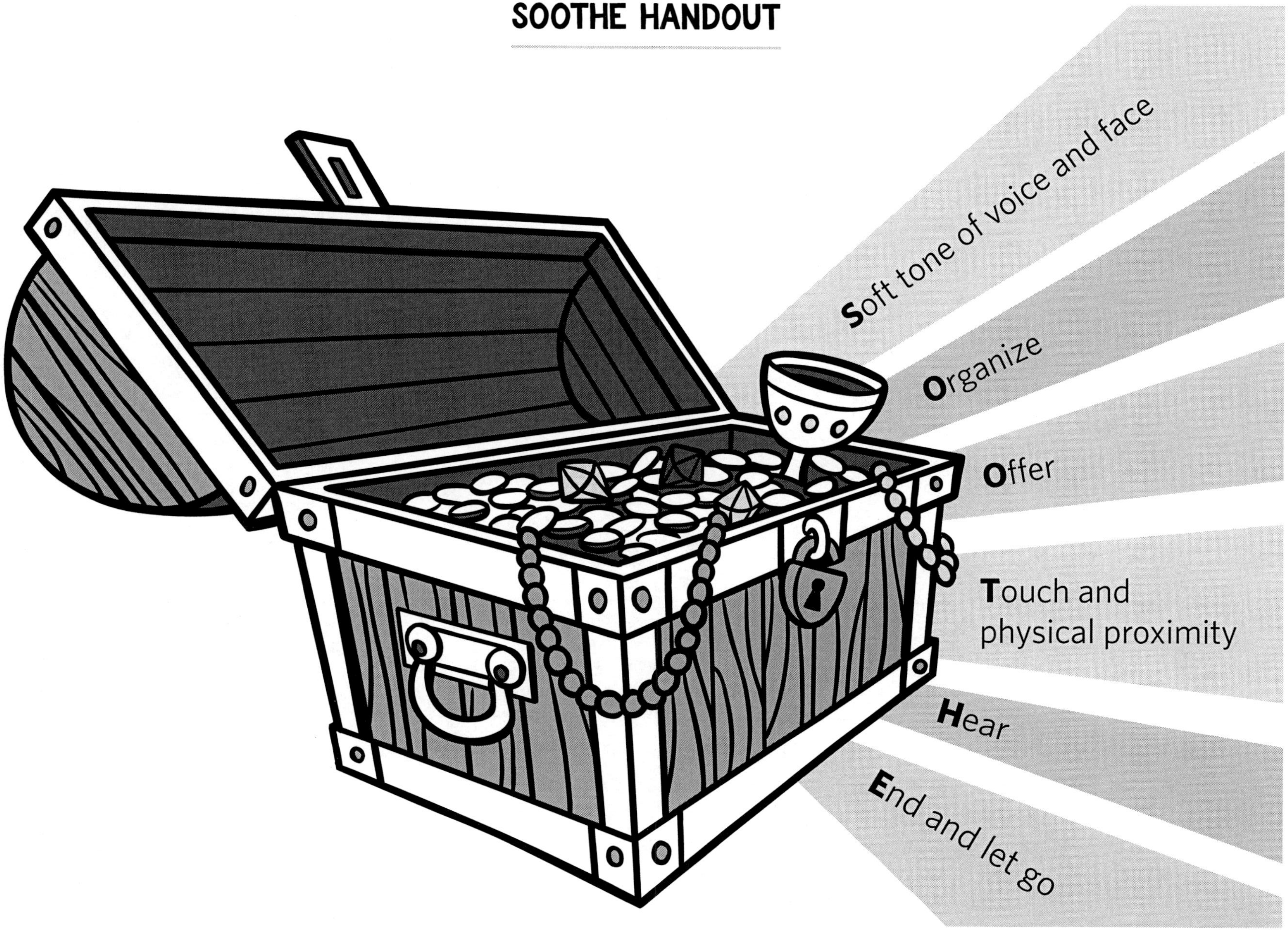

Copyright © 2026 Paris Goodyear-Brown, *Big Behaviors in All Containers*. All rights reserved.

SOOTHE TRACKING TOOL HANDOUT

Please record any moments over the course of the week when you use a SOOTHE strategy to calm your child. Write a few words that will help you remember that event and how the child responded to your intervention. Describe how helpful the strategy was using the following scale:

1 = Not at all helpful   2 = A little bit helpful   3 = Somewhat helpful   4 = Very helpful   5 = Extremely helpful

S **Soft tone of voice**	**O** **Organize**	**O** **Offer**	**T** **Touch**	**H** **Hear**	**E** **End**
Day: **Event:** **How helpful?** ________	**Day:** **Event:** **How helpful?** ________	**Day:** **Event:** **How helpful?** ________	**Day:** **Event:** **How helpful?** ________	**Day:** **Event:** **How helpful?** ________	**Day:** **Event:** **How helpful?** ________
Day: **Event:** **How helpful?** ________	**Day:** **Event:** **How helpful?** ________	**Day:** **Event:** **How helpful?** ________	**Day:** **Event:** **How helpful?** ________	**Day:** **Event:** **How helpful?** ________	**Day:** **Event:** **How helpful?** ________
Day: **Event:** **How helpful?** ________	**Day:** **Event:** **How helpful?** ________	**Day:** **Event:** **How helpful?** ________	**Day:** **Event:** **How helpful?** ________	**Day:** **Event:** **How helpful?** ________	**Day:** **Event:** **How helpful?** ________

Copyright © 2026 Paris Goodyear-Brown, *Big Behaviors in All Containers*. All rights reserved.

5.2 3D FACE

DESCRIPTION:

This intervention unpacks the first co-regulation strategy codified in the SOOTHE strategies: soft tone of voice and face. Caregivers have the power to de-escalate a child simply by the way they talk and the facial expressions they convey. For example, when a parent's brow is wrinkled or their jaw is tightened, children may interpret this as anger or judgment. The simple practice of relaxing their eyebrows or jaw can send signals of safety to the child. Similarly, a clipped and sharp tone of voice may arm a child's fear-based brain, while infusing warmth into the caregiver's tone of voice can send signals of safety to the child. By paying attention to their facial expressions and tone of voice in this manner, caregivers can become allies in providing cues of safety. In this intervention, caregivers will have an opportunity to identify any problematic facial expressions they may inadvertently give their child that convey fear or anger and practice softening their face to enhance their child's felt sense of safety.

TREATMENT GOALS:

- Educate the caregiver about the power of nonverbal communication
- Playfully explore the caregiver's angry and scared facial expressions

MATERIALS NEEDED:

- Three-dimensional dry-erase face
- Dry-erase markers in a variety of colors

DIRECTIONS:

1. Introduce the caregiver to research on how traumatized children perceive facial expressions. You can use the following script:

   "Scientists have done some fascinating studies to determine how traumatized children perceive facial expressions. They instruct a caregiver to make their most scared face and then take a picture of this facial expression. They then instruct the same caregiver to make their most angry face and take a picture of that expression. Then they morph these images by increments of 10 percent through some computer magic so that a card deck of sorts develops, where one image may be 80 percent angry and 20 percent scared, while another image of that same caregiver will be 20 percent angry and 80 percent scared. Then they show the whole set of images to a group of traumatized children and a group of typically developing children. Over and over again, the traumatized children see the anger in the caregiver's face sooner in the progression from scared to angry than the typically developing children do. This makes sense when you remember that trauma has caused your child to constantly scan the environment for any signs of danger."

Copyright © 2026 Paris Goodyear-Brown, *Big Behaviors in All Containers*. All rights reserved.

2. Invite the caregiver to reflect on what they know about their child's trauma history. How could the caregiver's facial expressions activate the child's internal alarm system and make them believe that they are in danger? For example, perhaps they crinkle their forehead, grit their teeth, or squint their eyes when they are angry.
3. Ask the caregiver to draw their angry face on the dry-erase face. Reflect on what it might convey. Erase this face and then invite them to draw their scared face on the dry-erase face.
4. If you are working with two caregivers, it is important that they feel like they are on the same team, since you will be asking them to highlight each other's problematic facial expressions. In healthy-enough parenting partners, this piece of the exercise can be helpful.
5. In some cases, you can do this work with the caregiver and child together. In this case, they might each draw the way they think their face looks when they are angry or scared, or they might draw their impression of the other person's face when they are angry or scared.
6. End the intervention by inviting the caregiver to practice making relaxed facial expressions that convey curiosity and care to the child.

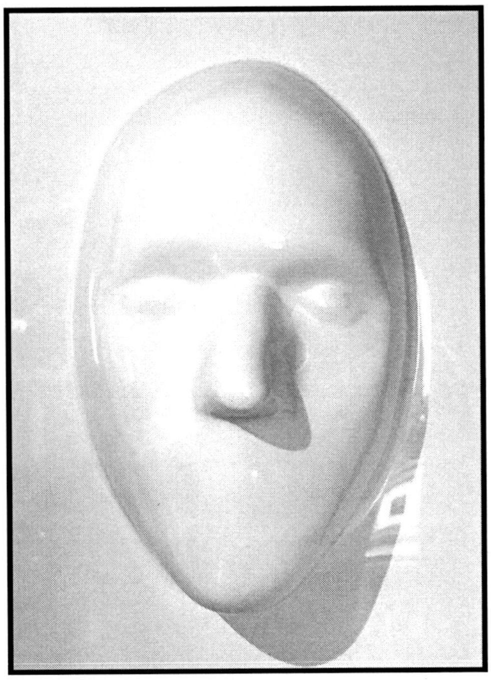

Copyright © 2026 Paris Goodyear-Brown, *Big Behaviors in All Containers*. All rights reserved.

5.3 MIRROR, MIRROR ON THE WALL

DESCRIPTION:

This intervention is meant to explore the role that mirror neurons play in helping caregivers either escalate or de-escalate a child through their facial microexpressions. Tied to the *S* in the SOOTHE strategies, this exercise helps caregivers look at their own reflection in a literal mirror, with a view toward how their face may communicate anger, frustration, confusion, concentration, and so on. When a parent speaks angrily to a child while drawing their eyebrows together, squinting their eyes, and pinching their mouth, the child's mirror neurons can engender a sense of anger or frustration within the child. On the other hand, when a parent smiles and delights in their child, oxytocin (the bonding chemical) and dopamine (the joy chemical) are released in the child's body, which mirrors the parent's felt sense of delight and closeness. This exercise is meant to explore and play with various facial states as the parent and child take turns drawing facial expressions on each other's reflection in a handheld mirror.

TREATMENT GOALS:

- Educate the caregiver about the power of nonverbal communication
- Playfully explore the caregiver's facial expressions and how they are perceived by the child
- Explain the role of mirror neurons in signaling cues of safety

MATERIALS NEEDED:

- *Mirror, Mirror on the Wall* handout
- Two handheld mirrors
- Dry-erase markers in a variety of colors

DIRECTIONS:

1. Explain to the parent and child that our facial expressions communicate powerful messages to each other. This nonverbal cuing can be just as impacting to our sense of felt safety or felt danger as our words.
2. Offer a handheld mirror to the caregiver and ask them to hold the mirror at arm's length. Explain that today, they are going to be playing with facial expressions.
3. Begin by asking the caregiver to make their silliest face. Invite the child to trace the parent's expression on the reflection in the mirror with a dry-erase marker. The child might draw raised eyebrows, wide eyes, or a protruding tongue.
4. Then ask the caregiver to make their angriest face. The child might draw angry eyebrows, pursed lips, or a scowl on the mirror.

Copyright © 2026 Paris Goodyear-Brown, *Big Behaviors in All Containers*. All rights reserved.

5. In safe-enough family systems, you can reverse the roles, with the caregiver then drawing additions to the child's reflection.
6. Alternatively, you can create an element of challenge by giving each participant their own mirror and asking them to draw the way they think their face looks when they are angry or scared. On the count of three, have the child and caregiver show their faces to each other. (Be prepared for laughter.)
7. Offer the *Mirror, Mirror on the Wall* handout and have one participant make an extreme emotion face while the other mimics it. Have them decide whose face is the most scared or most shocked and draw that face in the paper mirror.
8. If there is enough safety in the dyad, you might ask each person to draw their impression of the other person's face when the other person is angry, scared, or sad.

 Copyright © 2026 Paris Goodyear-Brown, *Big Behaviors in All Containers*. All rights reserved.

MIRROR, MIRROR ON THE WALL HANDOUT

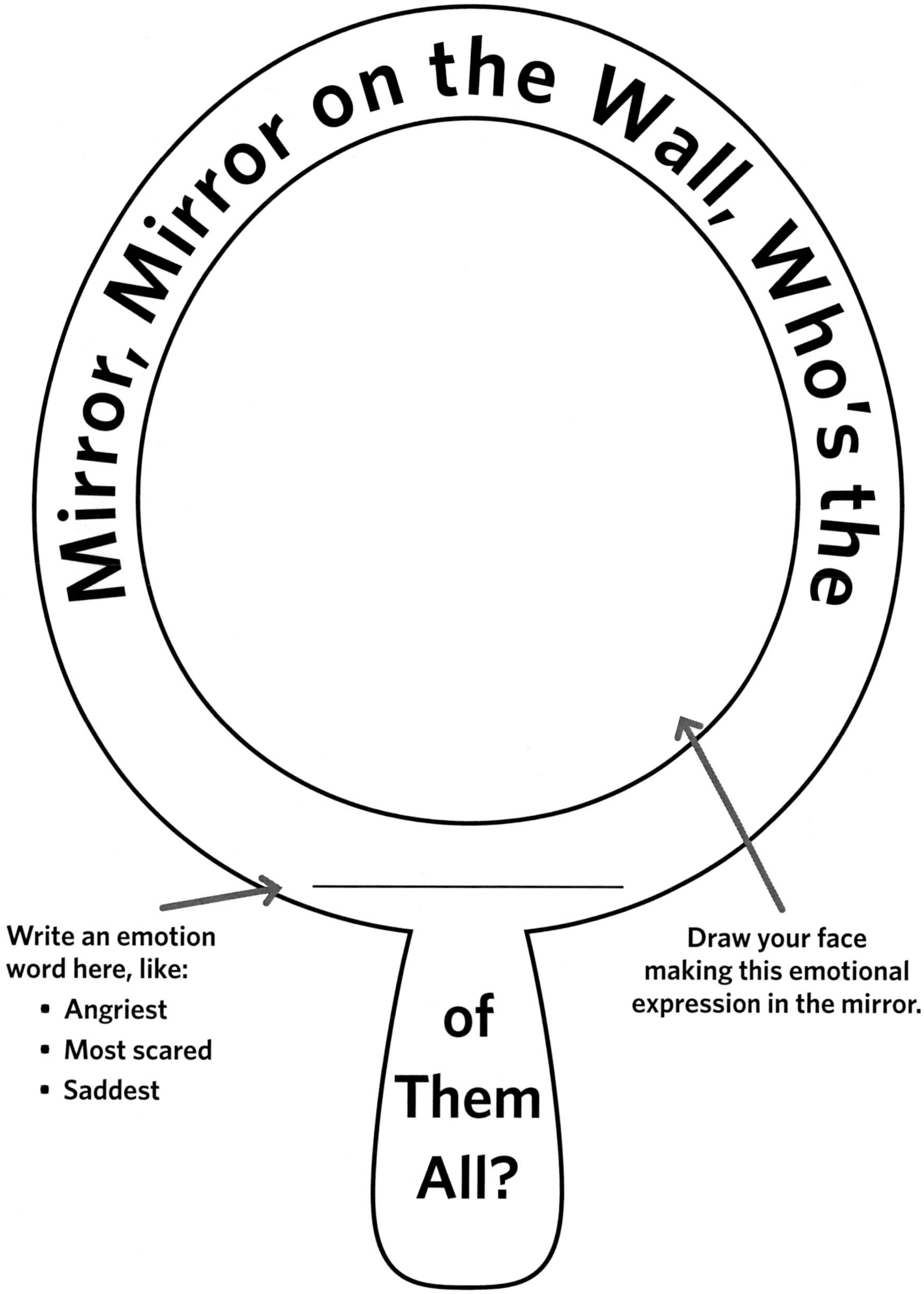

Copyright © 2026 Paris Goodyear-Brown, *Big Behaviors in All Containers*. All rights reserved.

5.4 PICTURE PEOPLE SCHEDULING TOOL

DESCRIPTION:

This intervention dives deeper into the second SOOTHE strategy: organize. This strategy has to do with providing routines for children who become easily dysregulated. The picture people scheduling tool offers a playful way to concretize a child's daily routine, as many children benefit from visual reminders and schedules. When they have a physical copy of their schedule that they can refer to, the caregiver does not have to spend as much time and energy repeating the schedule or nagging the child to complete tasks. It is preferable if the caregiver and child work together to create a collaborative scheduling tool, but if a child is very young or might respond negatively to reminders of parts of the schedule that are no fun, the caregiver can create the schedule on their own in session.

TREATMENT GOALS:

- Educate the caregiver on the importance of creating a schedule and routine for their child
- Concretize the child's daily schedule in a playful way

MATERIALS NEEDED:

- *Pictorial Scheduling* template
- Different colored paper
- Scissors
- Binder ring
- Hole puncher
- Coloring utensils (e.g., crayons, markers)

DIRECTIONS:

1. Explain to the caregiver that children with big behaviors are often soothed by more structure. They thrive on schedule and routine. Transitions can be hard for children who get easily dysregulated, and this tool will offer a playful way for children to move through transitions from one activity to the next.
2. Prior to meeting with the caregiver-child dyad, make a variety of gingerbread body cutouts using the *Pictorial Scheduling* template. I recommend copying them on a variety of different colored paper.
3. Offer the set of gingerbread cutouts to the caregiver-child dyad. Explain that you are going to draw a picture for each part of the child's day on each of the bodies.

 Copyright © 2026 Paris Goodyear-Brown, *Big Behaviors in All Containers.* All rights reserved.

4. Ask the dyad what the child does when they wake up. If they go to the bathroom first, they might draw a picture of a potty on the first body. Perhaps next they eat breakfast. If so, they can draw a bowl of cereal on the next body.
5. As each body is completed, invite the child to punch a hole in the top of the body's head and thread the body onto the binder ring.
6. Continue step-by-step through the child's day with as much specificity as possible.
7. When you are done, explain that the child can hang this from a belt loop, hook it onto their backpack, or place it wherever they will have easy access to it. As they complete each task in their schedule, they can flip that body to the bottom of the stack.
8. Encourage the caregiver to create additional surprise body cutouts they can intersperse in their child's schedule. These cutouts might have messages on them like "Thinking about you" or "We're having your favorite for dinner—spaghetti!" or "I love you." These surprise punctuations in the child's schedule can serve as moments of enhanced connection between the caregiver and child when they are apart.

Copyright © 2026 Paris Goodyear-Brown, *Big Behaviors in All Containers*. All rights reserved.

PICTORIAL SCHEDULING TEMPLATE

Copy off as many as you need on colored paper.

Copyright © 2026 Paris Goodyear-Brown, *Big Behaviors in All Containers*. All rights reserved.

5.5 BOTTOM-UP BOARD GAME

DESCRIPTION:

This intervention dives deeper into the second SOOTHE strategy: organize. In particular, this game offers a playful yet concrete way for caregivers and children, particularly those who are at home together all day (e.g., preschoolers, homeschoolers) to move through their daily schedule. This exercise will refresh caregivers on bottom-up brain development, provide a simplified heuristic of the triune brain as a way to work with the child's daily schedule, and offer a tracking tool to help maintain accountability.

TREATMENT GOALS:

- Provide psychoeducation regarding bottom-up brain development
- Concretize the child's daily schedule in rhythms that work with the triune brain

MATERIALS NEEDED:

- *Triune Brain* handout
- *Bottom-Up Board Game* handout
- Ziploc bags
- Sticky notes in different colors
- Air-dry clay
- Paints or paint markers

DIRECTIONS:

1. Explain to the caregiver that children with big behaviors are often soothed by structure. They thrive on schedule and routine. When we inform the rhythms of a child's schedule based on our understanding of bottom-up brain development, we provide repetitions of regulation, connection, and learning in brain-building cycles.
2. Introduce the three generalized parts of the triune brain on the *Triune Brain* handout: the reptilian brain, the limbic brain, and the neocortex. The reptilian brain is always seeking regulation. It is always asking the question *Am I safe?* The limbic brain seeks connection in order to thrive. It is always asking the question *Am I loved?* Only if these two lower-brain regions answer their questions with a resounding *YES!* can the thinking brain do its job of asking, *What can I learn from this?*
3. Offer the *Bottom-Up Board Game* handout to the dyad.
4. Invite the dyad to choose a color for regulation, a color for connection, and a color for thinking (or learning).
5. Instruct them to color in a three-block pattern over and over again in the board game template. If they choose blue for regulation, pink for connection, and yellow for learning, for example, then the pattern on the game board would go blue, pink, yellow from Start to Finish.

Copyright © 2026 Paris Goodyear-Brown, *Big Behaviors in All Containers*. All rights reserved.

6. Offer three Ziploc baggies. Label one "regulation," the second "connection," and the third "learning." Then instruct the dyad to name as many regulation activities as they possibly can. These might include eating breakfast, taking a hot bath, riding a bike, jumping on a trampoline, drinking some lemonade, and taking a nap. Write each one on a sticky note that matches the color the dyad chose for the game board (e.g., blue for regulation) and add it to the Ziploc bag for regulation.
7. Repeat the same process for connection and learning. Examples of connection activities may include snuggling, reading a book together, going on a walk together, or playing cards together. Examples of learning activities may include independently reading, putting a puzzle together, playing an educational game, or doing a school assignment.
8. Introduce the air-dry clay and paint markers and encourage each family member who will be using the board game to create a game piece for themselves.
9. Lead discussion around what time interval the family wants each space to represent. For example, if a 10-year-old is using the board game, each space might represent an hour. If the child is a 4-year-old, each space may just represent 15 or 30 minutes.
10. To begin playing, place all the board game pieces at Start and have the family set a timer for the length of the agreed-upon interval that each space represents.
11. Beginning with a regulation space, have the child choose a regulation activity from the Ziploc bag (or perhaps breakfast is always the first regulation activity of the day, as it meets the hunger need). The timer is started, and when the time interval ends, players move their game piece to the next space. This pattern is repeated across the three categories—regulation, connection, and learning—throughout the day.

Copyright © 2026 Paris Goodyear-Brown, *Big Behaviors in All Containers*. All rights reserved.

TRIUNE BRAIN HANDOUT

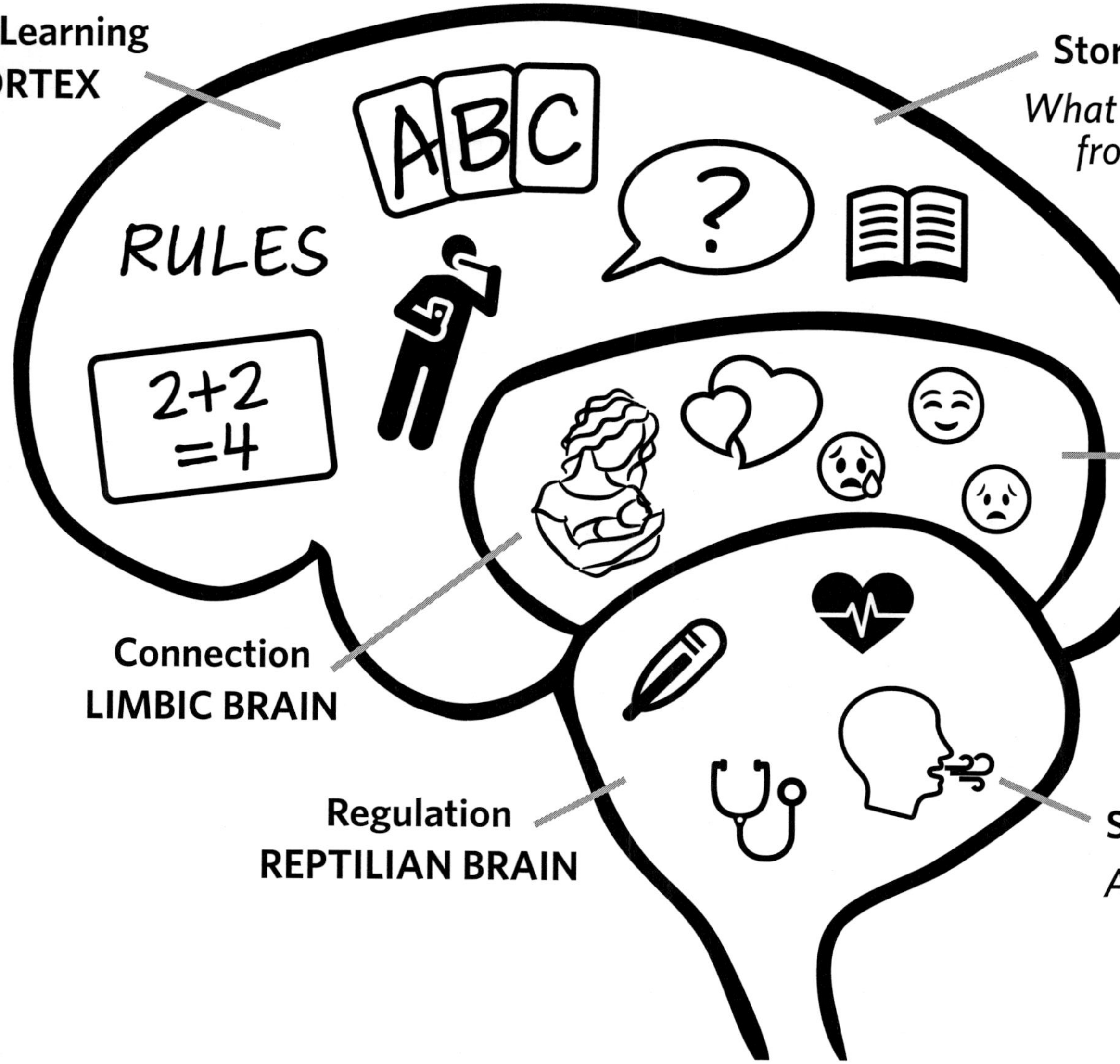

Copyright © 2026 Paris Goodyear-Brown, *Big Behaviors in All Containers*. All rights reserved.

BOTTOM-UP BOARD GAME HANDOUT

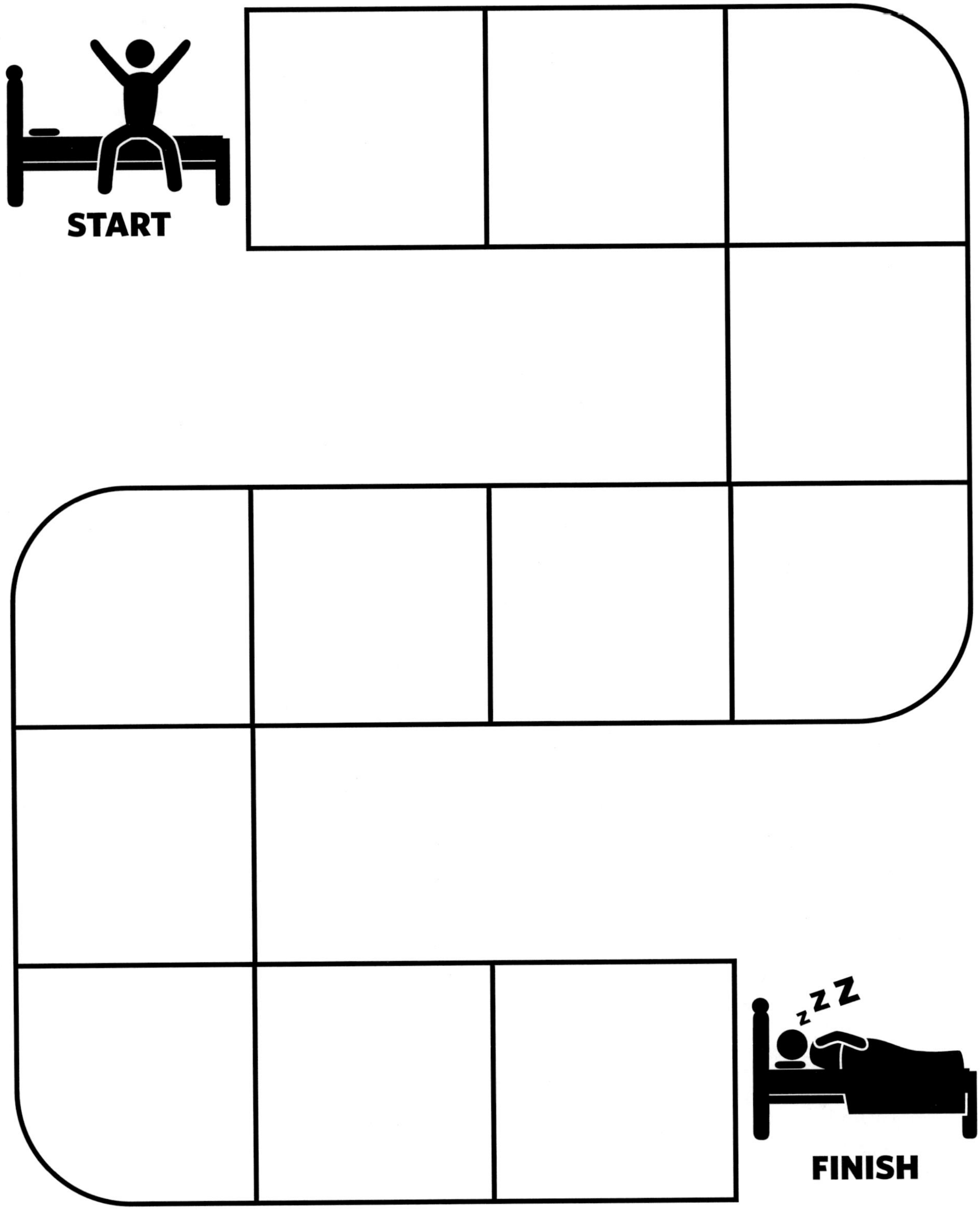

Copyright © 2026 Paris Goodyear-Brown, *Big Behaviors in All Containers*. All rights reserved.

PERSONALIZED BOTTOM-UP BOARD GAME EXAMPLE

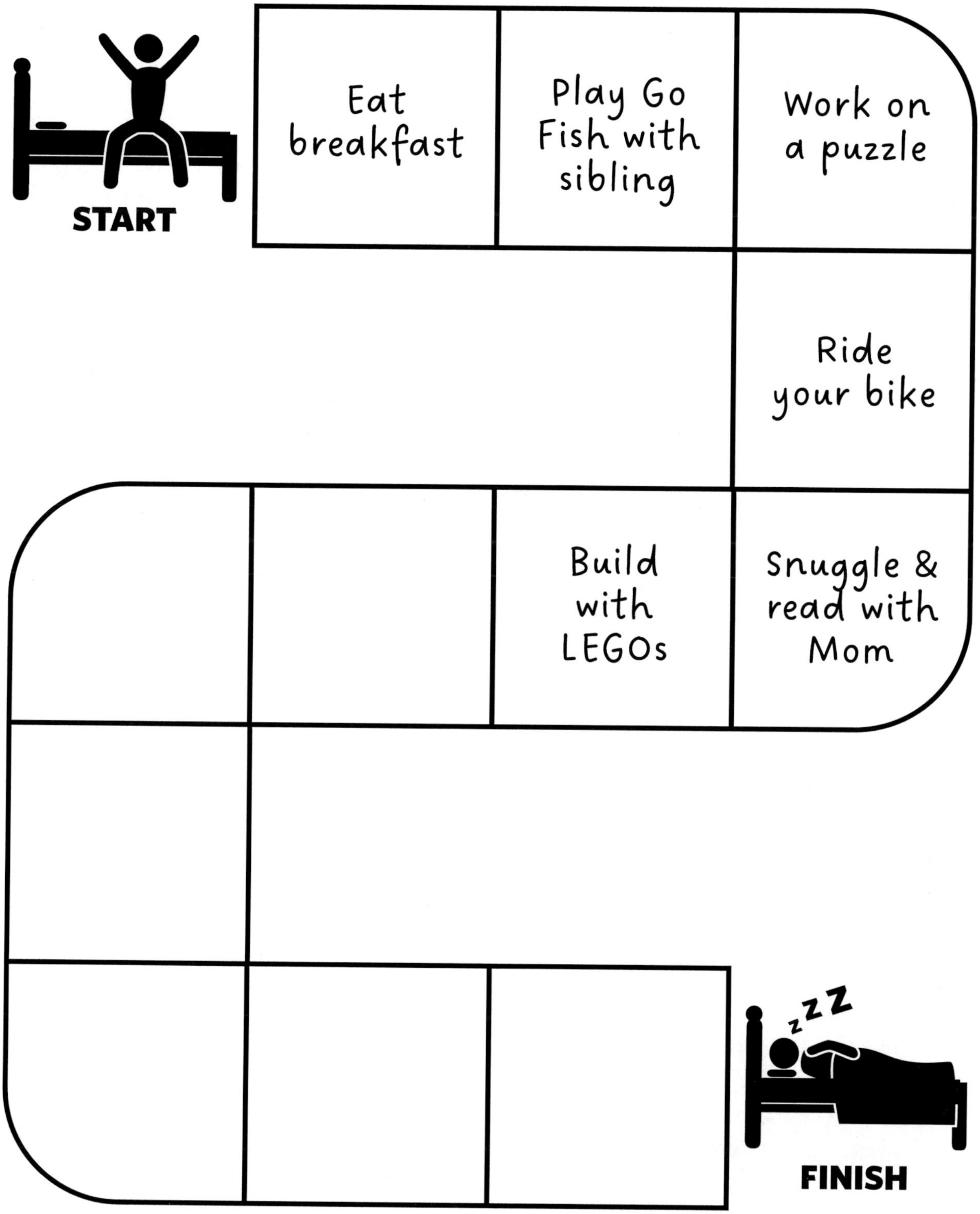

Copyright © 2026 Paris Goodyear-Brown, *Big Behaviors in All Containers*. All rights reserved.

5.6 LOWERING THE LADDER

DESCRIPTION:

This intervention supports the third SOOTHE strategy: offer. In particular, the focus is on helping the caregiver learn to *offer a way out* to the child who has dug themselves into a hole with their big behaviors. When a child or teen is engaged in a big behavior, many caregivers often feel a powerful pull to become even bigger themselves and enter into a power struggle with the dug-in child. This exercise helps caregivers shift the way they view their child's behavior—no longer seeing the behavior as a purposeful attempt to hurt them but rather as an indication that the child is trapped within their behavior. This paradigm shift serves to reopen the caregiver's capacity to extend compassion to the child and help them find a way out of the hole.

TREATMENT GOALS:

- Provide a paradigm-shifting metaphor when approaching big behaviors
- Identify specific co-regulation techniques the caregiver can use with the child in times of dysregulation

MATERIALS NEEDED:

- *Lowering the Ladder* handout
- Scissors
- Coloring utensils

DIRECTIONS:

1. Explain that when a child or teen is dug into a big behavior, they may not know how to get out of it. When a child says, "I will not!" and crosses their arms after having been given a direction, we usually view them as just being defiant. What if when we see that behavior, we instead imagine that the child has fallen into a 10-foot-deep, clay-packed hole? The walls are smooth and slippery, and there is no way out unless the caregiver builds a staircase or throws in a ladder. In these times, the caregiver will need to assume the role of a Safe Boss and offer a way out.
2. Offer the *Lowering the Ladder* handout to the caregiver and ask them to identify a recent time when their child seemed dug into defiant behavior.
3. Become curious about what sorts of co-regulating opportunities the caregiver could have provided in this moment to get their child out of the hole. They could have named the emotions underneath the seeming defiance, softened their tone of voice, injected humor into the situation, offered a connecting activity, or worked to meet an underlying need (e.g., hunger, thirst). Ask the caregiver to write down these co-regulating behaviors on each rung of the ladder.

Copyright © 2026 Paris Goodyear-Brown, *Big Behaviors in All Containers*. All rights reserved.

4. Remind the caregiver that regulation and connection precede a child being able to learn anything new from a situation. It is only through the caregiver's co-regulating actions that they can build a ladder—rung by rung—that gives the child an opportunity to climb out of the hole and back into connection.
5. If the caregiver is open to it, offer a guided imagery exercise in which they imagine their child at the bottom of a 10-foot hole. Invite them to notice what they feel in their body when they view their child as defiant versus when they view their child as trapped.

Copyright © 2026 Paris Goodyear-Brown, *Big Behaviors in All Containers*. All rights reserved.

LOWERING THE LADDER HANDOUT

RUNG BY RUNG

List five co-regulating behaviors you can choose to lower the ladder to your child.

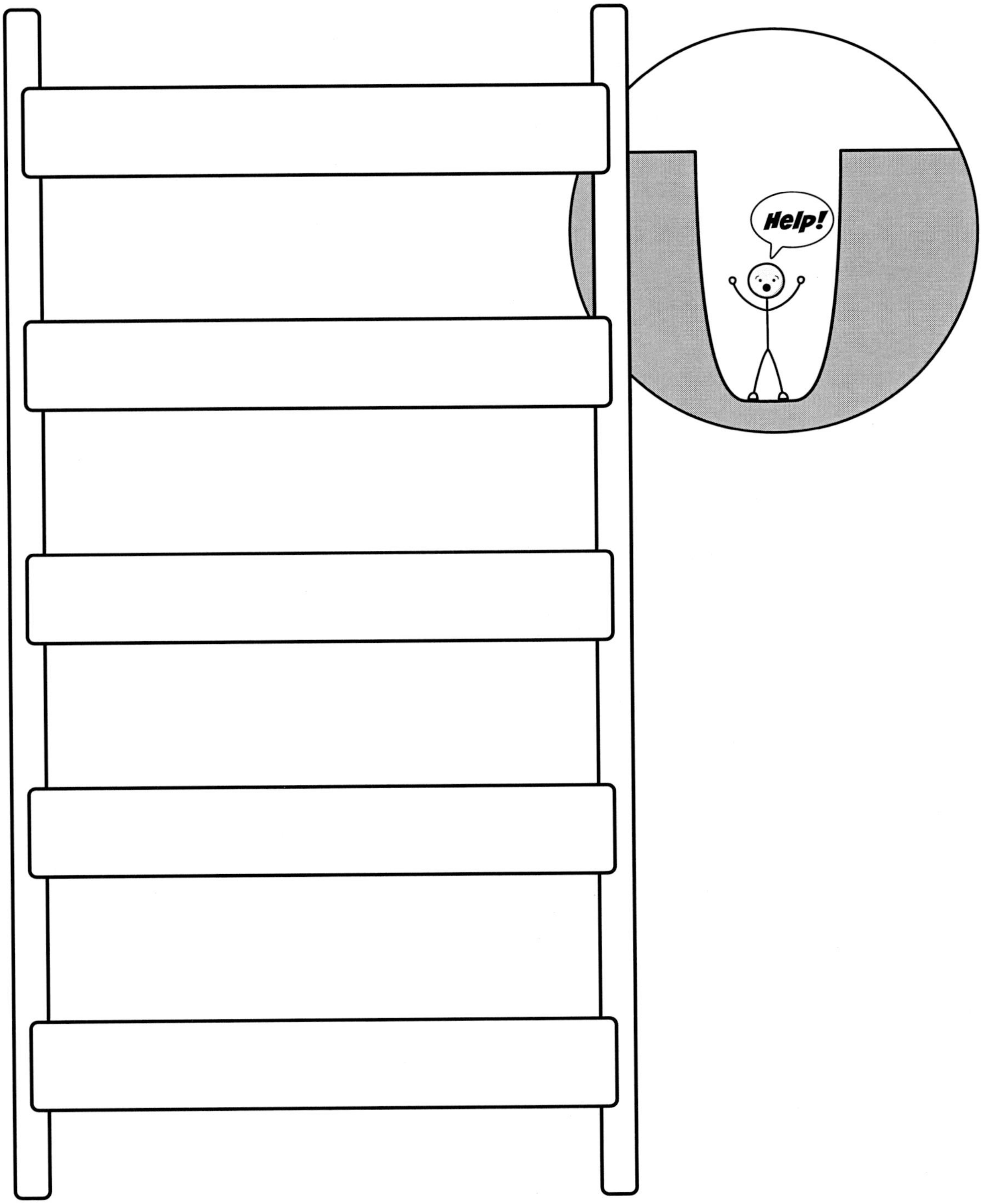

Copyright © 2026 Paris Goodyear-Brown, *Big Behaviors in All Containers*. All rights reserved.

5.7 TITRATIONS OF TOUCH

DESCRIPTION:

This intervention supports the fourth SOOTHE strategy: touch and physical proximity. Touch is one of the primary ways that oxytocin (the bonding chemical) is released between humans. However, some children have been hurt so deeply by the time they are adopted by a Safe Boss that they have trouble receiving nurture directly and may need some vicarious ways to receive nurturing touch. They may also need smaller doses of nurturing touch than a child who has grown up in a secure attachment relationship with their primary caregiver. This exercise helps caregivers reflect on the importance of physical touch in building healthy attachments and soothing the physiology, while also considering the unique dynamics of the child in their care.

TREATMENT GOALS:

- Educate the caregiver on the importance of touch in building healthy attachments
- Titrate doses of touch based on the child's trauma history, sensory needs, or other neurodivergences
- Identify at least five titrations of touch the caregiver can offer to their child

MATERIALS NEEDED:

- *Titrations of Touch* handout

DIRECTIONS:

1. Explain that physical touch is one of the primary ways we communicate love and care for infants. When a child has a good-enough caregiving system in early childhood, they get lots of healthy, nurturing touch that allows them to develop a secure attachment framework. However, when a child doesn't get this kind of touch, they can actually fail to thrive and die. Similarly, when a child has received only unkind or hurtful touch, they may need small doses of safe touch with their new caregiver while they are building trust. Children with neurodivergences or sensory processing issues may also need only certain kinds of touch or certain contexts for touch.
2. Offer the *Titrations of Touch* handout.
3. Explain that for one child, a tight, 20-second hug may be just the right touch to help their body relax, while for another child who does not enjoy hugs at all, this type of touch might be stressful. In this case, the child may benefit from feeling connected to their caregiver in some other way—for example, by high-fiving when the caregiver and child have achieved something together.
4. Help the caregiver identify five specific titrations, or doses, of touch that the child in their care will receive well. These might include fist bumps, side hugs, back rubs, or snuggles while reading a book or watching TV.
5. Instruct the caregiver to write one kind of touch in each finger on the handout.

Copyright © 2026 Paris Goodyear-Brown, *Big Behaviors in All Containers*. All rights reserved.

TITRATIONS OF TOUCH HANDOUT

Write a type of touch that your child receives well in each finger of the hand.

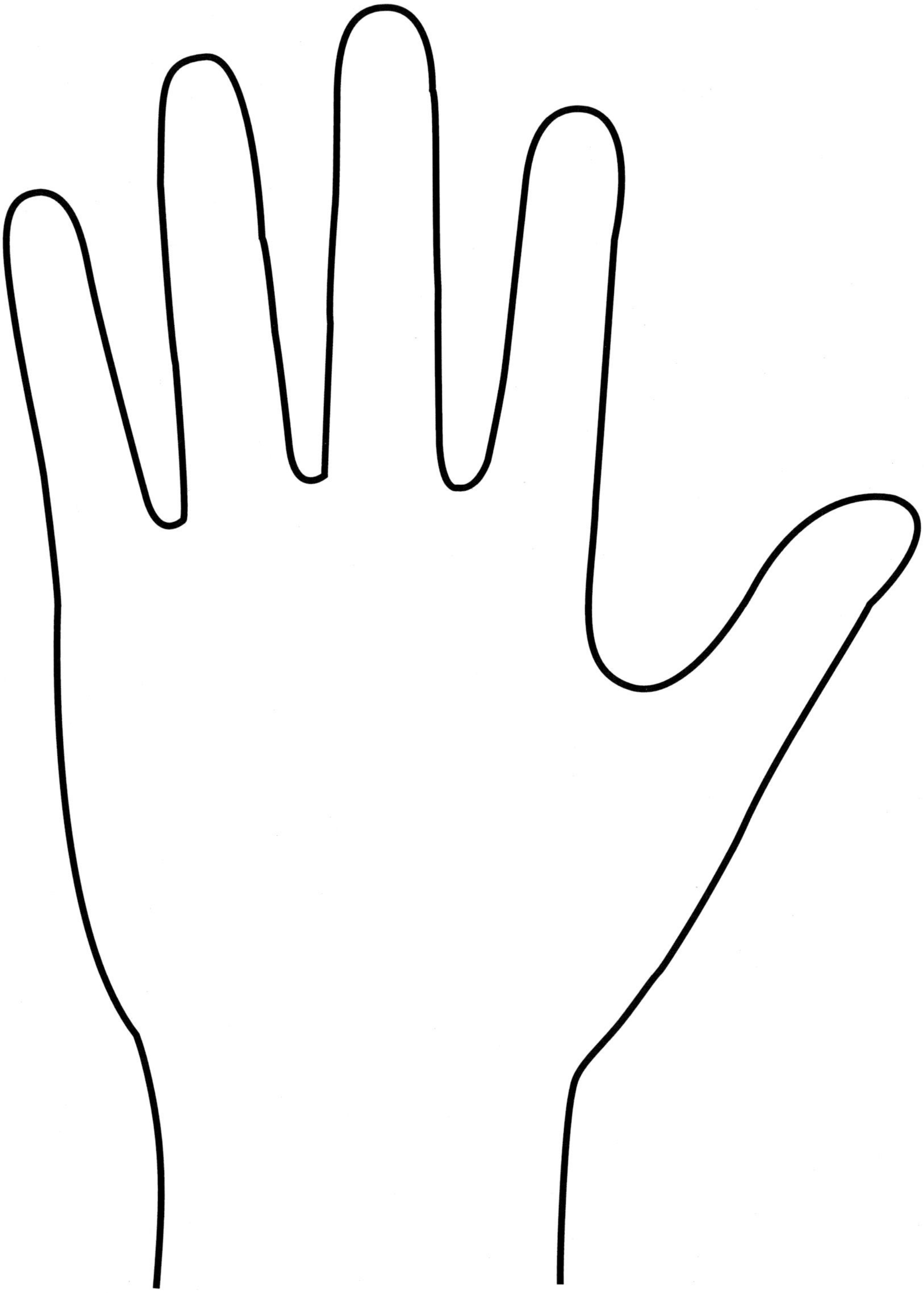

Copyright © 2026 Paris Goodyear-Brown, *Big Behaviors in All Containers*. All rights reserved.

5.8 THE PATHWAYS OF PROXEMICS

DESCRIPTION:

This intervention dives deeper into the fourth SOOTHE strategy: touch and physical proximity. While most children are co-regulated by nurturing touch, some children don't respond well to touch due to sensory issues, neurodivergences, or trauma histories. There are also some contexts in which touch can enhance the neuroception of safety, and other contexts in which it can further exacerbate the neuroception of danger that a child might already be sensing. This exercise gives caregivers a reflective space to explore the situations in which they may need to use physical proximity to a child instead of touch.

TREATMENT GOALS:

- Educate the caregiver on the nuance of touch versus the use of physical proximity
- Offer a paradigm shift around how touch may be helpful in some contexts but not in others
- Identify situations where the caregiver may need to utilize physical proximity instead of touch

MATERIALS NEEDED:

- *The Pathways of Proxemics* handout

DIRECTIONS:

1. Explain to the caregiver that, for many children, physical touch is a primary way that they receive love and soothing when they are upset. However, for a small subset of children, physical touch can actually be aversive. For example, a sensory-defensive child can perceive a back rub as irritating, a child who doesn't like to be extra warm may experience an uncomfortable absorption of body heat during extended snuggles, or a teenager who is self-conscious about their body might only want to engage in side hugs as opposed to full frontal hugs that make them uncomfortable.
2. Discuss that some traumatized children also have contexts in which they feel safe and can receive nurturing touch, and other contexts, even in the same environment, when they don't want touch. For example, a child who lives in a home environment characterized by interpersonal violence may be happy to give fist bumps and side hugs at school when they are feeling safe and connected. However, if that same child is under threat at school—if, for example, a teacher is having to provide some discipline (such as asking them to throw away their paper because they copied a friend's paper)—touch of any kind by the teacher may trigger a further escalation. In these times, it may be wisest to offer physical proximity instead of touch.

Copyright © 2026 Paris Goodyear-Brown, *Big Behaviors in All Containers*. All rights reserved.

3. Offer *The Pathways of Proxemics* handout and explain the concept of proxemics. The amount of space each of us needs when navigating physical proximity to others may vary based on situation, relational dynamics, and how we are feeling emotionally and physically as we negotiate physical space with others.
4. Explain that when a child's stress response is already armed, it can be helpful to use a sideways approach instead of a head-on approach. In certain circumstances, it may even be wiser to find a back doorway to approach the child or teen.
5. Ask the caregiver to think of a situation that arises in which the child's stress response may become armed. Ask the parent to identify which sort of pathway they use to approach the child in that situation and why.
6. This handout can be used and referenced in multiple sessions as parents bring difficult parenting moments.

Copyright © 2026 Paris Goodyear-Brown, *Big Behaviors in All Containers*. All rights reserved.

THE PATHWAYS OF PROXEMICS HANDOUT

Which pathway of approach is the wisest in different situations with your child? How close would you sit to this upset child? Place a mark somewhere on the dotted line to represent where you might physically place yourself on the bench as you work to co-regulate the child.

Copyright © 2026 Paris Goodyear-Brown, *Big Behaviors in All Containers*. All rights reserved.

5.9 BEAUTIFUL HANDS

DESCRIPTION:

This intervention dives deeper into the fourth SOOTHE strategy: touch and physical proximity. Sometimes, the most effective way to offer healthy touch to a traumatized child is to facilitate an activity in which touch is a necessary part of creating or accomplishing something else. In this exercise, the caregiver and the child will read the book *Beautiful Hands* and then paint each other's hands as part of creating art together. Both the child and the caregiver leave this activity with a visual image reminding them of what their teamwork can create and frequently report feeling more closely connected to each other at the end of the session.

TREATMENT GOALS:

- Educate the caregiver on the traumatized child's need for healthy touch experiences
- Titrate the experience of receiving healthy touch through the creation of an art piece

MATERIALS NEEDED:

- The book *Beautiful Hands* (Baumgarten, 2015)
- Large butcher paper
- Finger paint

DIRECTIONS:

1. Invite the caregiver to sit (and snuggle, if appropriate) with the child and read the book *Beautiful Hands.*
2. After they have finished reading it together, explain that they will make a beautiful art piece like the ones in the book using their own hands.
3. Invite them to peruse the book a second time and brainstorm what they might re-create together.
4. If the dyad has trouble deciding, you might offer the idea of making a butterfly. The caregiver's handprints can be the upper wings of the butterfly, as they are normally larger, and the child's handprints can be the lower wings of the butterfly. They might also decide to make a garden of flowers, a rainbow, a dragon, or little creatures like ladybugs and caterpillars.
5. Have the caregiver and child paint each other's hands and then invite them to press their hands or fingers down in the patterns that will create the picture. They can take turns.
6. Remind the dyad to use their asking words to communicate which colors they would like to have on their fingers or palms.
7. When the fingerpainting creation is complete, I often invite the dyad to title their artwork. I also often rehearse the TraumaPlay mantra after this intervention: *When we stick together, we can do hard things.*
8. Give the dyad the choice to take the art piece home and display it or to leave it with you.

Copyright © 2026 Paris Goodyear-Brown, *Big Behaviors in All Containers*. All rights reserved.

5.10 ANIMAL HANDS

DESCRIPTION:

This intervention dives deeper into the fourth SOOTHE strategy: touch and physical proximity. Touch is one of the primary ways that caregivers communicate love to their children, especially infants and toddlers. However, when a child has experienced maltreatment or neglect, they have been robbed of the healthy touch experiences that allow them to grow. Children who have experienced abuse may even associate touch with hurt, pain, or deceit. These children may need to receive touch in small titrations and in the midst of activities that offer novelty. In addition, pairing touch with new, fun experiences can trigger the release of dopamine (the joy chemical) and oxytocin (the bonding chemical) to counter the stress hormones in their bodies. This exercise offers the caregiver an opportunity to become a Nurturer to the child while also being a Storykeeper.

TREATMENT GOALS:

- Offer nurturing, healthy touch experiences to the child
- Provide a way for the caregiver to nurture the child while the child experiences novelty
- Co-create narratives about cooperation and nurturing care experiences

MATERIALS NEEDED:

- Temporary animal tattoos
- Water
- Paper towels
- Puppet theater (optional)

DIRECTIONS:

1. Invite the caregiver and child to explore the available animal tattoos.
2. Instruct them to each choose one tattoo for themselves or to decide together which tattoos they would like to apply to one another.
3. Have the caregiver apply the tattoo to the child first, gently holding the chosen tattoo on the child's hand while pressing a moist paper towel to both, until the tattoo has transferred to the child's hand.
4. Invite the child to follow the same process to apply the chosen tattoo on the caregiver's hand.
5. Ask the caregiver and child to create a puppet play for their animals to perform. Give parameters to the story, such as "The story should have a beginning, a middle, and an end. Also, something should happen in the story—something that requires the animals to work together and take care of each other."
6. You may decide to play the role of an antagonist, choosing an animal tattoo for yourself or a hand puppet that becomes a threat to the animal family in some way.

Copyright © 2026 Paris Goodyear-Brown, *Big Behaviors in All Containers*. All rights reserved.

This can offer the parent and child a shared experience of working together to protect themselves from danger.

7. You may also offer a puppet theater in which they can perform their story. With the dyad's consent, you may videotape the story for them to watch afterward.

Copyright © 2026 Paris Goodyear-Brown, *Big Behaviors in All Containers*. All rights reserved.

5.11 REROUTING

DESCRIPTION:

This intervention dives deeper into the fifth SOOTHE strategy: hear the underlying anxiety. Children with big behaviors often respond to directions with an automatic NO! Some of these children may be expressing their will, while others may be protesting because the task being asked of them is triggering an underlying anxiety. For example, the caregiver may have set the bar too high and given the child a direction that was too difficult to follow. Caregivers often believe that once they give a direction, the child must follow through and obey the direction. However, what if the developmental expectation is misattuned? Should caregivers shift their expectations? Can they revise a directive they've given the child after giving it? Yes, and in fact this can be good leadership. This intervention helps encourage caregivers to reroute when necessary.

TREATMENT GOALS:

- Determine when an expectation the caregiver has for the child may be developmentally inappropriate
- Offer an alternative when the bar has been set too high

MATERIALS NEEDED:

- *Rerouting* handout

DIRECTIONS:

1. Explain to the caregiver that when a child says no to a directive or avoids doing something asked of them, this is often a reflection of their underlying anxiety:

   "Let's imagine that you have two children in the same preschool classroom. The teacher says, 'Children, please put your shoes on, it is time to go play outside.' Two children say no. The first child just doesn't want to go outside, and when they are offered the *Two-Choice Procedure* [4.10], they put on their shoes and go outside. However, the second child is really saying, *I don't know how to tie my shoes, and I feel insecure and incompetent when confronted with this task.* If the caregiver can hear the underlying anxiety in this situation and respond as a Storykeeper, they might say, 'I'm remembering that you are still learning to tie your shoes. You put them on your feet, and I will help you tie them.' This allows the child to be supported at their current developmental capacity."

2. Reiterate that when a caregiver demands that their child do something that they are not developmentally ready for, the fallout of enforcing that command is likely to cause a rupture in the caregiver-child relationship. It also reinforces feelings of incompetence and anxiety in the child. Instead, it is important to become a Storykeeper in these moments, pulling back to take a more aerial view of the situation and offering another

Copyright © 2026 Paris Goodyear-Brown, *Big Behaviors in All Containers*. All rights reserved.

option for compliance that is more developmentally appropriate. This is known as *rerouting* the situation.

3. The advent of navigation apps can help you further teach this concept. If you are committed to driving a certain route to work but the GPS tells you that there will be a two-hour delay if you insist on staying on this road, you'll likely reroute around the delay. Similarly, if a caregiver can recognize that the directive they have given their child is too difficult to follow, they can reroute with a different directive.
4. Ask the caregiver to identify a time when their child could have benefited from rerouting—a time when the caregiver may have overestimated what the child could do.
5. Offer the *Rerouting* handout and invite the caregiver to write down the revised direction they can offer to their child in the future.

Copyright © 2026 Paris Goodyear-Brown, *Big Behaviors in All Containers*. All rights reserved.

REROUTING HANDOUT

Write your revised direction for the child on the rerouted pathway.

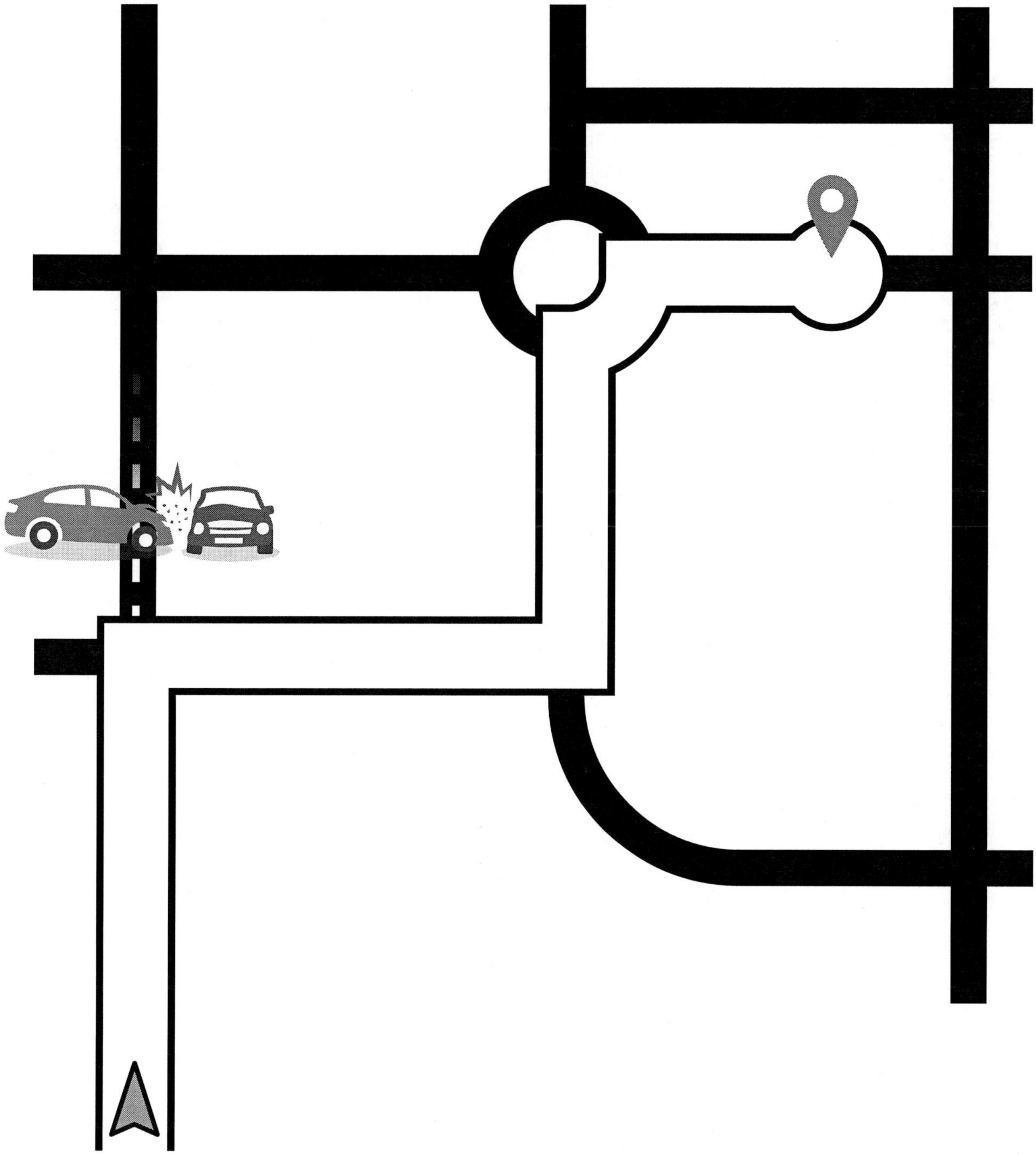

Copyright © 2026 Paris Goodyear-Brown, *Big Behaviors in All Containers*. All rights reserved.

5.12 SETTING THE BAR FOR SUCCESS

DESCRIPTION:

This intervention dives deeper into the fifth SOOTHE strategy: hear the underlying anxiety. Caregivers often have very high standards for their child's behavior. When a child is capable of reaching those standards, this can have a satisfying payoff for both the caregiver and the child. For example, if a caregiver expects their child to get an A on their math test and they do, the child feels proud of the accomplishment and the caregiver feels good about their leadership. Sometimes, though, caregivers set the bar impossibly high, which can cause toxic ruptures between the caregiver and child. For example, a teacher may expect the child to get up and recite a memorized poem in front of the class, but the child has an expressive language delay that makes the task incredibly difficult. Sometimes, the very best strategy for reestablishing a caregiver as a Safe Boss is to help them adjust the bar they are setting for a child's behavior to a realistic level.

TREATMENT GOALS:

- Assess the caregiver's developmental expectations of their child
- Reset the bar for the child's behavior to a developmentally realistic height

MATERIALS NEEDED:

- *Setting the Bar for Success* handout

DIRECTIONS:

1. Explain the importance of setting the bar at an appropriate developmental level for the child in their care:

    "When we are in the role of Safe Boss and we ask the child in our care to do something that is simply beyond their capacity at this moment in time, we injure the relationship and can damage the child's belief in their own competence. For example, if you ask your child to sit at the kitchen table and do math homework for an hour when their current attention span is closer to 15 minutes, relational ruptures are likely to result."

2. Introduce the idea of the *easy ask* to the caregiver: "What's a behavior that your child can complete every time you ask them to, with no additional help from you?" Write this example in the Easy Ask section of the *Setting the Bar for Success* handout.
3. Introduce the idea of the *supported ask* to the caregiver: "What's a behavior that your child can complete about half of the time, as long as you are nearby to help?" Write this example in the Supported Ask section of the handout.
4. Introduce the idea of the *impossible ask* to the caregiver: "What's a behavior that you ask your child to complete, but they are rarely able to do so without your help? Let's

Copyright © 2026 Paris Goodyear-Brown, *Big Behaviors in All Containers*. All rights reserved.

reflect on why this may be so difficult." Write this example in the Impossible Ask section of the handout.

5. Help the caregiver reflect on how they can better balance their use of easy asks with supported asks and limit their use of impossible asks that are simply too hard for the child right now.

Copyright © 2026 Paris Goodyear-Brown, *Big Behaviors in All Containers*. All rights reserved.

SETTING THE BAR FOR SUCCESS HANDOUT

Sometimes parents are asking their children to do things they simply aren't capable of doing yet.

In the lowest rung, identify one task that your child can do on their own. In the middle rung, identify one task that your child can do with your help. In the top rung, identify a task that may simply be too hard for your child to do consistently right now.

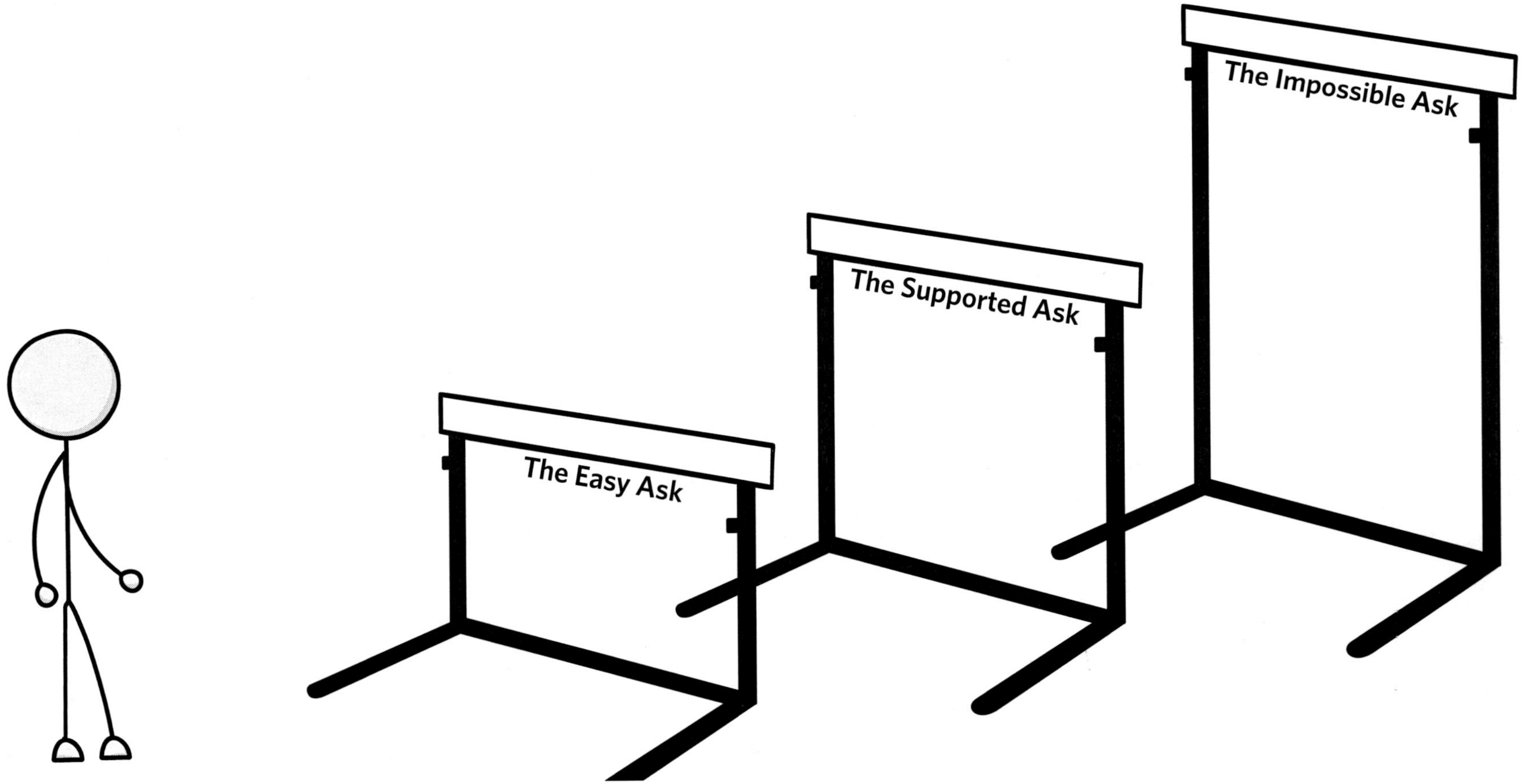

Copyright © 2026 Paris Goodyear-Brown, *Big Behaviors in All Containers*. All rights reserved.

5.13 RHYTHMIC READING

DESCRIPTION:

This intervention explores the sixth SOOTHE strategy: end and let go. Caregivers often correct a child's big behavior with their own big behavior (e.g., yelling, harsh consequences), and the fear this engenders in the child ceases the big behavior. However, this is often just a temporary bandage that quiets down the household for a period of time, as the reality is that the child has actually not been co-regulated back to baseline. As a result, the big behavior is likely to resurface. Once the child "erupts" and gets it all out, they are likely to feel more regulated. However, all that chaotic energy is now in the environment, leading the caregiver to feel exhausted and need a time out for themselves. This intervention is meant to help the caregiver remain connected with their child as the dyad regulates together after a behavioral storm.

TREATMENT GOALS:

- Propose a way for the caregiver and child to co-regulate together even when the caregiver is dysregulated
- Create a list of children's books that allow for easy rhythmic reading

MATERIALS NEEDED:

- *Rhythmic Reading Library* handout

DIRECTIONS:

1. Explain to the caregiver that children with big behaviors often have so much stress, anxiety, anger, or energy (whatever you decide to call this!) built up in their bodies that they almost have to "blow" to get it all out, but once they have had the escalation, they often feel better and recalibrated. However, they may have wreaked so much havoc in the environment that the caregiver now needs time for themselves. But here's the thing: The moment that traumatized children are coming down off a big behavior is when they are most accessible to new learning, so it is crucial for them have a co-regulating caregiver available during that time. It may seem counterintuitive, but these children may be able to receive nurture differently and connect at deeper levels than they would on a day when they are completely regulated.
2. Discuss that you have come up with a very simple way for the caregiver to stay present with their child after an escalation. It is called the rhythmic reading library. Each book on this list has a rhythmic cadence, a kind of repetition that helps regulate our brain and body.
3. Ask the caregiver whether they've ever read a children's book out loud and while they're reading, their mind is elsewhere. The books on this list do not require the caregiver to be fully present, just physically present and willing to stick together with the child as they both regroup from the behavioral storm.

Copyright © 2026 Paris Goodyear-Brown, *Big Behaviors in All Containers*. All rights reserved.

4. Any book that follows a patterned rhythm could be added, but some favorites are listed below:
   a. *Brown Bear, Brown Bear, What Do You See?* (Martin, 2011)
   b. *The Napping House* (Wood, 2005)
   c. *This Is the House That Jack Built* (Taback, 2002)
   d. *There Was an Old Lady Who Swallowed a Fly!* (Colandro, 2014)
5. Help the parent and child decide which books they want to read together in moments when they are working to regulate.
6. Offer the *Rhythmic Reading Library* handout to the dyad.
7. Invite them to write the names of the books they want to include in the blank book spines on the handout.
8. It will be helpful if you have hard copies of each of these books in your office. Support the caregiver in reading each of them to the child in your playroom prior to asking the caregiver to implement this strategy at home.

Copyright © 2026 Paris Goodyear-Brown, *Big Behaviors in All Containers*. All rights reserved.

RHYTHMIC READING LIBRARY HANDOUT

Write the name of at least one additional rhythmic book you can read with your child while regulating together after a behavioral storm.

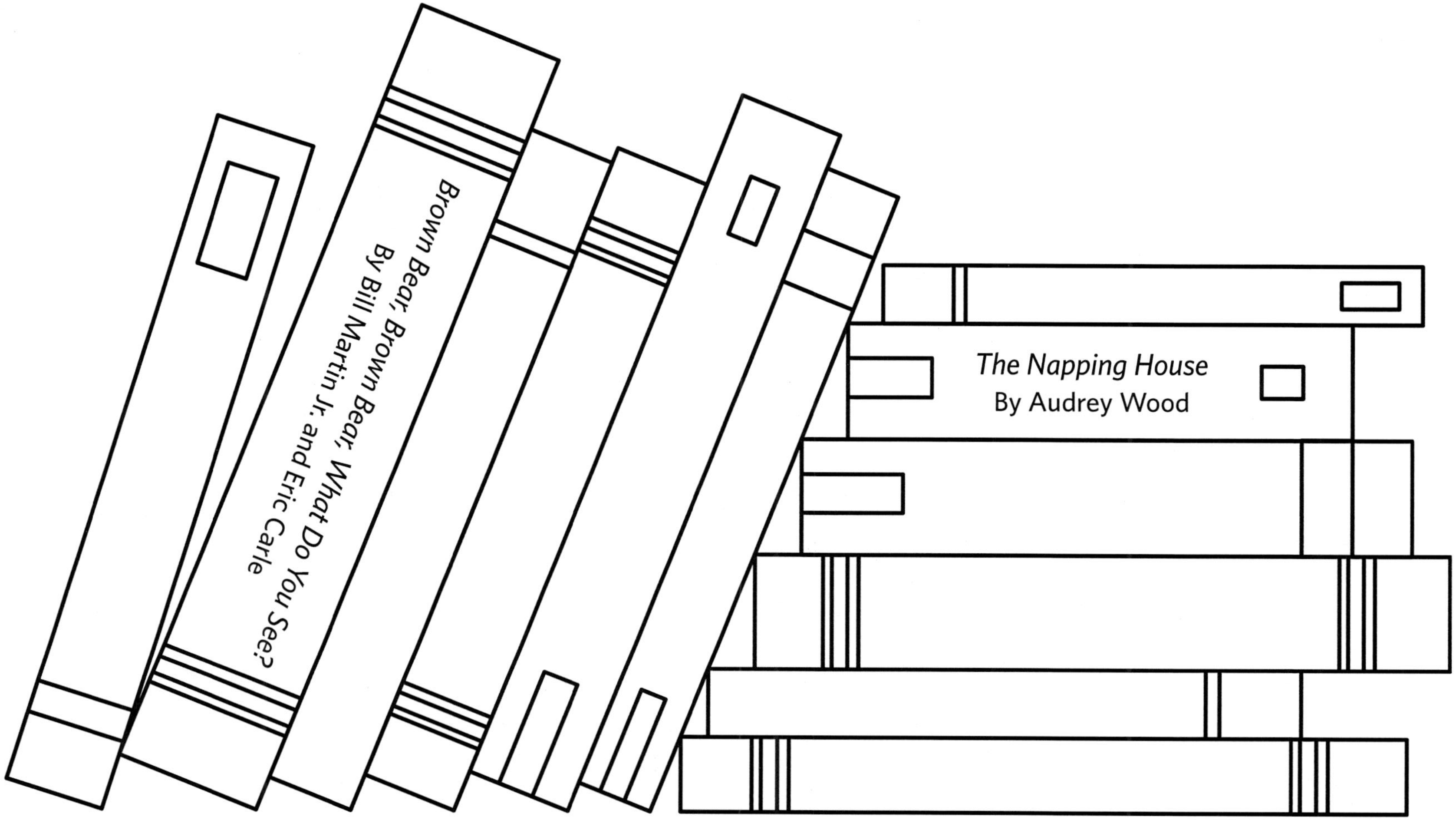

Copyright © 2026 Paris Goodyear-Brown, *Big Behaviors in All Containers*. All rights reserved.

six

Becoming a Safe Boss: Increasing Trust Through Need Meeting

Children with big behaviors often engender reactivity in their caregivers. For example, a child squeals in a high-pitched voice, and their caregiver (who can't stand that sensory experience) screams for the child to stop it. What has been modeled is a *matching* of the child's dysregulation instead of a meeting of the child's distress. This unconscious matching gets in the way of the parent or teacher asking, *What is the need underlying this behavior?*

From the first moments after a baby is born, good-enough caregivers begin to learn what the infant is needing when they cry. Children have limited abilities to tell us what they need. Babies come out of the womb wired to scream and cry when they feel uncomfortable. The good-enough parent spends the first weeks of the newborn's life figuring out which cry communicates which need. Are they hungry? Are they tired? Are they cold?

After thousands of repetitions of need meeting, caregivers begin to discern the difference between the cry that signals "I'm hungry" and the cry that signals "My diaper is full, and I need to be changed." These serve-and-return volleys of communication wire the brain of the infant to anticipate that when they express a need, it will be met. This is a working definition of trust.

When a little one has their needs consistently met over the first several years of life, they develop a trust foundation. However, when a little one cries because they are hungry, wet, or in need of some other care and no one responds, what develops instead is a control foundation. Alongside this control foundation, the following core belief takes root: *I must control everything at all costs because I can't trust anyone else to meet my needs.* In fact, over time, a child whose needs are not predictably met by their caregiver can develop an even more entrenched belief: *I must control everything at all costs, or I'll die.*

This chapter is full of interventions that help parents meet the underlying needs of the children in their care. These needs may include safety, limit setting, nurture, delight, skills practice, co-regulation, or storytelling. Some interventions are meant to help caregivers shift their paradigms to seeing themselves as the *need meeter* for the child in their care. The more dysregulated the child becomes, the more the caregiver embodies the roles of Safe Boss, Nurturer, and Storykeeper to interpret the distress and meet the underlying need.

6.1 ANCHORING BELOW

DESCRIPTION:

This exercise builds on the *Coping Kite* (3.4) and *Catch the Current* (3.5) interventions by enhancing the caregiver's role as an attachment anchor. In healthy attachment relationships, the caregiver functions as a Safe Boss, remaining grounded and offering co-regulating assistance when a child is dysregulated. Foster and adoptive caregivers may be in particular need of support when learning the ways in which they can enhance cues of safety for a traumatized child in their care. This activity is meant to help expand the caregiver's understanding of their role as an attachment anchor, while also reinforcing to the child that their caregiver will remain tethered to them and provide them with grounding even in the midst of the buffeting waves of life.

TREATMENT GOALS:

- Reinforce the caregiver's role as a grounding, co-regulating force for their child
- Identify safety cues the caregiver can provide the child

MATERIALS NEEDED:

- *Anchor* handout

DIRECTIONS:

1. Explain to the caregiver that the most effective way to help a dysregulated child come back to baseline is to remain grounded themselves. Become curious with the caregiver about the specific warning signs they see in their child that indicate the child is escalating. For example, perhaps the child begins to tap their foot, clench their hands, or use a more demanding or whiny tone.
2. Ask about the caregiver's own reactions to their child's escalation signals. For example, the caregiver may mention that they clench their jaw or tense their muscles when their child begins to whine.
3. Ask the caregiver to name some things a sailor might do to keep a ship safe when a big storm comes up. For example, they might tie a rope around themselves and anchor it to the mast so that if they get thrown overboard, they can be hauled back in. Or they might send up distress signals to hail a bigger ship nearby that might come and help them.
4. Help the caregiver translate these anchoring behaviors to practical strategies they can use to ground an escalated child. For example, the caregiver might breathe in and out in a certain rhythm, maintain a soft face, slow the cadence of their words, deepen the tone of their voice, speak in smaller sentences, and so on.
5. Offer the caregiver the *Anchor* handout and ask them to write down the behaviors that help them remain grounded and have the best chance of de-escalating their child.

Copyright © 2026 Paris Goodyear-Brown, *Big Behaviors in All Containers*. All rights reserved.

ANCHOR HANDOUT

Write at least three things you can do to provide cues of safety to your child. Being a grounded anchor during your child's behavioral storms is one way to show up as a Safe Boss.

Copyright © 2026 Paris Goodyear-Brown, *Big Behaviors in All Containers*. All rights reserved.

6.2 KITES, ANCHORS, AND CO-REGULATION

DESCRIPTION:

When a child is in the midst of a full-blown big behavior, it is not uncommon for caregivers to respond with their own big behaviors, making the situation worse. We want to train caregivers to see the verbal and nonverbal cues that tension is present in their little one *before* the child is unreachable. Caregivers do this best when they can regulate themselves and then work to co-regulate their child with strategies like soft eye gaze, gentle tone of voice and face, open body postures, and so forth. This intervention builds on the *Coping Kite* (3.4) and *Anchoring Below* (3.5) exercises by bringing the child and caregiver together in a joint session aimed at helping the child better understand their own escalation signals and helping the caregiver name specific behaviors they will use to co-regulate in response.

TREATMENT GOALS:

- Rehearse the ways in which our bodies give off cues of danger or safety
- Identify body signals that indicate the child is becoming dysregulated
- Enhance the caregiver's ability to co-regulate a child in distress

MATERIALS NEEDED:

- Paint
- Paintbrush
- Paper
- Scissors
- String
- Stick

DIRECTIONS:

1. Invite the caregiver to paint their child's hand while you talk about dysregulation and the need for Safe Bosses to help with co-regulation. Use the following script:

   "We're going to create a kite together. Your [*the child's*] handprint will be the kite itself, and the string will connect you and your mom or dad together. Kids get to run and play, but their Safe Bosses stay close by in order to help them stay safe. When you get upset, your body might sometimes feel like a kite being blown around by the wind. Your parent might need to pull you closer to the ground, out of the fiercest wind. Other times, they may need to let out the string so you can fly higher. Can you identify a time when you got so upset that you needed your Safe Boss to help you? Tell me about it."

2. The parent, child, or both can talk about times when the child became dysregulated and needed the co-regulation of the parent.
3. When the caregiver is done painting their child's hand, invite the child to make a handprint on a piece of paper. Allow it to dry while you continue the session.

Copyright © 2026 Paris Goodyear-Brown, *Big Behaviors in All Containers*. All rights reserved.

4. Explain that when kids are feeling unsafe, caregivers can either help the child feel safer or (without even meaning to) make them feel worse. For example, if a grown-up yells at a child who is already upset, or completely ignores the child, this can make a child feel less connected and less safe. Instead, remind the client that their role is to function as a Safe Boss in these times by serving as a grounding anchor for their child:

   "You can think of your child as a kite and yourself as the grounding anchor. When your child is way up high and being tossed around by the wind, you might need to bring them closer to get out of the chaos, or you might need to give them some more space so they can find the air current above."

5. Invite examples of the child's behaviors that may require the parent to bring the child closer or to give the child more space and process as needed.
6. Help the caregiver identify some of the child's body signals that indicate their child is needing to be brought closer, as well as body signals that indicate the child is needing more space. For example, if the child is beginning to talk really fast, it may be helpful for the parent to step closer and rub the child's back. If the child is crossing their arms in front of their body or clenching their fists, they may be giving a nonverbal cue that they need a little physical space between themselves and the parent. This can be a conversation with both the caregiver and the child, offered with playful curiosity. Ask the caregiver to write down each of these on the dried handprint.
7. When they're done, cut out the child's handprint and attach it to a string, wrapping the other end around a stick or dowel rod.
8. Ask the caregiver to name cues they can give their own body that they are safe, even when the child is feeling unsafe. Ask also what cues their own body can give to the child to communicate safety. The caregiver can write these on small strips of paper and wrap them around the dowel.

Copyright © 2026 Paris Goodyear-Brown, *Big Behaviors in All Containers*. All rights reserved.

6.3 TRUST AND TENSION: WALKING A FINE LINE

DESCRIPTION:

When a child client has experienced multiple adverse childhood experiences, these can manifest as a fierce independence—an *I can do it my own self!* stance. Children who have had multiple caregiver disruptions are especially prone to this response and may reject help of any kind from their foster or adoptive parent. In these cases, one of the first goals is to encourage the child to risk vulnerability (defined here as admitting that they could benefit from a caregiver's help, often followed by asking either verbally or nonverbally for the caregiver's help in some way). To work toward this goal, there is a slackline in the backyard of Nurture House that is often the first place I invite a parent and child to play, because the child will jump up on the slackline and want desperately to cross it. However, it is very wobbly and has yet to be entirely crossed without some help. The child must navigate the internal tension between wanting to conquer the slackline and deciding whether to trust their caregiver to help them get to the other side. The following intervention also uses a slackline to help children walk this fine line between trust and tension.

TREATMENT GOALS:

- Offer body-based play experiences that create competency surges for the client
- Identify the caregiver as a secure base who can help the child take risks as needed
- Enhance the attachment relationship by allowing the child to risk vulnerability

MATERIALS NEEDED:

- Slackline
- Open space to set up the slackline

DIRECTIONS:

1. Bring the child and caregiver to the slackline area and invite the child to cross the slackline if they would like.
2. As the child tries to cross it, remind the caregiver that their job is to stay near the child and wait for any cues from the child that indicate they need help. For example, you might say:

   "Mom, I can see that Johnny is trying really hard to cross the slackline by himself. His body is big and strong and so wise for him. His body will tell him if and when he needs your help. Why don't you just walk alongside him with your arm extended? He will grab it if he needs it."

3. As the child begins to lose balance, they will naturally reach out to their caregiver, who will be right there to support them. You might say, "Mom, Johnny's body is so wise for him. His body knew just what he needed."

Copyright © 2026 Paris Goodyear-Brown, *Big Behaviors in All Containers*. All rights reserved.

4. Allow the child to decide whether it is worth it to cross all the way to the other end of the slackline or whether they choose to jump down and play elsewhere. Either response offers valuable information to you about how entrenched the child's belief is that they have to do everything on their own or that it is dangerous to trust anyone else for help.
5. If the child makes it to the other side of the slackline, celebrate their success for working together as a team.
6. Brainstorm other ways the caregiver can create similar success scenarios in their own home or playground. Prescribe titrated doses of activities that build their sense of working together as a team.

Copyright © 2026 Paris Goodyear-Brown, *Big Behaviors in All Containers*. All rights reserved.

6.4 HOT AND COLD HIDE-AND-SEEK

DESCRIPTION:

From the first moments of peekaboo between an infant and their caregiver, there is excitement and risk in the game of hiding yourself from another and then being found. In fact, you can enhance attachment by playing with cycles of separation and return, which makes hide-and-seek a useful game for deepening security in the attachment relationship. A child with attachment wounds may have learned to mask their needs because the expressed need made their caregiver feel uncomfortable or resulted in some sort of punishment. For example, a child whose biological parent was uncomfortable with neediness may have learned to feign indifference when their caregiver would leave and return. However, if you were to put a heart rate monitor on that child, you would see that their heart rate is going wild at the moments of separation and reunion. They have just learned to mask their neediness. This hide-and-seek intervention helps children and their caregivers develop clear nonverbal cues they can use with each other in pursuit of a shared moment of celebration (i.e., finding the hidden item).

TREATMENT GOALS:

- Rehearse congruent serve-and-return communications between the child and caregiver
- Teach the caregiver and child to accurately read each other's cues
- Enhance healthy attachment behaviors between the child and caregiver

MATERIALS NEEDED:

- Any small objects that can be easily hidden

DIRECTIONS:

1. Invite the caregiver and child to choose a small object to hide in the room.
2. Decide which person will hide the object first and which person will seek it. Explain that as the seeker begins to move about the room, the hider's job is to say "Colder" if the seeker is moving away from the object, "Warmer" if the seeker is moving toward the hidden object, and "Hot!" when the seeker is right on top of the hidden object. The hider guides the ultimate success of the seeker in finding the hidden object.
3. In some cases, it may soothe an anxious child to have their caregiver hide the object first. In other cases, the child may want to hide the object first. In this case, you may need to support the child in giving verbal cues of hot and cold.
4. Have the caregiver and child switch roles and make sure they each get a turn to be the hider and the seeker.
5. Once the dyad feels proficient in the verbal cuing, increase the challenge level by creating a nonverbal cue to communicate hot, warm, and cold. At first, these

Copyright © 2026 Paris Goodyear-Brown, *Big Behaviors in All Containers*. All rights reserved.

nonverbals may be big and playful. For example, they might shiver their body to indicate cold, wiggle their body to indicate warm, and pretend to swipe at their sweaty forehead or fan themselves to indicate hot.

6. As the dyad feels successful at reading these bigger nonverbal cues, encourage them to make smaller cues, like winking their eyes to communicate hot or raising an eyebrow to communicate cold.
7. When the object is found, celebrate with the dyad by exclaiming, "You all read each other's cues so well that you found that object in record time!"

Copyright © 2026 Paris Goodyear-Brown, *Big Behaviors in All Containers*. All rights reserved.

6.5 A SAFE BOSS FOR BABY YODA

DESCRIPTION:

This intervention was the outgrowth of my work with an adopted child who was born addicted to methamphetamines. In the NICU, he was on the highest doses of morphine allowable to manage his withdrawal but was still inconsolable. He simply hurt for the first full month of his life, even as his adoptive mother struggled to comfort him. The in utero injuries he experienced, as well as the abrupt separation from his biological mother and the intense period of prolonged pain, all contributed to a foundation of control and distrust. It took years of work with his adoptive mother to establish a secure attachment. At one point along the way, he had received a stuffed Baby Yoda as a present and began to carry it around everywhere. Baby Yoda slept with him and ate with him, and when the child went to school, he would instruct his mom on the proper care and handling of Baby Yoda. Children will naturally move into this kind of play as they heal, choosing some toy or symbol to become the self-object and then nurturing it themselves or requesting that their caregiver or therapist (or both) nurture it. This is a process worthy of supporting deeply.

TREATMENT GOALS:

- Normalize the process of an attuned caregiver learning their baby's cues
- Support the child as they nurture a self-object and ask the caregiver to do the same

MATERIALS NEEDED:

- Baby Yoda (or any other stuffed animal that makes multiple unintelligible sounds)
- *Cries, Cues, and Clues* handout

DIRECTIONS:

1. Ask the child to bring in a stuffed animal or other lovey from home.
2. Invite the child and caregiver to tell you about the stuffed animal, asking questions like "What is their name?" "Did they live somewhere else before they came to live with you?" and "What do they need to feel safe and cared for here in the playroom?"
3. Ask to hear all the sounds that the stuffed animal makes. For example, the adopted child who brought Baby Yoda to session explained that he made four different sounds. I admitted that I didn't know what these sounds meant and normalized that good-enough parents learn what their baby's sounds mean, even though they are not saying real words. My client looked at me intently for a moment and then said, "Exactly! I can tell you what each of his sounds mean." He proceeded to proudly play each sound for me, while communicating what the sound meant. The communications ranged from "I'm hungry" to "I'm bored."

Copyright © 2026 Paris Goodyear-Brown, *Big Behaviors in All Containers*. All rights reserved.

4. Offer the *Cries, Cues, and Clues* handout and record the child's interpretations of their stuffed animal's sounds. If the dyad is able to do this work, ask the caregiver what kind of sounds or signals the child gave them (when they were younger) when they were bored, hungry, tired, and so forth.
5. Celebrate the child for being able to communicate their needs effectively, even without articulated words, and celebrate the caregiver's ability to understand these communications and meet the child's underlying needs.

Copyright © 2026 Paris Goodyear-Brown, *Big Behaviors in All Containers*. All rights reserved.

CRIES, CUES, AND CLUES HANDOUT

Listen and watch carefully. Can you find a clue in the communication? What does the baby's cry mean? What does the dog's bark mean?

What does it mean?

What does it mean?

What does it mean?

What does it mean?

Copyright © 2026 Paris Goodyear-Brown, *Big Behaviors in All Containers*. All rights reserved.

6.6 STRONG EYES

DESCRIPTION:

Traumatized children often have difficulty reading other people's nonverbal cues. One of my first clients was an adopted child who was also on the autism spectrum and had lots of trouble making eye contact with others. He told me that it made him feel nervous and weak to look into people's eyes. I needed to find a way to help him feel strong while taking risks to make himself vulnerable with his caregivers. This intervention was born out of that juxtaposition. It offers a playful way for the child and caregiver to practice sending and receiving accurate cues, attuning to one another and extending moments of eye contact.

Disclaimer: Traumatized children who have experienced abuse or witnessed interpersonal violence may not be the best candidates for this intervention. However, many children who have been hurt benefit from self-defense classes and an embodied sense of being able to protect themselves. Use your clinical discretion to decide whether this exercise is appropriate for your client.

TREATMENT GOALS:

- Enhance attachments between the caregiver and child
- Facilitate attunement through nonverbal serve-and-return communications

MATERIALS NEEDED:

- At least two pairs of boxing gloves (real or pretend)

DIRECTIONS:

1. Introduce the gloves to the caregiver-child dyad and explain that they will be engaging only in slow-motion punches and blocks for this intervention.
2. Teach the dyad several basic kickboxing moves, including a jab, a hook punch, and an upper cut. Then teach them several countermoves that will block each punch, including upper blocks and side blocks. If you are not familiar with kickboxing moves, watch several appropriate YouTube videos together before beginning the slow-motion practice.
3. Allow the child to practice a hook punch multiple times. (Children who feel the need to be strong in their bodies may ask to practice the punches and the blocks over and over again.) Then invite the caregiver and child to decide together on a nonverbal cue (maybe it is winking the left eye) that signals to their sparring partner that a hook punch will be coming from their left side. Invite the client to make the signal in slow motion and the caregiver to block the left hook punch in slow motion.
4. Move through each of the punches and blocks with the dyad, helping them work together to agree upon and practice signals for whichever kind of punch is coming.

 Copyright © 2026 Paris Goodyear-Brown, *Big Behaviors in All Containers*. All rights reserved.

5. Invite each partner to practice giving the nonverbal signal and then slowly offering the punch.
6. Give time and space for the other partner to block the punch.
7. Invite the child and caregiver to switch roles so they can each experience the roles of both puncher and blocker.
8. Celebrate both the parent and the child for being able to work together to agree upon nonverbal cues, read them appropriately, block them appropriately, and keep everyone safe in the process.

Copyright © 2026 Paris Goodyear-Brown, *Big Behaviors in All Containers*. All rights reserved.

6.7 SAFETY SIGNALS

DESCRIPTION:

This exercise is a very simple and concrete way to teach very young children and their caregivers about their bodies' cues of danger and safety. *Interoception* (listening to our bodies from the inside out) and *exteroception* (listening to how our bodies respond to the environment around us) are processes worthy of exploring, even with preschoolers. In this exercise, a distinction is made between "doing" safety signals (which are specific behaviors the caregiver completes that help the child feel safe) and "being" signals (which may include innate qualities or sensory experiences of the caregiver, such as the smell of their hair or their soft tone of voice, that contribute to safety). This exercise is meant to help each partner in the dyad rehearse the aspects of the other that contribute to their sense of felt safety. It also helps them identify any behaviors that make them feel unsafe in the relationship.

TREATMENT GOALS:

- Identify cues of safety for the caregiver and child
- Identify cues of danger for the caregiver and child

MATERIALS NEEDED:

- *Safety Signals* handout
- *Danger Signals* handout

DIRECTIONS:

1. Introduce the *Safety Signals* handout and ask the child, "How does [*caregiver's name*] make you feel safe?" The child client might answer, "They feed me, read to me, smile at me," and so on. Write or draw these responses under the "doing" stoplight on the handout.
2. Then ask the child, "What is something about your parent that helps you feel safe?" The child's answers may include specific sensory experiences, such as "The smell of Mommy's hair" or "The strength of Daddy's arms around me." Write or draw these responses under the "being" stoplight on the handout. Caregivers are often sweetly surprised by the cues of safety they provide their child just by being themselves.
3. Slow the session down enough to have some feel-good moments in the session, which may include inviting the dyad to hug each other, snuggle with each other, or feed each other. (If you are EMDR trained, these moments can be further installed through bilateral stimulation.)
4. Once you've created a felt sense of safety and connection between the caregiver and child, they should have enough bandwidth to become curious about signs of danger.

Copyright © 2026 Paris Goodyear-Brown, *Big Behaviors in All Containers*. All rights reserved.

5. Introduce the *Danger Signals* handout and ask the child, "How does [*caregiver's name*] make you feel unsafe?" The child might answer, "When they have a grumpy face. When they yell. When they talk through their teeth." Write or draw these responses in the blank stop signs on the handout.
6. Repeat this same process with the caregiver, becoming curious about the cues of safety and danger their child offers them.

Copyright © 2026 Paris Goodyear-Brown, *Big Behaviors in All Containers*. All rights reserved.

SAFETY SIGNALS HANDOUT

"Doing" Stoplights

What is something your caregiver does that makes you feel safe?

Write or draw one example in each light.

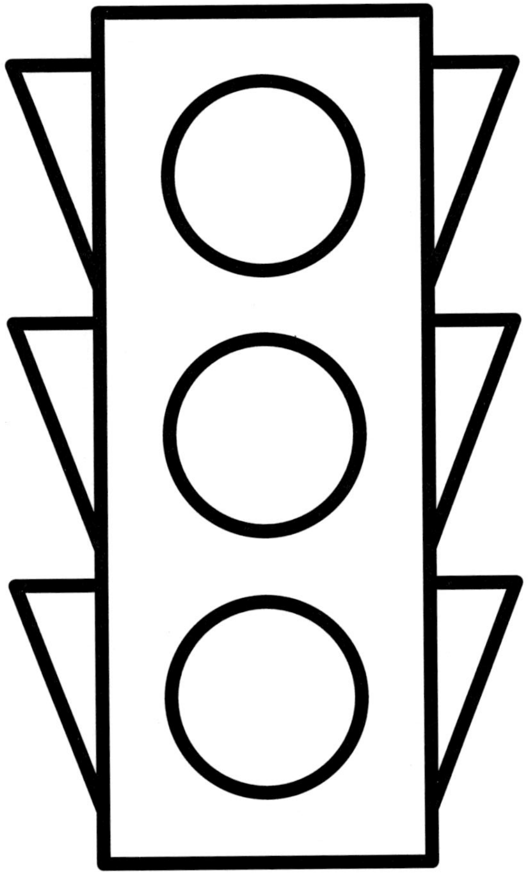

"Being" Stoplights

What is something about your caregiver that makes you feel safe?

Write or draw one example in each light.

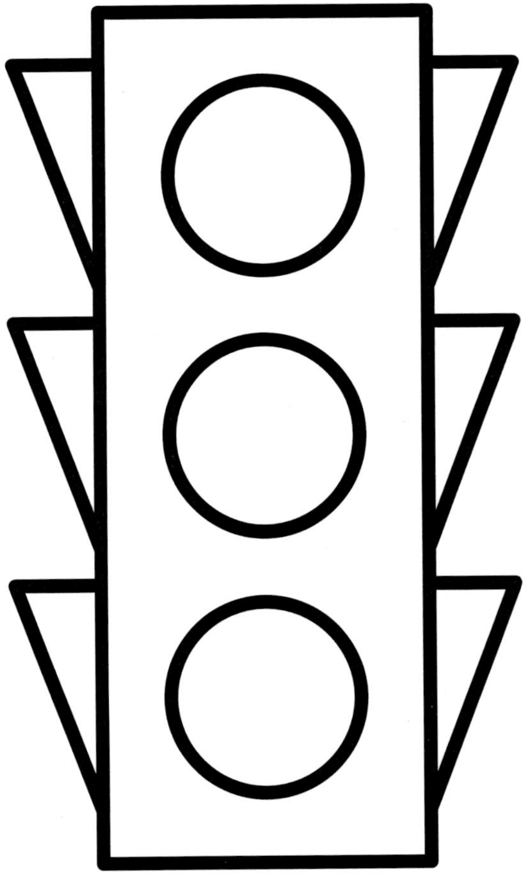

Copyright © 2026 Paris Goodyear-Brown, *Big Behaviors in All Containers*. All rights reserved.

DANGER SIGNALS HANDOUT

What is something your caregiver does (or what is something about your caregiver) that makes you feel unsafe? Write or draw one example in each stop sign.

Copyright © 2026 Paris Goodyear-Brown, *Big Behaviors in All Containers*. All rights reserved.

seven

Becoming a Nurturer: Delighting-In Games to Enhance Attachment

One of the three core attachment roles embedded in TraumaPlay is the role of Nurturer. Although it is often assumed that caregivers have innate nurturing abilities, this is not the case. Many caregivers grew up in environments where their own parents did not nurture them, so they never learned what it means to provide affection and attention to a child in their care. If you hope to help caregivers embody the Nurturer role, you must begin by nurturing them in the same ways you want to see them nurture their child. For example, when you use a warm tone of voice when communicating with the caregiver, it models to them how they should speak to the child in their care. When you experience genuine delight while greeting the caregiver in the lobby, it serves as a titrated dose of nurture that provides the caregiver with the building blocks needed to become that Nurturer themselves. As a clinician, you must embody the role that you want the caregiver to absorb. In other words, you may need to reparent the parent.

During the assessment phase, TraumaPlay therapists are always asking two simultaneous questions: *What's it like to be the child of this caregiver?* and *What's it like to be the caregiver of this child?* When the answer to the first question seems obvious (in that the child does not feel delighted in), it is likely that the answer to the second question is the same (in that the caregiver does not feel appreciated for all they do for the child). Loops of disconnection, misunderstanding, and rejection can become habitual for families, with neither the caregiver nor child being able to find a way out of the cycle. In these cases, you hold the hope for the dyad as you begin to craft experiences of delight between the caregiver and child. This includes designing Nurture Nooks and other safe spaces where you offer delighting-in games that support attunement, playfulness, connection, and joy.

Caregivers can also experience deep shame when confronted with the truth that nurturing their child feels awkward or unnatural. In these situations, you may need to do discrete skill building by training the caregiver to identify the needs underlying their child's big behaviors. Remember that children often act out when an underlying need is not met (e.g., hunger, thirst, rest, sensory input). Just as you can teach caregivers to home in on their child's needs, you can support caregivers in checking in with their own needs. You can nurture both the child and caregiver simultaneously through a parallel process in which you offer to meet some simple needs in session (e.g., offering blankets for warmth, a juice box for thirst, a crunchy snack for hunger, a gumball for oral gratification or proprioceptive and vestibular needs that can be met through chewing).

In some cases, a caregiver may already be a very strong Nurturer, but the child in their care has a need for control and a core distrust of all grown-ups. Sometimes, this distrust is related to betrayal traumas, like physical or sexual abuse in the previous home. Other times, this distrust may be related to an insecure attachment pattern that developed between the caregiver and child early in life as the caregiver struggled to welcome the child in moments of distress. In either case, the caregiver and child will need your support in providing doses of in vivo need meeting, while offering games that encourage both parties to delight in the other while still feeling safe in themselves.

7.1 DESIGN A NURTURE NOOK

DESCRIPTION:

When working to enhance attachment between a traumatized child and their caregiver, it is useful to have a separate space in your office for this purpose. TraumaPlay therapists have what's called a Nurture Nook, which is often a corner of the room that is defined by a large circular cushion of some sort (papasan chair cushions are an excellent option). It also contains pillows of various fabrics, shapes, and sizes as well as at least one blanket. This protected space becomes a dedicated area to conduct nurture work with a caregiver and child. The nurture work may include therapist-facilitated feeding games, storytelling prompts, EMDR work, and coherent narrative building. Once the dyad has experienced your Nurture Nook in session, this activity helps them create one at home.

TREATMENT GOALS:

- Provide a protected space for focused attachment work between the caregiver and child
- Help the dyad design their own protected space for attachment-enhancement work at home
- Practice attachment-enhancement games within a defined therapeutic space

MATERIALS NEEDED:

- A Nurture Nook within your own treatment space (containing a circular cushion, pillows, blanket)
- *Design a Nurture Nook* handout

DIRECTIONS:

1. Introduce the dyad to your Nurture Nook and explain the purpose of this space: "This is where you, your parent, and I will play fun games together. We will practice taking care of each other and working together as a team while having fun."
2. Spend some time engaging in several nurture-based exercises in the Nurture Nook. Basic nurturing activities (like putting bandages or lotion on hurts, brushing hair, or reading books while snuggling) can all happen in the Nurture Nook. You can find more specific interventions aimed at enhancing the attachment relationship in *Big Behaviors in Small Containers* (Goodyear-Brown, 2022) and later in this chapter. Feeding games, cooperative games, and games that encourage the child to risk allowing themselves to be nurtured in order to receive a powerfully pleasurable payoff can also be played in the Nurture Nook.
3. Explain to the dyad that they will have an opportunity to create their own Nurture Nook at home. Provide them with the *Design a Nurture Nook* handout and ask them to brainstorm what items they would like to include in this space. Let the dyad know that they don't need to purchase new items for their nook. Instead, help them identify what

Copyright © 2026 Paris Goodyear-Brown, *Big Behaviors in All Containers*. All rights reserved.

items they already have at home that they can commandeer for this new space (e.g., pillows, blankets).

4. Discuss where in the family's home would be the best place to put the Nurture Nook. In some families, the nook may need to be constructed and deconstructed after each use due to their need for space or the availability of certain items. Support them in designing something realistic within their space and economic constraints.
5. Become curious about what sorts of supplies (e.g., water bottle, favorite stuffy, soothing essential oil, special snack) should be present in the Nurture Nook.
6. Help the dyad decide how much time (i.e., what dose of nurture work) they would like to spend in their Nurture Nook each day, or how many days of the week they will use the nook. For example, some families with young children may spend just 5 minutes a day each day in their Nurture Nook. Other families may spend 15 minutes in the Nurture Nook every other day. Help the dyad work out an achievable rhythm and "dosage" of time in this space. Explain that you will be offering different activities for them to do at home during these times.
7. Encourage the dyad to take a picture of their nook and bring it to the next session, as you will be helping them create something to add to it.

 Copyright © 2026 Paris Goodyear-Brown, *Big Behaviors in All Containers*. All rights reserved.

DESIGN A NURTURE NOOK HANDOUT

Circle the items you need in your Nurture Nook.
Draw any other items you might need to include.

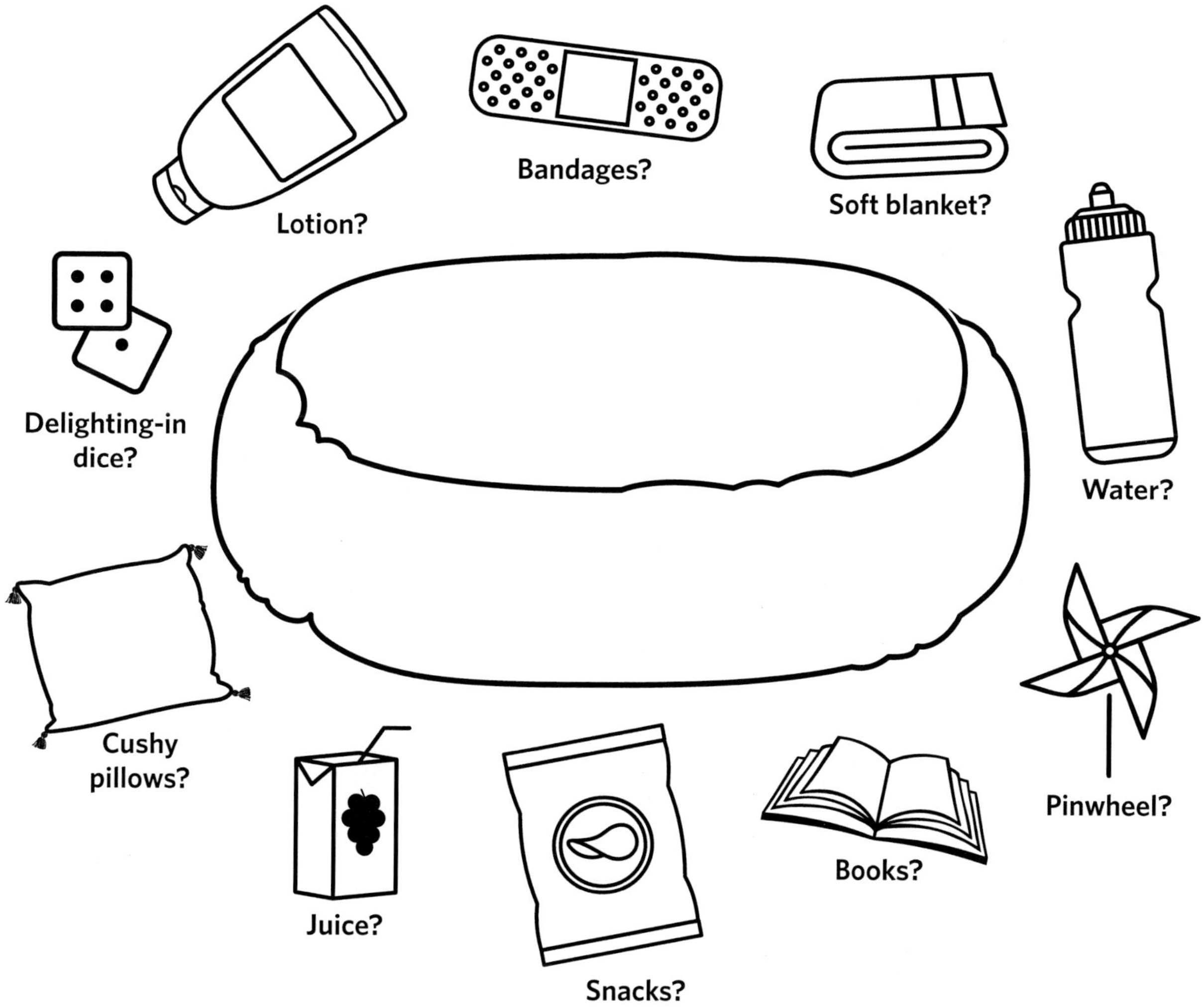

Copyright © 2026 Paris Goodyear-Brown, *Big Behaviors in All Containers*. All rights reserved.

7.2 A SAFE CIRCLE

DESCRIPTION:

Inviting a caregiver to read a book out loud to their child, usually while snuggling, is one activity that we strongly encourage in the Nurture Nook. Children who have experienced multiple caregiver disruptions before coming to foster or adoptive care may have very little experience being tucked in next to a Safe Boss who is reading to them. One book that can be read in the Nurture Nook is a bibliotherapy tool called *A Safe Circle for Little U*. This story is the journey of Little U, whose first caregiver leaves him. It chronicles Little U's loneliness, confusion, distrust, and courageous risk to trust a new caregiver. The story ends with Little U and Capital Q becoming a trusting team together. The safe circle in the story naturally lends itself to a discussion of which grown-ups might be in the child's safe circle.

TREATMENT GOALS:

- Enhance the attachment relationship between the caregiver and child
- Identify people who feel safe to the child

MATERIALS NEEDED:

- The book *A Safe Circle for Little U* (Goodyear-Brown, 2016)
- Paper plate
- Coloring utensils (e.g., crayons, markers)
- Modeling clay
- Circular sand tray
- Sand tray miniatures

DIRECTIONS:

1. Introduce the idea of having the caregiver read a story to the child. Explore whether and how they read books at home together. Then invite them to snuggle (or arrange themselves physically in a way that is comfortable to both of them) in your office Nurture Nook. You might ask, "Johnny, do you want to be on Dad's lap? Or tucked up next to him?"
2. You might consider having a blanket available and offer to tuck the dyad in under the blanket together. Sometimes, both the parent and child appreciate this sort of caretaking by the therapist.
3. Have the caregiver read *A Safe Circle for Little U* to their child.
4. After the story is complete, highlight how hard it was for Little U to lose his first safe circle and what a brave risk it was for him to allow a new caregiver to take care of him. Highlight the ways in which Little U and his new caregiver, Capital Q, teamed together to accomplish cool tasks.

Copyright © 2026 Paris Goodyear-Brown, *Big Behaviors in All Containers*. All rights reserved.

5. Offer a paper plate to each partner and have them draw pictures of the people who make up their safe circle. Alternatively, they can create these figures out of modeling clay, or you can offer the client a circular sand tray and have them choose miniatures to represent each of their support people.
6. Reflect on the qualities these people have in common. This discussion can highlight that people in their safe circle are kind and trustworthy, follow through on their word, do not make fun of each other, help each other, and so on.
7. Invite the child to choose a miniature for themselves and have them put it in the middle of their circle of support people. Explore how it feels for them to be surrounded with safety.

Copyright © 2026 Paris Goodyear-Brown, *Big Behaviors in All Containers*. All rights reserved.

7.3 CUSHIONING THE CONNECTION

DESCRIPTION:

Intimacy of any kind can be threatening for traumatized children. For these children, it can help to facilitate delighting-in games in session, which are interventions that offer both the child and parent powerfully pleasurable payoffs for cooperating, negotiating, nurturing each other, or simply being silly and laughing together. These games may involve painting each other's nails, eating a piece of licorice to the middle, or moving across the room with a pipe cleaner between their two bodies. The goal is that both the child and caregiver feel supported while taking risks to nurture each other. Since games like this require intimacy, trust, and risk-taking, it helps to have a whole set of games that children can choose from. This intervention offers a visual tracking tool, drawn to look like a Nurture Nook, to document the games that the dyad has played. The completed tracking tool can be given to the dyad, posted in their comfy corner at home, and serve as a guide for doses of delighting-in game play.

TREATMENT GOALS:

- Provide a tool to track which delighting-in games are most fun for the parent-child dyad
- Encourage rehearsal of delighting-in games in the home environment

MATERIALS NEEDED:

- *Cushioning the Connection Tracking Tool* handout

DIRECTIONS:

1. Complete the *Design a Nurture Nook* exercise (7.1) with the parent and child prior to using this tool.
2. Have a copy of the *Cushioning the Connection Tracking Tool* handout with you as you lead the dyad through a variety of delighting-in games in your office Nurture Nook. Each dyad will have different clinical needs, so some will prefer nurture-based activities, others will prefer high-challenge activities, and still others will prefer storytelling games.
3. As you are wrapping up the portion of your clinical session that focuses on these attachment-enhancement games, ask the dyad which activities they enjoyed the most.
4. Invite them to write the names of these activities in the cushions drawn on the *Cushioning the Connection Tracking Tool* handout.
5. Instruct them to take the tracking tool with them and post it in their home Nurture Nook to guide daily practice. Even a five-minute dose of delighting-in games daily can help enhance connections between parents and children.
6. They can bring the handout back and add to it week after week, or you can provide a new one at each session, depending on how high the dyad's needs are for novelty.

Copyright © 2026 Paris Goodyear-Brown, *Big Behaviors in All Containers*. All rights reserved.

(Some families will want to rehearse the same games over and over, while others will feel more buy-in if they are offered at least one novel exercise during each session.) The more repetitions of delighting-in games at home, the faster the dyad will lay down new neural pathways for connection to one another.

Copyright © 2026 Paris Goodyear-Brown, *Big Behaviors in All Containers*. All rights reserved.

CUSHIONING THE CONNECTION TRACKING TOOL HANDOUT

What were your favorite delighting-in games today?
Write the names of each game in the individual cushions.

Copyright © 2026 Paris Goodyear-Brown, *Big Behaviors in All Containers*. All rights reserved.

7.4 PILLOWS FOR PLAYTIME

DESCRIPTION:

This intervention invites the creation of a concrete reminder (a pillow) of the comforting, connecting activities that the child and caregiver are practicing in the Nurture Nook. Children benefit from concrete, three-dimensional anchors that reinforce the therapeutic learning they have been doing in session. They also benefit from getting their sensory needs met. One way to achieve both of these goals is to help them construct a small pillow, with the help of their caregiver, that they can use to remember each attachment-enhancement game they play in session. They can take this pillow home as a transitional object and use it to further decorate their homemade Nurture Nook. This pillow also serves as a physical reminder of the nurturing interactions they have practiced with their caregiver in session, which they can rehearse at home.

TREATMENT GOALS:

- Create a three-dimensional anchor for the therapeutic experience
- Rehearse attachment-enhancement experiences in between sessions

MATERIALS NEEDED:

- *Cushioning the Connection Tracking Tool* handout from previous session (7.3)
- Fabric and stuffing
- Craft materials (e.g., felt, sequins, ribbons)
- Glue
- Fabric pens
- Needle and thread (only offered with adult supervision)

DIRECTIONS:

1. Prior to the session, sew three sides of a pillow together but leave one side open.
2. Explain to the dyad that you will be helping them make a pillow that they can take home. Invite them to add stuffing to the pillow while explaining, "Some people like pillows with lots of fluff, while others like their pillows to be flat. Mom, which kind of pillow does your child like most?" This exploration encourages the parent to move into the Storykeeper role and narrate out loud what they remember about the child.
3. Invite the caregiver to help the child sew up the final edge of the pillow, explaining that since needles can hurt us, the child needs their Safe Boss to supervise the task.
4. Ask the child to name a fun activity that they have played in a previous session with their caregiver in the Nurture Nook. For example, a child might say, "That game where you and Mom rocked me in the blanket and sang to me." If so, help the caregiver facilitate further rocking in the blanket during this session.

Copyright © 2026 Paris Goodyear-Brown, *Big Behaviors in All Containers*. All rights reserved.

5. When the dyad has finished playing the game, record the name of the game on the *Cushioning the Connection Tracking Tool* handout from the previous session (7.3). In this example, the Theraplay game Rock the Blanket would be written on the pillow.
6. Introduce the craft materials to the dyad and invite them to explore different textures. Help them decide on which type of materials they'd like to glue (or sew) onto their pillow to help them remember this game. For example, if the attachment game they played involved decorating each other with sticky jewels or ribbons, they might choose to sew a ribbon onto their reminder pillow.
7. Each week, invite the dyad to choose different sensory materials to decorate their pillow with. They might choose a soft, furry material one week and a rough, burlap surface the next.
8. As a fun addition, the child and caregiver can write affirming notes or words to each other on the pillow, which represent how it felt to play together.
9. When the pillow is complete (this will take several weeks), instruct the dyad to take the pillow home and add it to their Nurture Nook.

Copyright © 2026 Paris Goodyear-Brown, *Big Behaviors in All Containers*. All rights reserved.

7.5 RITUALS, RESOURCE, AND RELATIONSHIP

DESCRIPTION:

Children who have endured multiple adverse childhood experiences are often lacking in trust with their caregivers. If children have survived several caregiver disruptions, they may have very few daily rituals that help them connect to their caregivers. Foster and adoptive parents can feel at a loss for how to connect with the child they are now caring for, as they are often missing lots of the history. Therapists can facilitate the development of new rituals between the dyad as one way to begin building a shared history between them. For example, during COVID-19, I had one dyad who created their Nurture Nook in the "mommy/daddy bed" with a specific fuzzy blanket, a scented candle burning on the bedside table, and a cup of coffee for the mom and a cup of chocolate milk for the child. When they would join me on the screen for their telehealth session, we would engage in a ritual in which the child poured a little bit of her chocolate milk into her mom's coffee to create a mini version of a mocha latte. At the end of the session, the child and mom would clink their cups together three times while saying, "We stick together."

TREATMENT GOALS:

- Invite repetitions of nurturing care between the parent and child
- Pair the relationship between the parent and child with access to resources, recapitulating early dyadic attachment behaviors

MATERIALS NEEDED:

- None needed

DIRECTIONS:

1. Explain to the caregiver:

   "When babies are born, they have no ability to feed themselves. They are wholly dependent on their caregiver for nourishment. Good-enough parents hold their babies, engaging in nurturing touch and making loving eye contact while they nurse the baby or feed them a bottle. In each feeding session, relationship and resource are paired. The child in your care did not get those thousands of repetitions of a safe, reliable caregiver providing a needed resource. So we are going to design at least one ritual that you and your child can have together that will encourage this kind of pairing."

2. Invite the caregiver to name the kinds of activities that encourage the pairing of a relationship and a resource. Examples might include reading a bedtime story, making cookies together, or cutting with scissors.

Copyright © 2026 Paris Goodyear-Brown, *Big Behaviors in All Containers*. All rights reserved.

3. Design one ritual that can be practiced each day in the dyad's home. For example, the parent and child might start making a smoothie together each morning. The steps of this activity can be ritualized: The caregiver pours a cup of milk into the blender. The child counts out five frozen strawberries and adds those in. The caregiver puts the lid on the blender and plugs it in. The child presses the button. Once the smoothie is done, they pour it into special matching cups that are later cleaned for use again the following morning.
4. Part of the benefit of designing a ritual like this is that you can ask the dyad to rehearse the steps of this ritual with you. As children's attachments to their new caregivers grow, they can become very proud of the shared storykeeping they have with their caregiver around how these unique family rituals work.

Copyright © 2026 Paris Goodyear-Brown, *Big Behaviors in All Containers*. All rights reserved.

7.6 MOMMY AND ME

DESCRIPTION:

This intervention is another attachment-enhancement intervention that can be done in the Nurture Nook. Many of the traumatized children we see in practice have separation anxiety and benefit from concrete reminders of the connection between themselves and their caregiver, especially when they are apart. This intervention begins with a reading of the classic children's book *The Kissing Hand* and finishes with the caregiver and child labeling a letter M in each of their hands, which connects them in a playful, tangible way. I first did this intervention with a child who was adopted interracially at birth and who was delighted the first time I found the M lines in both his hand *and* his adoptive mother's hand. He behaviors had long been asking the questions *Do I belong with you? Do you belong with me? Are we the same?* As I traced the M-shaped lines of his palm with a Sharpie, he worriedly asked, "What if it comes off when I wash my hands?" His mother responded with reassurance that they would simply draw them on again. This client asked his mother to redraw the matching "Mommy and Me" M-shaped lines every day for the next several weeks.

TREATMENT GOALS:

- Increase connection between the child and their caregiver
- Identify ways in which the child and caregiver are the same
- Offer concrete reminders of the caregiver-child connection during periods of separation

MATERIALS NEEDED:

- The book *The Kissing Hand* (Penn, 2007)
- Permanent and washable markers

DIRECTIONS:

1. Begin by inviting the caregiver to read *The Kissing Hand*, a beloved children's story in which Chester the Raccoon is headed off to his first night of school, which will mean separation from his mom. If you haven't read the book—spoiler alert—the story ends with his mother giving him a kiss in his hand that runs all the way up his arm and into his heart, keeping him warm and connected to her throughout his time away. It becomes even more poignant when Chester looks back at his mom, seems to understand intuitively that the separation may be hard for her as well, and runs back to give her a kiss in her hand before he scampers off to learn.
2. After reading the story, talk about the powerful ways in which our hands can be used to build connections—for example, hand holding, high fives, pats on the back, hugs, fist bumps, and so forth.

Copyright © 2026 Paris Goodyear-Brown, *Big Behaviors in All Containers*. All rights reserved.

3. Then ask the caregiver:

   "Do you know the other really cool thing about hands? Most of our hands have lots of lines in the palms. Can you take [*child's name*]'s hand and look at their palm? What shapes do you see? Can you trace the shapes as you see them?"

4. When you have supported the caregiver in exploring their child's hand, invite the child to hold the caregiver's palm and find as many shapes as they can find in the caregiver's hand.
5. This tracing of shapes in the palms of the hands was first introduced to me while training in the Theraplay model. In their version of this intervention, often the hands are coated with baby powder to make the lines, cracks, and crevices in the hands easier to see. In this adaptation, you look for three lines of any size and shape that can be traced together to form the letter M.
6. When you find the M in each palm, exclaim, "Wow! You each have an M in your hand. One for [*caregiver's name*], and the other for [*child's name*]. You two belong together. How cool!" Then trace the M in the color of their choice. Offer permanent and washable markers, although many children choose the permanent marker if their caregiver agrees.
7. Encourage the dyad to spend a few minutes in the Nurture Nook, each morning before school, retracing the M in each of their hands.

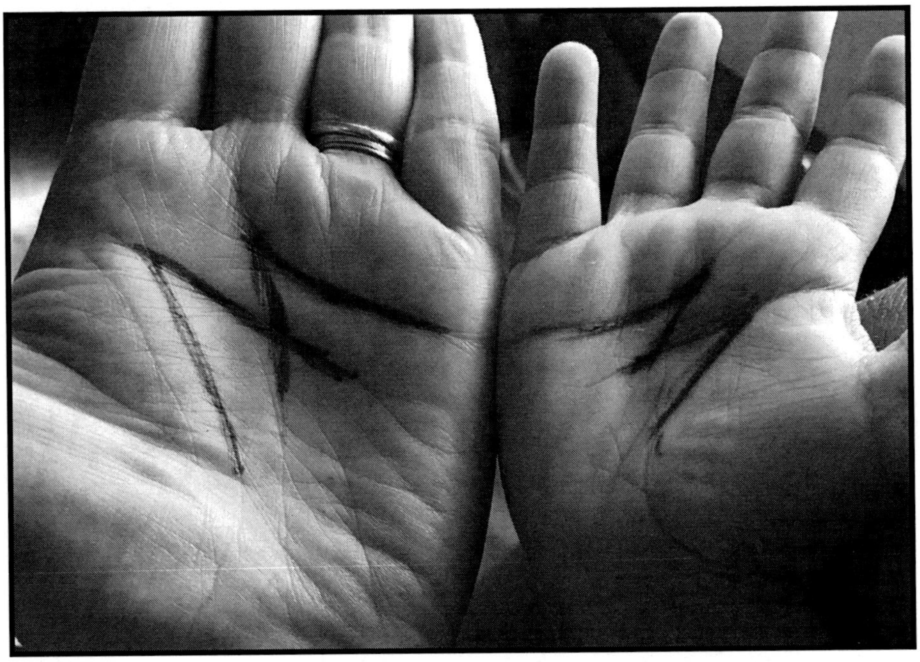

 Copyright © 2026 Paris Goodyear-Brown, *Big Behaviors in All Containers*. All rights reserved.

7.7 DELIGHTING-IN STORIES

DESCRIPTION:

One of the goals of TraumaPlay is to build coherent narratives within the family system of the hard things that have happened. However, telling stories about hard things is easier for parents to do if they have already practiced telling stories about positive experiences with their child. Telling positive stories has the added benefit of "dosing" the child with a moment of their parent's focused delight while also helping the parent practice giving developmentally appropriate narratives about pleasant content before introducing anything more difficult. This tool provides parents with some structure to engage in positive narration about their child, breaking down narrative prompts into the following areas: celebrations of new competencies, moments of shared humor from the week, prosocial choices or caretaking behaviors exhibited by the child, and times when the child used their voice to ask for what they need.

TREATMENT GOALS:

- Train the caregiver to tell a positive story about their child
- Practice caregiver verbalization of stories that celebrate the child in preparation for the later work of creating coherent trauma narratives

MATERIALS NEEDED:

- *Delighting-In Story Starters* handout

DIRECTIONS:

1. Invite the caregiver to an individual session and explain the following:

    "One of the pieces of work we will need to do is help you and your child share a story of the hard things that have happened in your family. But diving into stories about hard things can feel overwhelming for parents, so we like to practice storytelling first with positive stories about your child. We call these 'delighting-in stories.'

    "A delighting-in story is one that brags on your child in some way. It might be focused on a new competency your child is developing and sound like 'This week, my child tied their own shoes for the very first time!' Other stories might highlight a time when your child provided care for another member of the family, shared a toy with their sibling, or used their asking words for something they needed instead of demanding it."

2. Offer the parent a copy of the *Delighting-In Story Starters* handout, which gives lots of examples of stories the caregiver could tell in joint sessions with their child. Some parents like to have time to think about the story they want to tell in session during the week prior, so encourage the caregiver to write down any ideas they have in each of these categories.

Copyright © 2026 Paris Goodyear-Brown, *Big Behaviors in All Containers*. All rights reserved.

3. Explain that the caregiver will tell this delighting-in story in the next session after they and their child have played some delighting-in games in the Nurture Nook. The parent will narrate the story while the child enjoys a snack.
4. Some parents will need significant help in telling a story that is truly positive about their child, so you might consider vetting the stories before they are told. You will also want to be ready to amplify the delight if you are working with depressed caregivers who may show up with blunted affect or monotone voices while sharing their stories.

Copyright © 2026 Paris Goodyear-Brown, *Big Behaviors in All Containers*. All rights reserved.

DELIGHTING-IN STORY STARTERS HANDOUT

During each session, we will have you tell a story in which you get to do one of the following:

1. Celebrate a new competency that your child has developed or achieved. Examples include:
    a. Learning to ride a bike
    b. Reading for 20 minutes out loud
    c. Making their own breakfast or lunch
2. Rehearse a moment of humor or delight from the week. Examples include:
    a. A time your child told a joke
    b. A night your child did a silly dance before bed
    c. A time you played three rounds of thumb wars, and your child won every time
3. Give the details of a prosocial choice (or choice that required self-control that was clearly hard for your child, but they did it anyway). Examples include:
    a. A time your child came to you and told you their sibling was bothering them
    b. A time your child sat with you at dinner for a long time and then politely asked to be excused
    c. A time your child could have taken the last cookie, but they shared it with a sibling instead
4. Describe, in detail, a caretaking moment that occurred between you and your child. Examples include:
    a. A time your child had a boo-boo and came to you to take care of it
    b. A time you and your child both took care of a pet together
    c. A time you made food that your child liked, and they ate it all up
5. Describe a time when your child used their voice to ask for what they needed. Examples include:
    a. A time your child expressed that they were scared and asked for comfort vulnerably
    b. A time your child asked for a kind of food, drink, or resource (like screen time) with their asking words (this is especially important to rehearse if the child normally demands things)
    c. A time your child felt confused by a concept in school and asked appropriately for help with it (this is especially important if your child expresses frustration during homework time and refuses to complete assignments)

Copyright © 2026 Paris Goodyear-Brown, *Big Behaviors in All Containers*. All rights reserved.

Below are some prompts you can use to begin a delighting-in story about your child. How would you complete each of these stories for your own child? Be ready to share your own example in your next session with your child.

1. When you were a baby, I used to snuggle you, and you would . . .
2. I need to brag on Sally. She has been working so hard on ________ and just this week . . .
3. We had a super silly moment together earlier this week when Sally . . .
4. Sally and I baked cookies together. I broke the eggs, and she stirred in the flour.
5. Earlier this week, Sally really needed ________ and I wasn't understanding her yet, but she was able to use her good words to ask for what she needed.

Copyright © 2026 Paris Goodyear-Brown, *Big Behaviors in All Containers*. All rights reserved.

7.8 DELIGHTING-IN DICE

DESCRIPTION:

This intervention is a fun and concrete way to support the rehearsal of nurture within family systems. Children with attachment wounds often need significantly increased doses of nurturing care to shift their core belief that there is no one who will meet their needs and keep them safe. This exercise draws on Gary Chapman's (Chapman & Campbell, 2016) work on love languages by exploring the unique ways in which the child and caregiver receive love most deeply (Goodyear-Brown, 2021).

TREATMENT GOALS:

- Provide psychoeducation about the five love languages
- Identify the child and caregiver's primary love language
- Support the child and caregiver in expressing and receiving love

MATERIALS NEEDED:

- Large dry-erase die
- Dry-erase markers
- *Delighting-In Dice* handout
- Coloring utensils (e.g., crayons, markers)
- Two one-inch foam cubes (one for each client)

DIRECTIONS:

1. Invite the caregiver-child dyad into the Nurture Nook. Explain that today they will each be making "delighting-in dice" based on the five love languages.
2. Write one of the primary love languages on each side of the dry-erase die as you explain each one. The five classic love languages include physical touch, words of affirmation, quality time, acts of service, and gifts. You can simply label the sixth side of the die with "free choice."
3. Give each client a turn rolling the large dry-erase die, and whichever love language it lands on, ask them to give an example of it. For example, an act of service might be unloading the dishwasher. Physical touch might be a hug or high five. Keep rolling the die until at least one example has been stated for each love language.
4. Give each client a copy of the *Delighting-In Dice* handout and have them color in the die that represents their top love language. Support each person in generating and writing down six expressions of their love language on the worksheet.
5. Let each client choose a one-inch foam cube (make sure to have several colors available, as choice amplifies voice). Help them write an example of their primary love language on each side of the die. For example, a child whose primary love language

Copyright © 2026 Paris Goodyear-Brown, *Big Behaviors in All Containers*. All rights reserved.

is physical touch might write down the following six expressions: high five, fist bump, Eskimo kiss, pat on the back, hug, and hand massage.

6. Invite the dyad to set aside five minutes, at least three times a week, to take turns throwing the dice in their Nurture Nook at home and giving and receiving expressions of love.

 Copyright © 2026 Paris Goodyear-Brown, *Big Behaviors in All Containers*. All rights reserved.

DELIGHTING-IN DICE HANDOUT

Everybody has a primary way in which they give and receive love. Using the dice below, identify your primary portal for receiving delight.

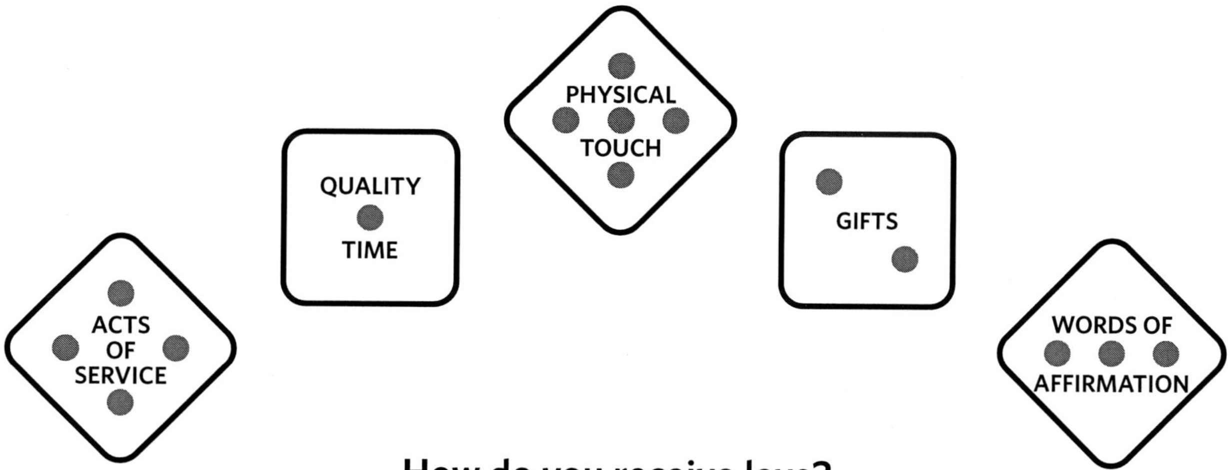

How do you receive love?

★ ______________________________ ★

List six specific ways others can love you:

1. ______________________________
2. ______________________________
3. ______________________________
4. ______________________________
5. ______________________________
6. ______________________________

Copyright © 2026 Paris Goodyear-Brown, *Big Behaviors in All Containers*. All rights reserved.

7.9 STICK TOGETHER SQUIGZ

DESCRIPTION:

One of the hallmarks of a Safe Boss is staying physically close enough to a child to keep them safe. The optimal distance between a caregiver and child depends on many factors, including the child's developmental level, ability to manage themselves, trust between the grown-up and child, and how dangerous the environment around them might be. For example, a Safe Boss might let their four-year-old run quite a distance away from them in a large grassy field but is likely to keep them much closer, and hold their hand, while walking in a busy parking lot. This intervention encourages caregivers and children to play with physical distance in various scenarios.

TREATMENT GOALS:

- Dramatize physical proximity between the caregiver and child as one aspect of Safe Boss behavior
- Identify situations that may require closer physical proximity or distance
- Identify behaviors that may encourage psychological proximity or distance

MATERIALS NEEDED:

- A set of Squigz (these are flexible silicone shapes with suction cups)
- Yarn or pipe cleaners
- *Stick Together Signals* handout

DIRECTIONS:

1. Offer the set of Squigz to the caregiver and child, inviting them to explore how they stick together.
2. Explain how the Squigz can be used as a metaphor for Safe Boss behavior:

   "One of the primary ways that kids stay safe is to stick together with their Safe Bosses. Today, we are going to see how you two stick together in different situations. These toys can stick to your body and stick to each other. Try sticking one to your forehead. Once you have them good and stuck, see whether you can stick them to each other."
3. Allow them to explore sticking one end of the Squigz to a body part (e.g., their forehead, their knee, the palm of their hand) and then connecting the Squigz to each other. Some dyads will be comfortable with being very close together as they play with the Squigz, while others may decide to make a long chain of Squigz between them.
4. Once the dyad has gotten the idea of making chains of different lengths between them, feel free to use yarn or chains of pipe cleaners to play with different physical distances

Copyright © 2026 Paris Goodyear-Brown, *Big Behaviors in All Containers*. All rights reserved.

between the caregiver and child based on examples that you generate. For example, you might say, "Show me how close you like to be physically when you are watching a movie, when you are grocery shopping, and when you are irritated with each other."

5. For some dyads, you might move from physical distance to psychological distance by generating examples of difficult moments that have happened between the caregiver and child (e.g., a child who withdraws to their bedroom whenever the caregiver asks about their day). Use the yarn or pipe cleaners to demonstrate different examples of withdrawal or intimacy.
6. Give each of them a *Stick Together Signals* handout. Invite them to write behaviors they exhibit (e.g., a smile, warm eye gaze, listening without judgment) or words they say that signal to others that they are safe to approach.
7. In a future session, you could build on the conversation about body language, becoming curious about which of the caregiver's nonverbal cues signal danger to others. (Strong therapeutic rapport must already be in place to support this kind of curiosity with a caregiver.)

Copyright © 2026 Paris Goodyear-Brown, *Big Behaviors in All Containers*. All rights reserved.

STICK TOGETHER SIGNALS HANDOUT

What signals do you give with your words or body language to let others know that it is safe to approach? Label each Squigz below with one of your *stick together* signals.

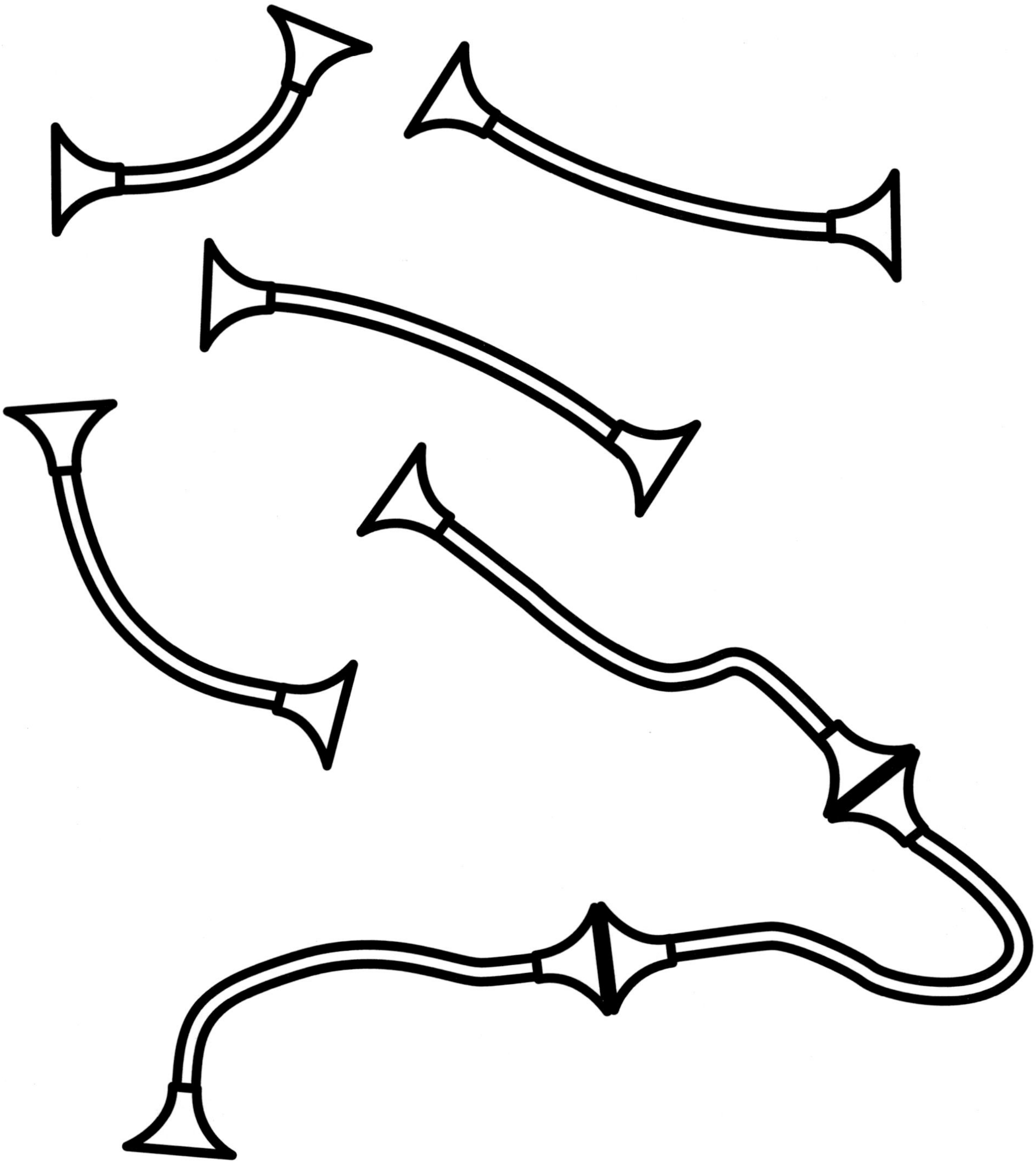

Copyright © 2026 Paris Goodyear-Brown, *Big Behaviors in All Containers*. All rights reserved.

7.10 MEET IN THE MIDDLE

DESCRIPTION:

Many young children experience nurture through healthy touch and feeding experiences that require the Nurturer and Safe Boss to gather food and offer it to their offspring. There is a famous moment in the Disney movie *Lady and the Tramp* in which Lady and Tramp are sharing a plate of spaghetti and meatballs. They each take an end of a spaghetti noodle and eat it to the middle, resulting in an unexpected and sweet kiss. This intervention harnesses the novelty and playful connection from this moment between caregivers and children in similar ways.

TREATMENT GOALS:

- Enhance the attachment relationship between the caregiver and child
- Increase positive communication within the dyad
- Practice compromise and negotiation

MATERIALS NEEDED:

- Long red licorice strings
- Yarn
- Scissors
- Sand tray miniature or other small object

DIRECTIONS:

1. Ask the dyad whether they have ever seen *Lady and the Tramp*, especially the scene where they eat the spaghetti noodle to the middle. If not, you might pull up that moment on video.
2. For younger children, offer the licorice string to the dyad. Instruct each to place one end in their mouths and have them chew toward the middle. This often comes with lots of laughter. As the candy string gets smaller and smaller, the child and caregiver negotiate who will get the last bite. They may decide to end with a kiss if the family finds this kind of physical affection comfortable and translates physical affection from a caregiver as a nurturing gesture.
3. For older children and teens, you can do a more challenging and nontouch version of this exercise by replacing the licorice with yarn. Cut a long piece of yarn and have the teen hold one end of the string while their caregiver holds the other end.
4. Invite the dyad to decide on one small object (usually a sand tray miniature) that they will pick up from its current location and move to another location using only the string between them.
5. The caregiver and child will need to wrap the yarn around the object and then pull it taut enough to pick it up together by pulling on each end of the yarn.

Copyright © 2026 Paris Goodyear-Brown, *Big Behaviors in All Containers*. All rights reserved.

6. Encourage verbal communication between the caregiver and child. For example, you might say:

   "Sometimes, the string needs to be tightened on both ends before the object can be picked up. It will help if you two communicate this verbally. Johnny, you might ask Dad whether he can pull his string tighter. Dad, you might offer a countdown to the moment the two of you pull hard on your ends of the string and pick up the toy. You might also need to talk together about the new location where you want to set the toy down."

7. Once they have picked up the object, celebrate their success by saying, "When you work together, you guys make a great team!"

Copyright © 2026 Paris Goodyear-Brown, *Big Behaviors in All Containers*. All rights reserved.

7.11 SWEET DREAMS LOTION POTION

DESCRIPTION:

When trauma—especially acute trauma, like a car accident or house fire—occurs within a family system, the sudden overwhelming distress can block the child from accessing positive childhood memories. In this exercise, you'll offer a multitude of scents to the child to see whether any might spark positive childhood memories. Trauma hijacks our senses—deeply encoding the sounds, smells, and tastes that remind us of the trauma—while whispering in our ears to avoid these sensory experiences at all costs. By pairing olfactory experiences with previous happy memories, you can provide some practical pathways to take back the territory stolen by trauma.

TREATMENT GOALS:

- Identify warm, happy, or nurturing family memories
- Rehearse the stories associated with these memories to increase coherence in the family narrative
- Mitigate bedtime stress and potential nightmares

MATERIALS NEEDED:

- A collection of scented lotions or essential oils
- A magical-looking basket
- Sand art or lotion bottles in different shapes
- Mixing bowl and spoon
- *Lotion Potion* handout

DIRECTIONS:

1. Present the dyad with a magical-looking basket full of essential lotions and oils. (My basket is made of gold wire.)
2. The child's natural curiosity may kick in right away, and they may spontaneously start smelling the items. If not, prompt the child and their caregiver to explore the scents in the basket together:

   "These lotions are here for you two to explore together. When something big and scary happens in a family, it can be hard to remember that you have each other now and that you had each other before the hard thing ever happened. Did you know that smells can take us right back to certain memories, good or bad? I thought we'd concentrate on good memories today. Feel free to open each lotion or oil, take a whiff, close your eyes, and see whether any happy family memories surface for you. My guess is that two or three of these smells will remind you of some fun times that you have shared. For example, the vanilla-scented lotion might remind you of baking sugar cookies together during the holidays."

Copyright © 2026 Paris Goodyear-Brown, *Big Behaviors in All Containers*. All rights reserved.

3. Make sure to give both the child and caregiver a chance to share their memories. For example, one of my four-year-old clients smelled the Stress Relief lotion from Bath and Body Works and immediately said, "This reminds me of when we were driving and saw a leaf pile on the side of the road. We stopped the car and all jumped in it. Remember, Mom?" Although his mother did not remember this experience, she did experience a resparking of previous joy as her son remembered.
4. Record each scent and accompanying memory on the *Lotion Potion* handout and add a squeeze of that lotion or oil to the mixing bowl. What emerges is a lotion potion that is unique to each family's set of positive memories.
5. Mix all the oils or lotions together and pour the finished lotion potion into a sand art or lotion bottle to give to the family.
6. Instruct the caregiver to take the lotion potion home and use it to do a short massage of the child's hands just before bed while rehearsing the positive memories represented in the potion. This can help reduce any trauma-related nighttime stress or nightmare.
7. Repeat until the lotion is gone.

Copyright © 2026 Paris Goodyear-Brown, *Big Behaviors in All Containers*. All rights reserved.

LOTION POTION HANDOUT

Scent

Vanilla

Story

I remember when . . .

Scent

Story

I remember when . . .

Scent

Story

I remember when . . .

Scent

Story

I remember when . . .

Scent

Story

I remember when . . .

Scent

Story

I remember when . . .

Copyright © 2026 Paris Goodyear-Brown, *Big Behaviors in All Containers*. All rights reserved.

7.12 SHAVING WITH DAD

DESCRIPTION:

This delightful activity is a playful way for dads and their kids to bond. In many cultures, as well as within the animal kingdom, family members perform hygiene tasks together, or for each other, as a way to express care. (Think about monkeys grooming each other.) Additionally, children who have experienced trauma often yearn to be grown-up already, envisioning that they will have more power as a grown-up. When children have survived several adverse childhood experiences, they have trouble trusting their caregivers and are less likely to engage in hygiene-related routines together. However, the novelty of learning to shave paired with knowledge that shaving is a pretty grown-up activity can increase the likelihood that a hurt child will participate in this exercise. While it can be done in the office, if you are an in-home therapist or can commandeer a singular restroom, that would be optimal.

TREATMENT GOALS:

- Enhance the attachment relationship between the caregiver and child
- Expand the child's window of tolerance for taking direction or receiving care from their caregiver
- Support cooperation within the dyad

MATERIALS NEEDED:

- Shaving cream
- Real razor for the grown-up
- Popsicle stick for the child
- Bowl of water
- Mirror
- Hand towels
- Tarp (optional)

DIRECTIONS:

1. Ask the child whether they have ever watched their dad shave. If the answer is yes, have them describe it to you. If the answer is no, ask Dad whether he would be willing to demonstrate.
2. Make sure a mirror, a basin of water, shaving cream, hand towels, and a razor are available. (Depending on whether you are doing this in your office, you might want to have a tarp too.)
3. Instead of having the dad apply shaving cream to himself, invite the child to apply it for him. Then invite the dad to put shaving cream on his child's face as well.
4. Explain that the child will pretend to shave their face while the dad shaves his. Offer a popsicle stick to the child and the real razor to the dad.

Copyright © 2026 Paris Goodyear-Brown, *Big Behaviors in All Containers*. All rights reserved.

5. You can heighten the challenge level in this activity by asking the child and dad to watch each other in the mirror and synchronize their movements, "shaving" the same parts of their faces and wetting their "razors" at the same time.
6. After they are finished, each participant can towel off the other person's face. If both parties agree, a soothing facial lotion could also be applied. If the child is willing to receive nurturing touch from the father figure, the dad could put the lotion on the child's face, and vice versa. In other dyads, each party might elect to put the lotion on themselves.
7. Celebrate the dyad's cooperation and care for one another as appropriate.

Copyright © 2026 Paris Goodyear-Brown, *Big Behaviors in All Containers*. All rights reserved.

7.13 POUCH JUMPING

DESCRIPTION:

In a healthy attachment system, the caregiver functions as a secure base and allows the child to explore their environment and practice gaining independence. When the child becomes tired, scared, sick, hungry, lonely, or distressed, they return to their caregiver, who then moves into the role of safe haven by welcoming the child back and comforting them in their distress or neediness. This pattern happens thousands of times in healthy attachment systems, but traumatized children may have had little experience with this pattern. This intervention provides a playful structure for helping a hurt child practice moving away from and returning to their caregiver in small degrees.

TREATMENT GOALS:

- Solidify the caregiver as a secure base for their child
- Support the caregiver in offering multiple repetitions of safe-haven behavior
- Enhance the attachment relationship between the caregiver and child

MATERIALS NEEDED:

- The book *Pouch!* (Stein, 2012)
- Hula hoop
- Sensory sack
- Large wooden die
- Hand puppets of predators (e.g., bear, wolf)
- *Joey Jumps* handout

DIRECTIONS:

1. Invite the caregiver-child dyad to snuggle in the Nurture Nook as the caregiver reads *Pouch!* to the child.
2. When they're done reading, have the dyad move to a larger space in your office or an outside area if available.
3. Explain that just like in the book, you are going to pretend that the child is a joey (a baby kangaroo) who stays in its mother's pouch for safety.
4. Ask the child, "How should we pretend that you are in her pouch?" Offer the hula hoops and sensory sack as possible options. For example, the dyad might decide to use the hula hoop to define the safe space that the joey jumps in and out of. They might decide to use the sensory sack by having the child stand very close to the caregiver inside the sensory sack. You can also invite a young child to stand on their caregiver's feet while the caregiver encircles the child with their arms.

Copyright © 2026 Paris Goodyear-Brown, *Big Behaviors in All Containers*. All rights reserved.

5. After deciding on a "pouch" the child will use, explain that the dyad will be playing a game in which the child rolls the die and whatever number comes up on the die will be the number of jumps that the child will take away from the caregiver. Each time the child jumps away from the caregiver, become curious about how this distance feels to them.
6. In some cases, the child client may enjoy pretending to become scared by something while they are exploring their environment. You might playfully "scare" the child with a variety of puppets (like a bear or wolf) as they jump away from their caregiver, leading them to jump back to their pouch as fast as they can. You can turn this into a challenge by encouraging the child to beat their previous time whenever they jump back to their secure base.
7. Facilitate a discussion about appropriate times the child might seek out their caregiver for help or comfort and write these on the *Joey Jumps* handout.

Copyright © 2026 Paris Goodyear-Brown, *Big Behaviors in All Containers*. All rights reserved.

JOEY JUMPS HANDOUT

When the joey gets scared, hurt, or tired, or just wants to snuggle, they return to their pouch.
Fill in each line between the jumps with a time you might need to return to your Safe Boss.

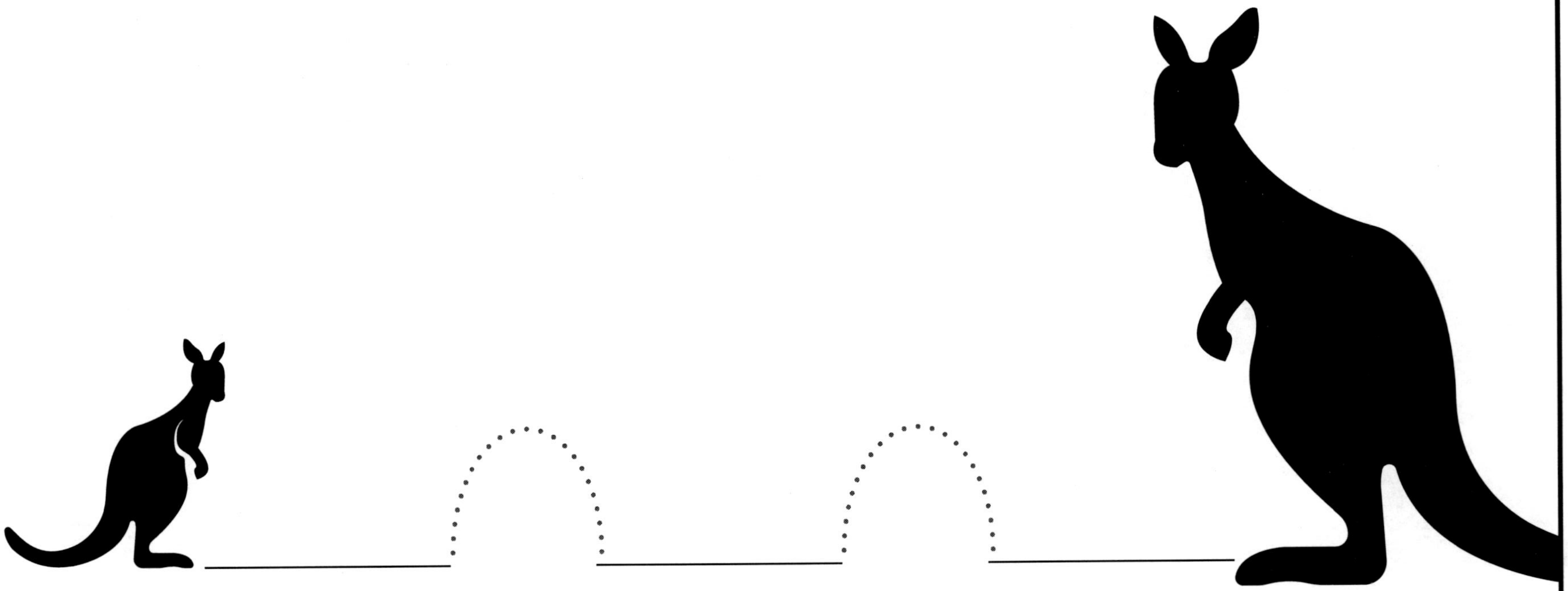

Copyright © 2026 Paris Goodyear-Brown, *Big Behaviors in All Containers*. All rights reserved.

eight

Working with Negative Activation of the Caregiver

Children with big behaviors often trigger problematic behaviors in their grown-ups. When exploring these problematic behaviors in session, it is important to assume that a caregiver always has positive intentions. Caregivers need to know that we like them. They need to have the felt sense of being enjoyed, understood, and maybe even delighted in before they will trust clinicians to work with the uncomfortable emotions, thoughts, and behaviors they wish they could avoid.

It is also important to understand that a caregiver's negative activation occurs along a continuum. Some caregivers will be able to quickly identify the pattern of escalation that occurs between themselves and their children. These caregivers will benefit from learning the Safe Boss discipline strategies discussed in chapter 4, which provide them with the internal structure needed to manage difficult situations with their child. Other caregivers may have internalized these discipline strategies but become dysregulated when they hear their child's high-pitched whine or see their teenager roll their eyes. These caregivers will benefit from learning self-regulation tools they can use when their equilibrium is challenged, many of which you can find in this chapter. This includes self-visualization techniques, mindful mantras, and distancing tools. They will also benefit from attunement strategies that use the power of oxytocin (the bonding hormone) to counter the effects of cortisol (the stress hormone).

In addition, several exercises in this chapter help caregivers explore their own window of tolerance and examine how they react when they're in a state of hyperarousal or hypoarousal. These interventions playfully prompt caregivers to reflect on how they experience themselves in various stress states and then take this work deeper by reflecting on how their child experiences them in each of these states. The reality is that caregivers feel pulled in too many directions—they work hard at their jobs and then come home and work even harder in their family lives—to remain in their window of tolerance all of the time. By making practical changes to their day-to-day rhythms, they can better remain in their window of tolerance and more easily return to baseline when they get kicked into a state of hyperarousal or hypoarousal. They can also learn to better manage their emotions by proactively identifying specific situations that engender stress so they can feel empowered to respond differently.

8.1 WOT ARE YOU DOING? FOR PARENTS

DESCRIPTION:

Parents are people first, and there are a variety of reasons they may get kicked out of their window of tolerance (WOT) into a state of hyperarousal or hypoarousal. However, when a child is dysregulated, their autonomic nervous system is very sensitive to the arousal state of their caregiver, which is why it is crucial for caregivers to understand their own stress response patterns. When caregivers can become aware of these patterns, they can more quickly return to their optimal arousal zone. This intervention is simply intended to help caregivers identify their own dysregulated behaviors when they are outside their window of tolerance.

TREATMENT GOALS:

- Provide psychoeducation about the window of tolerance
- Assess the caregiver's stress response patterns (hyperarousal or hypoarousal)

MATERIALS NEEDED:

- *WOT Are You Doing? for Parents* handout

DIRECTIONS:

1. Introduce the *WOT Are You Doing? for Parents* handout and explain the three basic arousal states (hyperarousal, optimal arousal, and hypoarousal) captured on the page.
2. Talk about the characteristics listed in the center column (the best parenting self) and invite the caregiver to share stories about times they have shown up for their child in these ways. Then ask them to think about times when they have been stressed and didn't respond this way.
3. Invite the caregiver to circle the behaviors they engage in most frequently when they are stressed. Based on the caregiver's response, it may become visually clear which stress response (hyperarousal or hypoarousal) they lean toward. If not, process the situations that engender either stress response. For example, some caregivers may move toward hypoarousal in the evenings, letting things like teeth brushing and bedtime slide because it feels like too much of a battle and their resources are depleted from the day. Other parents may find that the end of the day is when they tend to yell and criticize the most, and their fuse is shorter because of their depleted resources.
4. Explain that some of your work together will involve helping them learn to upregulate when they are in a state of hypoarousal and downregulate when they are in a state of hyperarousal.

Copyright © 2026 Paris Goodyear-Brown, *Big Behaviors in All Containers*. All rights reserved.

5. Set the stage for the work the parent will do over the next couple of sessions:

   "We will be exploring how it feels in your own body when you are outside your optimal arousal zone. We will also be exploring how your child may experience you when you are outside your optimal arousal zone. The more you explore your window of tolerance, the easier it is to be curious about what you need to come back into your optimal arousal zone."

Copyright © 2026 Paris Goodyear-Brown, *Big Behaviors in All Containers*. All rights reserved.

WOT ARE YOU DOING? FOR PARENTS HANDOUT

This exercise helps you reflect on your window of tolerance for stress and how you tend to react when you are kicked out of your optimal arousal zone. **Circle the behaviors you engage in most often.** What does this say about how you respond to parenting stress?

OVERRESPONDING	BEST PARENTING SELF	UNDERRESPONDING
Hyperarousal	**Optimal Arousal Zone**	**Hypoarousal**
Yelling	*Regulating my emotions*	*Withholding attention*
Barking out orders	*Giving clear, positive instructions*	*Withholding affection*
Slamming doors	*Setting clear, kind limits*	*Sleeping a lot*
Stomping around	*Asking for what I need*	*Scrolling on my phone*
Speaking critically	*Listening with compassion*	*Giving up on rules*
Controlling my kids	*Seeking to understand*	*Sighing a lot*
Hovering	*Enjoying my child*	*Feeling fuzzy and unsure about how to respond*
Rushing around	*Feeling safe with myself*	*Shutting down*
		Zoning out

Copyright © 2026 Paris Goodyear-Brown, *Big Behaviors in All Containers*. All rights reserved.

8.2 WOT ARE YOU DOING? FOR TEACHERS

DESCRIPTION:

Just like parents, teachers and childcare workers are humans who can get kicked out of their window of tolerance (WOT) for all sorts of reasons. And just like parents, a teacher's stress response patterns can impact the way a student learns in school. Therefore, this intervention is similar to the previous one in that it is simply intended to help teachers identify their own dysregulated behaviors when they are outside their window of tolerance. It is intended to be used during teacher in-services or professional development workshops. Teachers enjoy the normalization provided by the experiences of others within their school or administration.

TREATMENT GOALS:

- Provide psychoeducation about the window of tolerance
- Assess the teacher or childcare worker's stress response patterns (hyperarousal or hypoarousal)

MATERIALS NEEDED:

- *WOT Are You Doing? for Teachers* handout

DIRECTIONS:

1. Introduce the *WOT Are You Doing? for Teachers* handout and explain the three basic arousal states (hyperarousal, optimal arousal, and hypoarousal) captured on the page.
2. Talk about the characteristics listed in the center column (the best teacher self) and invite the teacher to share stories about times they have shown up for their students in these ways. Then ask them to think about times when they have been stressed out and didn't respond this way.
3. Invite the teacher to circle the behaviors they engage in most frequently when they are stressed. Based on the teacher's response, it may become visually clear which stress response (hyperarousal or hypoarousal) they lean toward. If not, process the situations that engender either stress response. For example, if the teacher reports yelling, barking out orders, and slamming doors (all behaviors associated with hyperarousal), invite them to share an example of a time when this occurred over the last week. You can ask questions like "What happened first?" "What happened next?" and "Then what happened?" These questions can help teachers reflect on their escalation patterns. The same process can be used when a teacher has circled hypoarousal symptoms like shutting down, withholding attention, or feeling fuzzy.
4. Explain that some of your work will involve helping them upregulate when they're in a state of hypoarousal and downregulate when they're in a state of hyperarousal.

Copyright © 2026 Paris Goodyear-Brown, *Big Behaviors in All Containers*. All rights reserved.

5. Set the stage for the work the teacher will do over the next couple of sessions:

   "We will be exploring how it feels in your own body when you are outside your optimal arousal zone. We will also be exploring how your students may experience you when you are outside your optimal arousal zone. The more you explore your window of tolerance, the easier it is to be curious about what you need to come back into your optimal arousal zone."

Copyright © 2026 Paris Goodyear-Brown, *Big Behaviors in All Containers*. All rights reserved.

WOT ARE YOU DOING? FOR TEACHERS HANDOUT

This exercise helps you reflect on your window of tolerance for stress and how you tend to react when you are kicked out of your optimal arousal zone. **Circle the behaviors you engage in most often.** What does this say about how you respond to teaching stress?

OVERRESPONDING	BEST TEACHER SELF	UNDERRESPONDING
Hyperarousal	**Optimal Arousal Zone**	**Hypoarousal**
Barking out orders	*Using kind tone*	*Ignoring classroom behaviors that should be addressed*
Giving directions more quickly than students can follow them	*Regulating my emotions*	*Letting the schedule/structure of the classroom slide*
Repeating myself over and over	*Having patience for students who take longer*	*Feeling fuzzy and unsure of how to respond*
Giving consequences quickly (time out, sending students to principal)	*Giving clear, positive instructions*	*Feeling numb, hopeless, or checked out*
Being impatient	*Setting clear, kind limits*	*Scrolling on my phone when students are working*
Correcting students in front of the class	*Connecting with my students*	
	Enjoying my classroom	

Copyright © 2026 Paris Goodyear-Brown, *Big Behaviors in All Containers*. All rights reserved.

8.3 THE FELT SENSE FOR YOU

DESCRIPTION:

After assessing the big behaviors that the caregiver exhibits when they are outside their window of tolerance, this intervention shifts the focus inward by helping the caregiver recognize their interoceptive cues that they are in distress. This includes cues such as a racing heartbeat, a clenched jaw, or butterflies in their stomach. By helping the caregiver hone their felt sense of hyperarousal, hypoarousal, and optimal arousal, they can better notice when they are beginning to escalate in their caregiving settings.

TREATMENT GOALS:

- Explore the caregiver's felt sense of different nervous system states
- Identify when the caregiver is moving out of their window of tolerance

MATERIALS NEEDED:

- *Felt Sense* handout
- Modeling clay
- Coloring utensils (e.g., crayons, markers)

DIRECTIONS:

1. Offer the caregiver the *Felt Sense* handout and invite them to create a symbol that represents how they experience themselves when they are in each nervous system state. They can use modeling clay to make these symbols or draw them directly on the handout. Some hyperarousal symbols that caregivers have created in their work with me include a ball with spikes on it, shrapnel, and a big, angry monster. Some hypoarousal symbols that caregivers have created in their work with me include a puddle, an empty cup, a very weighty bowling ball, and phone or computer screens (to represent bingeing whole seasons of a show or scrolling endlessly on social media).
2. In some cases, it can be useful for you to engage in some intentional self-disclosure, sharing the symbol you might create for yourself in a state of hyperarousal. For example, you might say:

   "When I become curious about my felt sense of hyperarousal, I often create a symbol of a hamster on a wheel. I feel like I am in frantic, constant motion but not getting anything done. So, I would create a hamster and a wheel in the column labeled hyperarousal. What would your symbol be for how you experience yourself in this state?"

Copyright © 2026 Paris Goodyear-Brown, *Big Behaviors in All Containers*. All rights reserved.

3. After the caregiver has created their symbols, invite a conversation about each state. Caregivers can be prompted with the following questions:
    a. Looking at the symbol you created, what are three adjectives that describe it?
    b. If your symbol could speak, what would it say?
    c. What does your symbol need in order to feel better?
4. Invite the caregiver to stand up and enact or embody each symbol in some way. Continuing with the previous example, you might say, "Remember when I mentioned my hyperarousal symbol is a hamster on a wheel? My embodiment of this felt sense is me running really fast in place. Like this."
5. It is important that you stand up and embody a pose yourself, both to model the posture for the caregiver and to maintain relationship with the caregiver through what might be an uncomfortable exercise for them.
6. Repeat this process for all three autonomic states.
7. Take a picture of the *Felt Sense* handout before removing the modeling clay (if that is the medium the caregiver chose to use).
8. Be sure to take a picture of the completed symbolic work. You may share the picture with the caregiver for further reflection or keep it for future sessions when you may revisit it.

Copyright © 2026 Paris Goodyear-Brown, *Big Behaviors in All Containers*. All rights reserved.

FELT SENSE HANDOUT

Create a symbol with clay or markers to represent yourself in each of these states.

OVERRESPONDING	BEST SELF	UNDERRESPONDING
Hyperarousal	**Optimal Arousal Zone**	**Hypoarousal**

Copyright © 2026 Paris Goodyear-Brown, *Big Behaviors in All Containers*. All rights reserved.

8.4 HOW DO THEY SEE ME?

DESCRIPTION:

The first exercises in this chapter focused on naming the big behaviors caregivers exhibit when they are outside their window of tolerance versus when they are in their optimal arousal zone. This exercise offers the caregiver a shift in perspective, asking them to explore how their child or student experiences them in each arousal state. When a Safe Boss is kicked up into hyperarousal or descends into hypoarousal, the child in their care may experience them as less safe. In fact, dysregulation in the grown-up can set off the child's amygdala alarm and engender dysregulation in the child. Taking the child's perspective can also encourage a parent or teacher's compassion well to be reopened, as the caregiver may be able to perceive the fear or distress that their arousal states may spark in the child.

TREATMENT GOALS:

- Invite a paradigm shift by asking the caregiver to take the perspective of the child on the receiving end of their autonomic states
- Identify when the caregiver is moving out of their window of tolerance

MATERIALS NEEDED:

- *How Do They See Me?* handout
- Modeling clay
- Sand tray and miniatures (alternative)

DIRECTIONS:

1. Invite the caregiver to put themselves in the position of the child or student in their care. Explain that children's nervous systems are always neurocepting the autonomic states of the grown-ups around them, meaning that they are constantly assessing whether the environment feels safe or threatening.
2. Offer the caregiver modeling clay and invite them to create a symbol for how their child experiences them in each state of arousal.* Some hyperarousal symbols that caregivers have created in their work with me include a knife (for how their words can cut), a bomb exploding, a mouth screaming, and a foot stomping. Some hypoarousal symbols that caregivers have created include a block of ice (for the child's experience of them as cold or frozen), a door (to represent the child's experience of the caregiver's withdrawal), and a blank screen (to represent the child's inability to read how the caregiver is feeling at all).

* If you did the previous *The Felt Sense for You* exercise (8.3) in one medium, consider doing this one in a different medium. For example, if the caregiver used clay to create symbols of their felt sense of themselves, you can offer a sand tray split into three sections and a wide range of miniatures to choose from for this exercise.

Copyright © 2026 Paris Goodyear-Brown, *Big Behaviors in All Containers*. All rights reserved.

3. In some cases, it can be useful for you to engage in some intentional self-disclosure, sharing the symbol you might create for how the children in your care might experience you in a state of hyperarousal. For example, you might say:

   "When I think about how my own children experience me when I am in a state of hyperarousal, I often create a symbol of a drill sergeant. I begin to bark out orders, and I may be less nurturing in my tone than I usually am. So, I would create a soldier out of modeling clay. What will you make?"

4. After the caregiver has created their symbols, invite conversation about each state. Prompting questions might include the following:
   a. Looking at the symbol you created, what are three adjectives that describe it?
   b. If your symbol could speak, what would it say to your child?
   c. What does your symbol need in order to come back into a just-right place?
5. Invite the caregiver to stand up and enact or embody each symbol in some way. Continuing with the previous example, you might say, "Since my children experience me as a drill sergeant when I am in a state of hyperarousal, my embodiment is a super rigid body saluting."
6. It is important that you stand up and embody a pose yourself, both to model the posture for the caregiver and to maintain relationship with the caregiver through what might be an uncomfortable exercise for them.
7. Repeat this process for all three autonomic states.
8. Take a picture of the *How Do They See Me?* handout before removing the modeling clay (or take a picture of their sand tray creation if that is the medium you used).
9. You may share the picture with the caregiver for further reflection or keep it for future sessions when you may revisit it.

Copyright © 2026 Paris Goodyear-Brown, *Big Behaviors in All Containers*. All rights reserved.

HOW DO THEY SEE ME? HANDOUT

When I am in HYPERAROUSAL, they see me as . . .

When I am in OPTIMAL AROUSAL, they see me as . . .

When I am in HYPOAROUSAL, they see me as . . .

Copyright © 2026 Paris Goodyear-Brown, *Big Behaviors in All Containers*. All rights reserved.

8.5 MINDFUL MANTRA

DESCRIPTION:

This exercise is designed to teach caregivers a mindful mantra that helps create physiological and emotional distance from their child's big behavior while the behavior is happening. Oftentimes, parents and teachers can feel like the distress is happening *to* them, when in fact the distress is happening *around* them. By using the mindful mantra *This is happening around me, not to me*, they can remind themselves that they are separate from their child and that they have choices in how they respond to a child in distress. This allows wider access to their executive functions and can reassure them that they can remain a Safe Boss even when their child is dysregulated.

TREATMENT GOALS:

- Improve the caregiver's ability to self-regulate in stressful movements
- Support the caregiver's feelings of groundedness during the child's big behavior
- Provide distance from a big behavior as it is happening

MATERIALS NEEDED:

- *Mindful Mantra* handout
- Glass of water
- Spoon
- Sand tray miniatures (including a life raft)

DIRECTIONS:

1. Explain how easy it is for our autonomic nervous systems to react when we're faced with a child who is dysregulated. When a child offers up a high-pitched, blood-curdling scream, it is likely that this will have an aversive effect on the caregiver, priming their nervous system to perceive the child's scream as a threat to their own safety. When adults feel under threat, it is difficult to access Safe Boss behavior.
2. Introduce the caregiver to the *Mindful Mantra* handout, which contains the mantra *This is happening around me, not to me*. Use the vortex analogy on the handout to explain the distancing effect this kind of self-talk can provide:

   "When a child is engaged in a big behavior, it's like they are trapped in a vortex. Our bodies often respond by feeling like we are spinning in the vortex with them. Using this mantra can help us see ourselves as on solid ground, outside the vortex. That way we can throw in a life raft and help the child climb out, instead of getting sucked into the vortex alongside them."

Copyright © 2026 Paris Goodyear-Brown, *Big Behaviors in All Containers*. All rights reserved.

3. Ask the caregiver to identify one big behavior their child exhibits that triggers a big reaction from the caregiver.
4. Invite the caregiver to visualize this scenario as they stir up a clear glass of water to create a vortex. Have them put sand tray miniatures representing themselves and their child inside the vortex. Be curious with the caregiver about what it's like to watch the miniatures spin around out of control.
5. Next, invite the caregiver to repeat the mindful mantra out loud as they remove their miniature from the vortex and place it on solid ground. They can then practice throwing a miniature life raft into the water to help their child's miniature out of the vortex.
6. Encourage the caregiver to pull up this imagery of standing on solid ground while helping their child as they practice the mindful mantra in real-life scenarios with their child.

 Copyright © 2026 Paris Goodyear-Brown, *Big Behaviors in All Containers*. All rights reserved.

MINDFUL MANTRA HANDOUT

THIS IS HAPPENING AROUND ME, NOT TO ME.

Repeating this to yourself during a child's big behavior may help you stay grounded.

Copyright © 2026 Paris Goodyear-Brown, *Big Behaviors in All Containers*. All rights reserved.

8.6 LIVING THE LIFE RAFT

DESCRIPTION:

This intervention is designed to help caregivers rehearse the mindful mantra from the previous exercise to create physiological and emotional distance from their child's big behavior. In this exercise, they will have an opportunity to practice pairing this mantra with the visual imagery of a life raft. This helps the caregiver shift their paradigm—seeing themselves as a Safe Boss and rescuer instead of a punisher when their child's physiology has been hijacked by a stress reaction.

TREATMENT GOALS:

- Improve the caregiver's ability to self-regulate in stressful movements
- Support the caregiver's feelings of groundedness during the child's big behavior
- Provide distance from a big behavior as it is happening
- Remind the caregiver to use the mindful mantra in their day-to-day life

MATERIALS NEEDED:

- *Mindful Mantra Lifesaver* template
- Scissors

DIRECTIONS:

1. Offer the caregiver several copies of the *Mindful Mantra Lifesaver* template.
2. Invite them to begin cutting out various lifesavers while you become curious about where their child's big behaviors tend to happen most frequently. It can be helpful to also ask about the times of day when these big behaviors most often happen.
3. Rehearse the mantra *This is happening around me, not to me* as the caregiver is cutting out the various images as well.
4. When they're done, ask them to display the lifesaver images wherever they need the most help remembering that their child's behavior is not happening to them, just around them. For example, if their child has the biggest tantrums in the car after school pickup, the caregiver might want to keep a copy of a lifesaver on their dashboard as a visual cue to use their mindful mantra during moments of upset.

Copyright © 2026 Paris Goodyear-Brown, *Big Behaviors in All Containers*. All rights reserved.

MINDFUL MANTRA LIFESAVER TEMPLATE

This mantra can function like a lifesaver for you and your child.

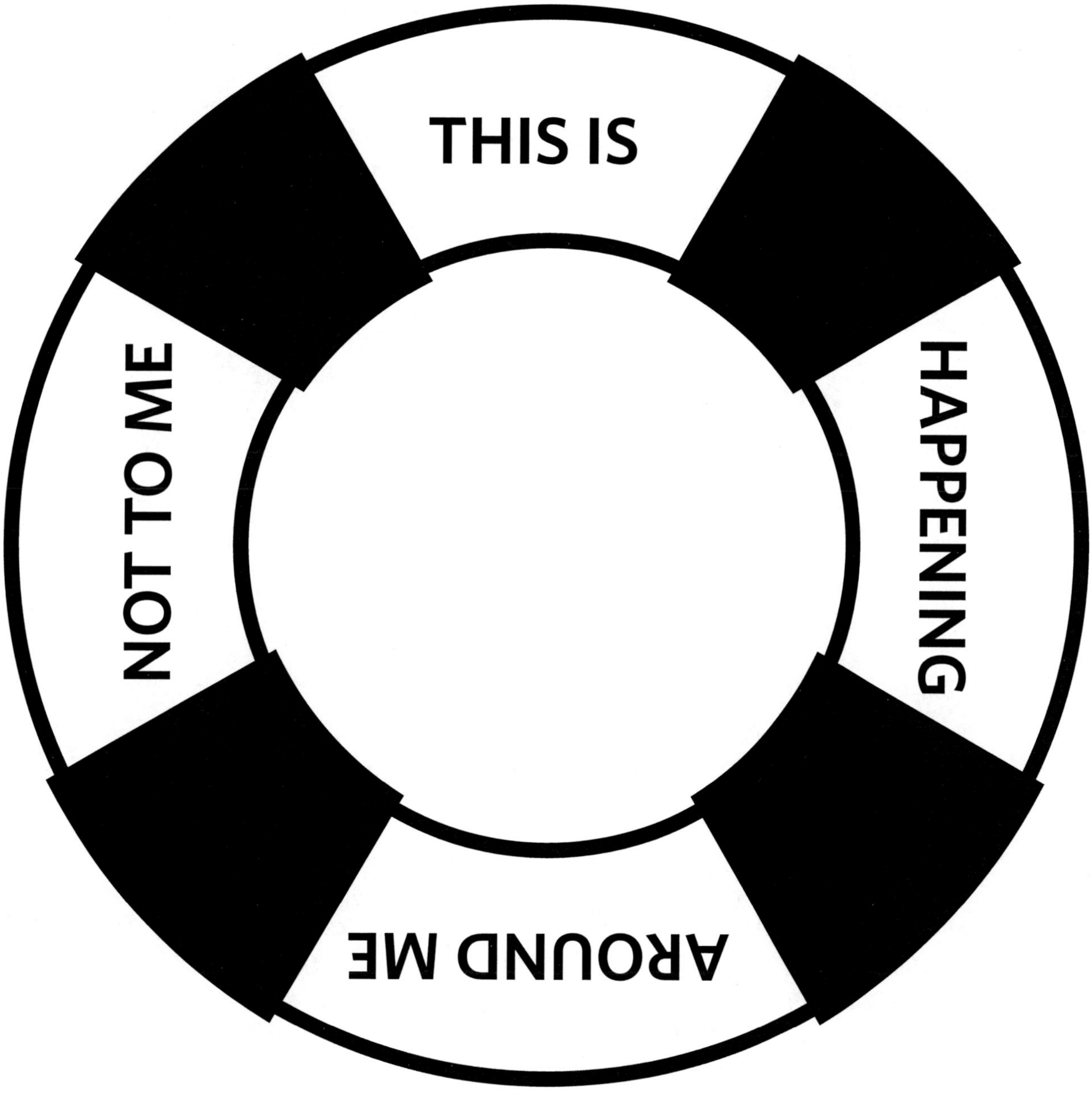

Copyright © 2026 Paris Goodyear-Brown, *Big Behaviors in All Containers*. All rights reserved.

8.7 DISTANCING DEVICE

DESCRIPTION:

This exercise is designed to teach caregivers a mindful mantra while also encouraging them to distance themselves from their child's big behavior when it is happening. Parents and teachers can feel trapped in the same autonomic nervous system response that their child is experiencing, but if they can maintain an awareness of the separate self, they can access their neocortex and make intentional choices about how they respond to a child's big behaviors. While the *Mindful Mantra* intervention (8.5) introduced the mindful mantra *This is happening around me, not to me* and supported this with visual imagery of a vortex, this intervention offers another metaphor for helping the caregiver remember their separateness from the dysregulated child so that they can operate more easily from the role of Safe Boss when the child is in distress.

TREATMENT GOALS:

- Improve the caregiver's ability to self-regulate in stressful movements
- Support the caregiver's feelings of groundedness during the child's big behavior
- Provide distance from a big behavior as it is happening

MATERIALS NEEDED:

- *Distancing Device* handout

DIRECTIONS:

1. Remind the caregiver of the mindful mantra *This is happening around me, not to me.*
2. Ask the caregiver to identify one big behavior their child exhibits that triggers a big reaction from the caregiver.
3. Invite them to draw the behavior on the "digital" screen embedded in the *Distancing Device* handout.
4. Lead the caregiver through a visualization exercise in which they imagine being with the child in the midst of this big behavior. Then have them repeat the mindful mantra as they imagine that they are watching this behavior play out on a screen. By visualizing the behavior as something that is separate from them rather than something that is happening to them, it can provide the necessary emotional and physiological distance for them to decide how to respond to the behavior instead of reacting to it.
5. You can adapt this imaginal exercise by asking the caregiver to imagine "pinching" the digital image of the big behavior with their fingers to shrink it on the screen, turning down the volume, or changing the image from color to black and white.

Copyright © 2026 Paris Goodyear-Brown, *Big Behaviors in All Containers*. All rights reserved.

DISTANCING DEVICE HANDOUT

Draw one triggering behavior on the "screen" below.

When your child is engaging in a big behavior, it can help to repeat this mantra: *This is happening around me, not to me.* Then imagine you are watching their behavior play out on your phone or iPad.

Copyright © 2026 Paris Goodyear-Brown, *Big Behaviors in All Containers*. All rights reserved.

8.8 CHANGE THE CHANNEL

DESCRIPTION:

Children and caregivers with big behaviors often wish that they could go back in time and handle a situation differently. However, they can both feel lots of shame when reflecting on their big behavior. This intervention supports children and their caregivers in reflecting on their challenging behavior while empowering them to envision the response they would like to have instead. They can then have the experience of immediately changing the image (i.e., changing the channel) to that outcome. They also get an immediate competency surge by watching things change at their command. Alternatively, this intervention is a powerful way to combat nightmares (a common trauma symptom), as it allows the child to envision one channel that has the nightmare and another channel where "the nightmare is all better."

TREATMENT GOALS:

- Expand the client's window of tolerance for working with shame-inducing behaviors
- Invite future template work related to how the client might engage in alternate behavior next time
- Increase the client's felt sense of personal agency

MATERIALS NEEDED:

- Cardboard box to use as a TV screen
- Scissors
- Paper
- Coloring utensils (e.g., crayons, markers)
- Novelty remote control

DIRECTIONS:

1. Explain to the dyad that you are going to make a TV together. Invite the parent and child to cut out one side of the box, leaving some room around the edges so that you can place paper behind it like an image on a television screen.
2. While they work to cut the box, ask them whether they've ever seen something on a screen that they wish they could unsee. Be prepared for the addition of new treatment targets if the child talks about terrifying content or sexually themed content that was confusing or uncomfortable.
3. Normalize the idea that we all have moments we wish we could forget, moments when we acted in a way that embarrassed us, hurt a relationship, or got us into trouble. Ask the parent and then the child to identify one such moment for themselves. You don't need to specifically name an incident for the child, unless they have been stuck in the avoidance symptoms of posttraumatic stress disorder for a long time. Most clients will move within their memory systems to a painful memory that they can tolerate working with today.

 Copyright © 2026 Paris Goodyear-Brown, *Big Behaviors in All Containers*. All rights reserved.

4. Ask them to draw the memory of this hard thing on a piece of paper.
5. Next, ask them to draw what they wish they had done or said instead. In cases where the trauma involved interpersonal violence, a natural disaster, or an accident over which the child had no control, the new image may be one in which they fantasize having enough power to get out of the situation, find safety within the threatening environment, or prevent the accident.
6. When they're finished with both drawings, introduce the remote control. Explain that today they get to change the channel on their experience. Offer the remote control to the child as you stand behind the makeshift TV. Hold the first image in place and when the child exclaims, "Change the channel!" (usually while pointing the remote at the TV), you shift to the second picture. Switching out the two different drawings helps the child feel how behaviors can shift over time.
7. Alternatively, if you are using this intervention individually with a caregiver who is reflecting on one of their own big behaviors, you would simply physically change the images on the TV after the caregiver has drawn their past behavior and the behavioral response they hope to have in the future.

Copyright © 2026 Paris Goodyear-Brown, *Big Behaviors in All Containers*. All rights reserved.

8.9 OXYTOCIN AND THE OXYGEN MASK

DESCRIPTION:

This exercise offers another metaphor to explain the importance of staying regulated in the midst of a child's big behaviors. Since co-regulation by a caregiver always precedes self-regulation for a child, grown-ups must remain competent and available during times of crisis. It is only when grown-ups take care of themselves first that they can most effectively harness the power of oxytocin, the neurochemical that bonds us together. In this intervention, the caregiver is invited to reflect on what it means to put their oxygen mask on first in situations that cause the most dysregulation in their child's environment.

TREATMENT GOALS:

- Identify self-care practices that keep the caregiver within their window of tolerance
- Identify self-regulation strategies that can ground the child in a crisis

MATERIALS NEEDED:

- *Oxytocin and Oxygen Mask* handout

DIRECTIONS:

1. Introduce the oxygen mask analogy to the caregiver:

   "Have you been on airplanes where the flight attendants tell the parents of small children to put their own oxygen masks on first in case of emergency? This can sound selfish or shocking, and it is certainly counterintuitive, as most parents want to secure their child's mask first. However, if there were a real emergency, it is likely that both the parent and child would be filled with stress hormones and feel deeply afraid. In this case, the parent needs to remain conscious and alert in order to remain a Safe Boss and co-regulator for their child. If the parent passes out, the child will have no one to help them or soothe their fears."

2. Explain that oxytocin is the neurochemical that is released between a mother and baby when a baby is nursing. It is meant to bond the mother and baby closer together, hence it is referred to as the bonding chemical. Reassure the parent that oxytocin can be stimulated and released through other forms of nurturing touch, as well as humor and play.
3. Offer the *Oxytocin and Oxygen Mask* handout to the caregiver.
4. Ask them what self-care practices they already engage in regularly. If they are unable to identify any, slow down and help them choose one self-care practice they will begin to implement this week. This may include practices like exercising, having quiet time, spending time with friends, taking a hot bath, practicing breath work, journaling, and so forth.

Copyright © 2026 Paris Goodyear-Brown, *Big Behaviors in All Containers*. All rights reserved.

5. Invite the caregiver to document three self-care practices they can commit to doing inside the larger oxygen mask on the handout.
6. Next, explore what the child might need to co-regulate during a crisis. For example, they might benefit from receiving a hug, holding hands, or taking deep regulating breaths in tandem with their caregiver.
7. Invite the caregiver to write three co-regulation strategies they might offer to their dysregulated child in a time of crisis.

Copyright © 2026 Paris Goodyear-Brown, *Big Behaviors in All Containers*. All rights reserved.

OXYTOCIN AND OXYGEN MASK HANDOUT

Caregiver

Write three self-care practices you can use in the mask on the left.

Child

Write three co-regulation strategies you can use with your child on the right.

Copyright © 2026 Paris Goodyear-Brown, *Big Behaviors in All Containers*. All rights reserved.

8.10 MY OPTIMAL WORK WINDOW

DESCRIPTION:

It is easy for caregivers to get kicked out of their window of tolerance when they are overworked. This exercise helps caregivers think about the amount of time they spend in a variety of work-related tasks. It encourages them to explore the following factors as they design their optimal work windows: (1) commute time to and from work, (2) hours spent at work, (3) hours spent working from home versus in an office space separate from home, and (4) time spent in client meetings versus on administrative tasks or special projects.

TREATMENT GOALS:

- Connect the caregiver's work dynamics to their current window of tolerance
- Identify the caregiver's desired work rhythms to establish a better work-life balance

MATERIALS NEEDED:

- *My Optimal Work Window* template
- Paper
- Writing utensil

DIRECTIONS:

1. Discuss how many caregivers balance their work demands with their family demands. Sometimes, the work demands are so intense that the family gets less time, which may leave both the caregiver and the family feeling depleted. Other times, a caregiver's work life might not be challenging enough for them, leaving them in a place that feels boring or even hopeless.
2. Offer the *My Optimal Work Window* template to the caregiver.
3. Explain that they will be designing a window, with each pane in the window representing one aspect of their work life. It might be an arch-shaped window, a rectangle, a triangle, an octagon, or any other shape they like.
4. Invite the caregiver to choose a window type from the template or to create their own window on a piece of paper, filling in each pane with a work activity frequency that they would find optimal. It may be useful to give an example from your own work life. For example, you might say:

   "I have found that when I see five or six clients a day and have breaks in between, I feel like I have the necessary energy and focus for each client but can still return home and have energy left for my family. If I have to see eight clients in a day, I am exhausted by the time I get home."

Copyright © 2026 Paris Goodyear-Brown, *Big Behaviors in All Containers*. All rights reserved.

5. It's okay if the caregiver's work window does not line up with their current work experience. Explain that we sometimes need visual images of the concrete goals we are working toward in order to create positive change.
6. Explore at least one aspect of work that the caregiver might begin to tweak in order to feel more congruent in their daily rhythms of work.

Copyright © 2026 Paris Goodyear-Brown, *Big Behaviors in All Containers*. All rights reserved.

MY OPTIMAL WORK WINDOW EXAMPLE

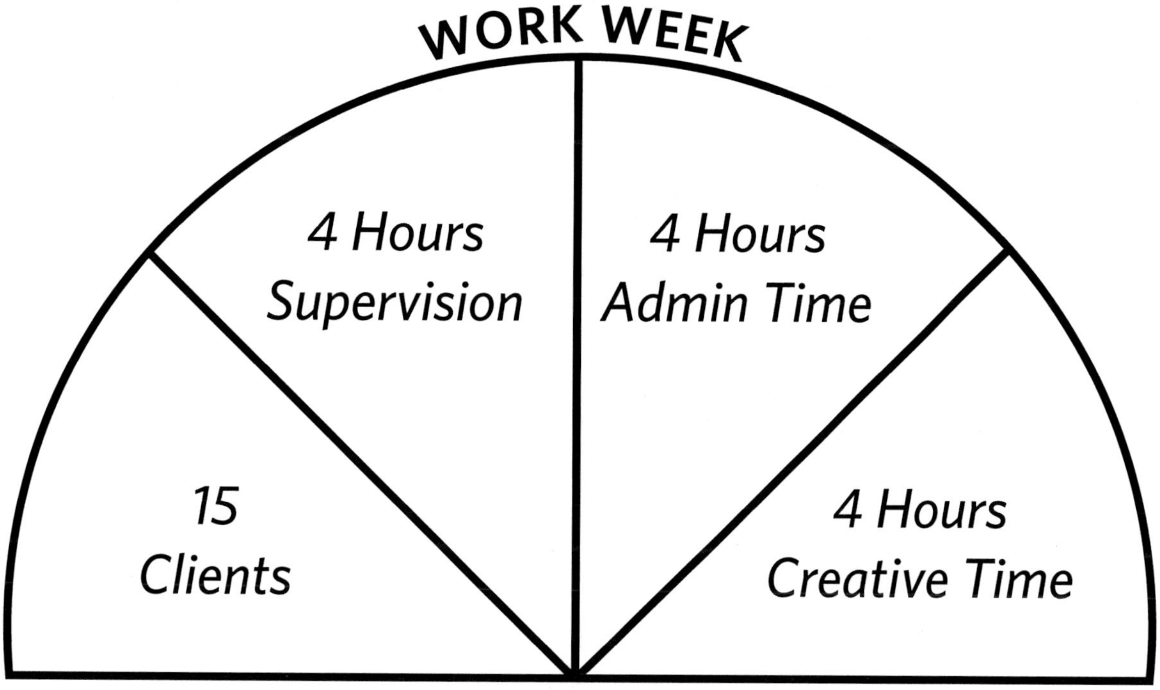

Copyright © 2026 Paris Goodyear-Brown, *Big Behaviors in All Containers*. All rights reserved.

MY OPTIMAL WORK WINDOW TEMPLATE

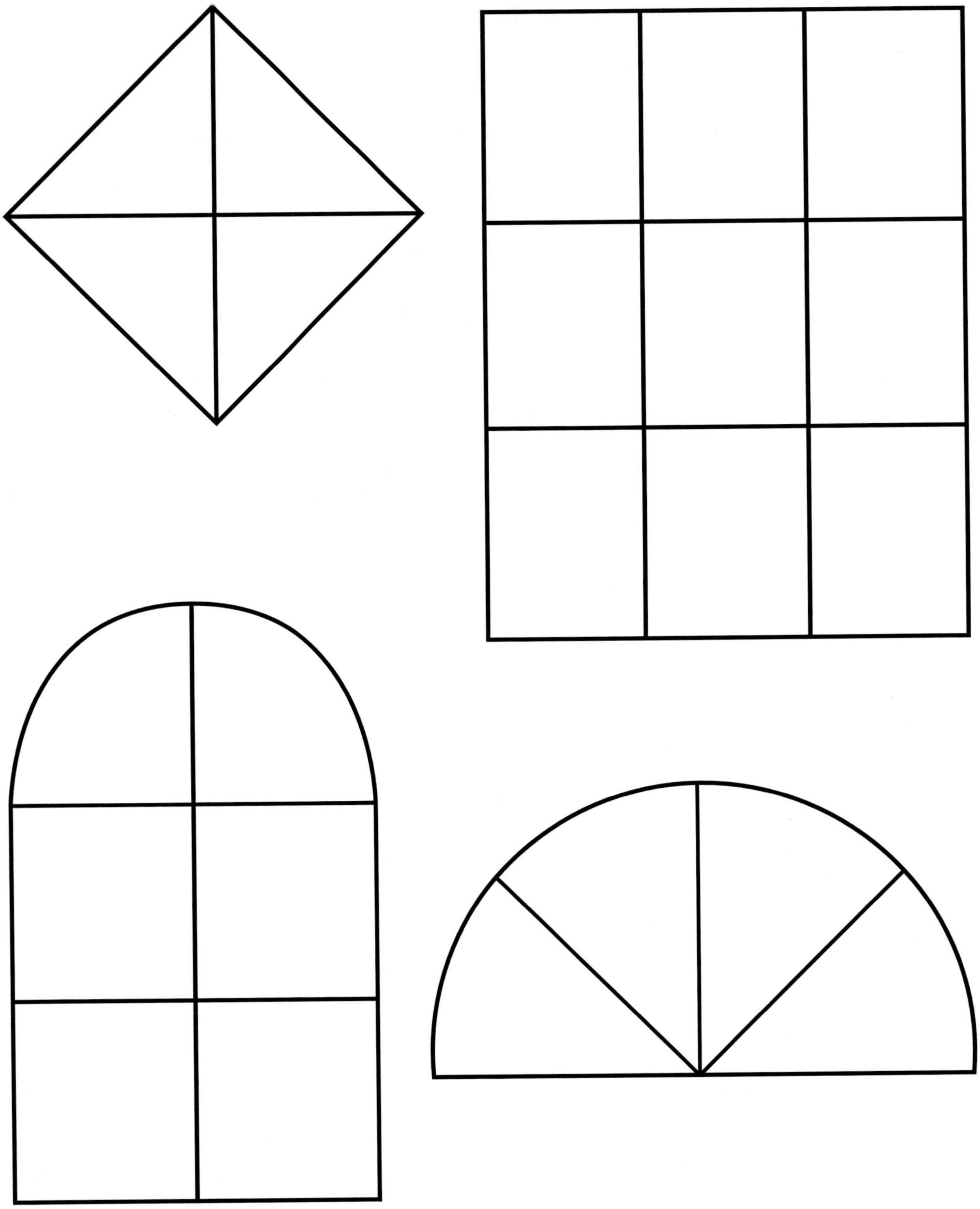

Copyright © 2026 Paris Goodyear-Brown, *Big Behaviors in All Containers*. All rights reserved.

8.11 MY OPTIMAL FAMILY WINDOW

DESCRIPTION:

Family rhythms can be challenging to maintain. At the start of the new year, many families commit to having family dinners regularly, doing some sort of spiritual practice regularly, having weekly date nights for the caregivers—and then life happens, and these best-laid plans can feel like they are being sabotaged. Sometimes, this is because the family set the expectations too high. For example, perhaps the caregivers decided that family dinner would happen five times a week at 6:30 p.m., not realizing that their teenage daughter's rehearsals wouldn't be done until 8:30 p.m. most nights. Caregivers need support in casting vision for a healthy balance of fun time, chores, homework, discipline, and so on. This exercise provides reflective space for them to review their current family rhythms and reorganize patterns as needed.

TREATMENT GOALS:

- Connect the family's dynamics to the caregiver's current window of tolerance
- Identify the caregiver's desired family rhythms to establish a better work-life balance

MATERIALS NEEDED:

- *My Optimal Family Window* template
- Paper
- Writing utensil

DIRECTIONS:

1. Discuss how many caregivers balance their work demands with their family demands: In some families, caregivers may feel pressured to have more quality family time, more quality one-on-one time with their partner, and more dedicated individual time with each child each week. However, the standards they set for themselves may be impossible to meet. In other families, caregivers may have given up on trying to have quality time together, and they may simply collapse into a heap in front of the TV each evening without any conversation.
2. Explain that neither extreme is helpful or sustainable. Therefore, this exercise is meant to help the caregiver dream about the good-enough family rhythms they would like to aim for in their own family.
3. Offer the *My Optimal Family Window* template to the caregiver.
4. Explain that they will be designing a window, with each pane in the window representing one aspect of their family life. It might be an arch-shaped window, a rectangle, a triangle, an octagon, or any other shape they like.

Copyright © 2026 Paris Goodyear-Brown, *Big Behaviors in All Containers*. All rights reserved.

5. Invite the caregiver to choose a window type from the template or to create their own window on a piece of paper, filling in each pane with an aspect of their family life that they would find optimal. For example, how many family dinners would they like per week? Do they want to make these as a family, take turns, or order takeout? How much time do they think each person needs to spend doing chores per day or week? Is there a family game night, family movie night, or family day?
6. It's okay if the caregiver's family window does not line up with their current family experience. Explain that we need visual images of the concrete goals we are working toward in order to create positive change.
7. Explore at least one aspect of family life that the caregiver might begin to tweak in order to feel more congruent in their daily rhythms of family life.

Copyright © 2026 Paris Goodyear-Brown, *Big Behaviors in All Containers*. All rights reserved.

MY OPTIMAL FAMILY WINDOW EXAMPLE

Family dinner four times per week	*Chores done daily by each person*
Individual time with each child twice per month	*Sunday family day/ date night*

Copyright © 2026 Paris Goodyear-Brown, *Big Behaviors in All Containers*. All rights reserved.

MY OPTIMAL FAMILY WINDOW TEMPLATE

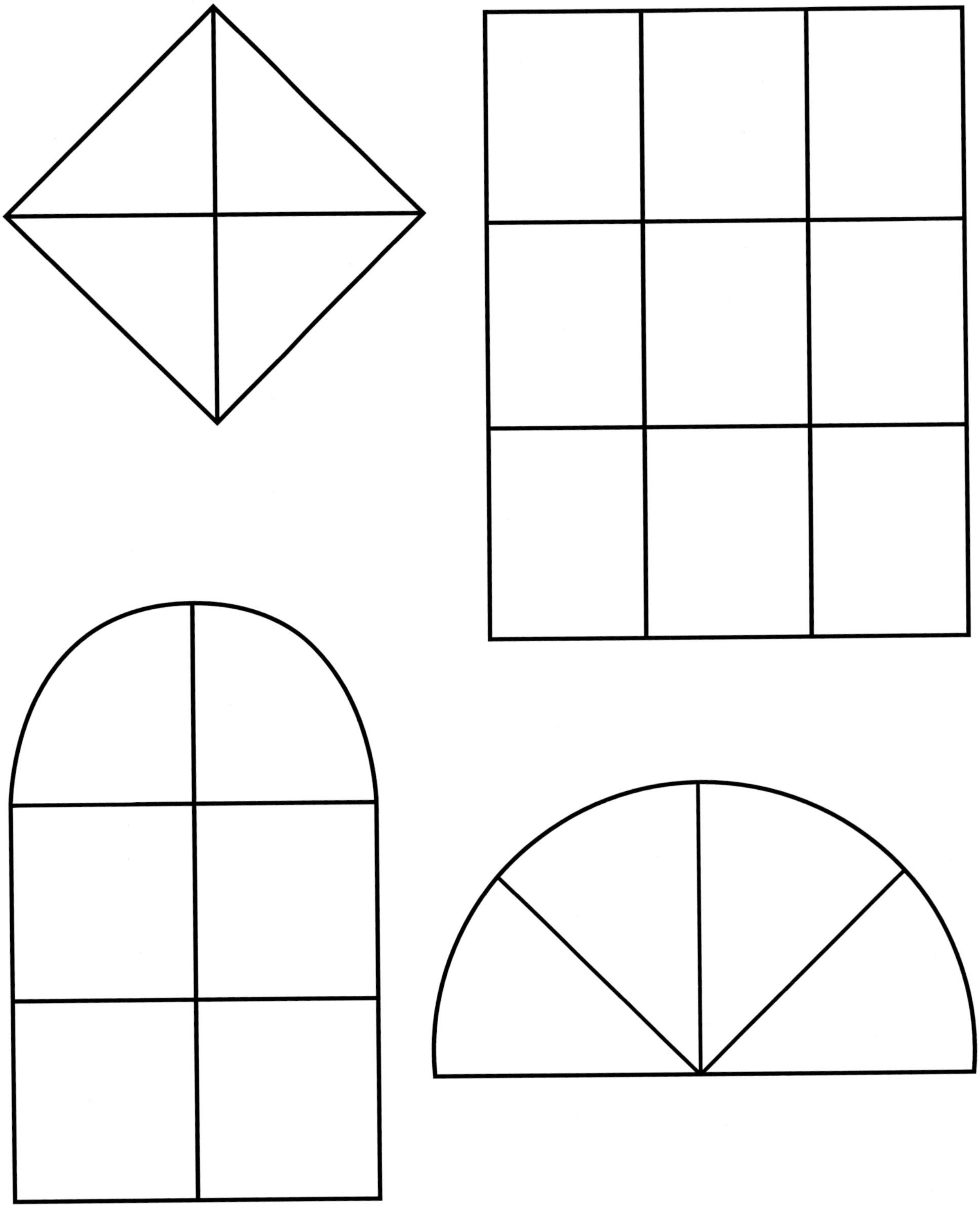

Copyright © 2026 Paris Goodyear-Brown, *Big Behaviors in All Containers*. All rights reserved.

8.12 HOME SECURITY THREAT LEVEL ASSESSMENT

DESCRIPTION:

This intervention is designed to help caregivers assess the level of autonomic threat they experience in response to a child's big behaviors. Oftentimes, when a caregiver perceives an autonomic threat, they begin to engage in their own big behaviors by yelling, withholding attention, giving extreme consequences, and so forth. As caregivers become more aware of their own activation as it is tied to their children's specific behaviors, it becomes easier to choose appropriate strategies for self-regulation at each level. When parents and teachers don't feel secure in the environments (whether they are in the home or in a classroom) where they are supposed to be a Safe Boss, a child's big behaviors can lead these grown-ups to neurocept danger and end up engaging in big behaviors of their own.

TREATMENT GOALS:

- Identify big behaviors that cause the caregiver's nervous system to neurocept danger or threat
- Assess the caregiver's perceived level of autonomic threat based on the child's behaviors

MATERIALS NEEDED:

- *Home Security Threat Level Assessment* handout

DIRECTIONS:

1. Use the analogy of the Homeland Security Advisory System to explain how a caregiver might perceive their child's threat level:

   "After 9/11 happened, the Department of Homeland Security implemented a color-coded advisory system to alert the public about the perceived level of security at airports. Five levels of threat were outlined to denote the possible risk of a terrorist attack: low (level 1, coded in green), guarded (level 2, coded in blue), elevated (level 3, coded in yellow), high (level 4, coded in orange), and severe (level 5, coded in red). We have come up with a similar rating system for how threatened our autonomic nervous systems feel by different behaviors exhibited by our children."

2. Offer the *Home Security Threat Level Assessment* handout.
3. Explain that the feeling of security we have in our homes on a day-to-day basis is influenced by our children's behaviors and our bodily response to them. The behaviors that upset us are unique to us. For example, while some adults might see it as extremely disrespectful for a teenager to roll their eyes, other adults might not see it as a big deal.

Copyright © 2026 Paris Goodyear-Brown, *Big Behaviors in All Containers*. All rights reserved.

4. Beginning at the bottom of the handout (level 1), ask the caregiver, "What's a behavior your child exhibits that is annoying but that doesn't really trigger your stress response system?" It can help to give examples, like chewing gum with their mouth open, leaving the toilet seat up, and so on. The key factor here is that the adult recognizes the behavior is annoying but easily manageable.
5. You may decide to ask for a second, slightly more irritating behavior for level 2, but you may also decide to stick with levels 1, 3, and 5 if this titration of the exercise is more appropriate for the caregiver.
6. Move to the middle of the handout (level 3) and ask the caregiver, "What's a behavior your child exhibits that stresses you out, but you have found a clear, boundaried way to handle it? It's a behavior you can correct or manage without you losing your cool." Examples might be a child whining, nagging, or taking things from siblings without permission.
7. You may decide to ask for a second, slightly more irritating behavior for level 4, but you may also decide to stick with levels 1, 3, and 5 if this titration of the exercise is more appropriate for the caregiver.
8. Move to the top of the handout (level 5) and ask the caregiver, "What's a behavior that is so upsetting to you that when it happens, you really lose it? You are abruptly thrown out of your window of tolerance and act in a way that you later regret."

Copyright © 2026 Paris Goodyear-Brown, *Big Behaviors in All Containers*. All rights reserved.

HOME SECURITY THREAT LEVEL ASSESSMENT HANDOUT

Each caregiver has different behaviors that trigger them. While some may see their child's eye-rolling as a level 1, others may see it as a level 5. Write your child's difficult behaviors in the boxes below based on how triggering or threatening they are to your sense of calm.

5 SEVERE RISK	
4 HIGH RISK	
3 ELEVATED RISK	
2 GUARDED (GENERAL) RISK	
1 LOW RISK	

Copyright © 2026 Paris Goodyear-Brown, *Big Behaviors in All Containers*. All rights reserved.

8.13 BOXING WITH THE BEST OF THEM

DESCRIPTION:

When children have experienced attachment trauma, caregivers can provide a powerful neurochemical cocktail with experiences that increase oxytocin (the bonding chemical) and dopamine (the joy chemical). This builds their attachment relationship with the child while countering cortisol hormones released during times of stress. TraumaPlay therapists see this process of offering caregiver co-regulation as a neurochemical boxing match. This exercise is meant to shift the caregiver's paradigm to seeing their power in this new way.

TREATMENT GOALS:

- Provide psychoeducation on the neurochemicals involved in the body's stress response system
- Amplify the power that the caregiver has to provide experiences that heal the brain

MATERIALS NEEDED:

- *Neurochemical Boxing Match* handout

DIRECTIONS:

1. Explain the role of different neurochemicals in the brain:

   "Our brains and bodies are amazing. We all have neurochemicals that help us gear up and get ready to fight, flee, or freeze in times of stress. This includes adrenaline, epinephrine, norepinephrine, and cortisol—the stress hormone. However, your child may release more than their fair share of cortisol when they are experiencing threat. In fact, they may see threats where none exist, causing this stress hormone to pump through their body at unexpected times or places and with surprising people.

   "Our brains and bodies also produce some other cool neurochemicals. One is oxytocin, which is a chemical released between a mother and baby during times of nursing. It serves to bond them closer together emotionally. For this reason, some people call it the bonding or love chemical. Dopamine is another neurochemical that's released when we are having fun. It's often called the joy chemical. We see the oxytocin-dopamine combo as a one-two punch to cortisol. When enough love and joy chemicals are on board, they can figuratively knock out the cortisol."

2. Offer the *Neurochemical Boxing Match* handout to further this analogy of the oxytocin-dopamine combo "knocking out" cortisol:

   "Have you ever seen a boxing match? There are two opponents in opposite corners, and each has a team of coaches helping to equip and take care of them in between rounds. Let's imagine that in one corner is Cortisol and in the other corner is Oxytocin. Cortisol, the stress hormone, is being coached by Adrenaline. Oxytocin is

Copyright © 2026 Paris Goodyear-Brown, *Big Behaviors in All Containers*. All rights reserved.

being coached by Dopamine. There are certain moves that Cortisol will try to make, such as screaming, hitting, or taunting you with hurtful words like 'I hate you' or 'You're not my parent.' If you can see past these moves and view them as cues that your child needs to release oxytocin and dopamine back into their brain and body, you can choose how you come out swinging.

"The next two activities, *Cortisol Cues* (8.14) and *Countering Cortisol* (8.15), will help you better understand your child's cues that cortisol has taken over and brainstorm ways you might counter this using your own powerful neurochemical cocktail."

Copyright © 2026 Paris Goodyear-Brown, *Big Behaviors in All Containers*. All rights reserved.

NEUROCHEMICAL BOXING MATCH HANDOUT

IN THIS CORNER OF THE RING:

Adrenaline: A stress hormone

Cortisol: A stress hormone

IN THIS CORNER OF THE RING:

Dopamine: The joy chemical

Oxytocin: The bonding or love hormone

 Copyright © 2026 Paris Goodyear-Brown, *Big Behaviors in All Containers*. All rights reserved.

8.14 CORTISOL CUES

DESCRIPTION:

This intervention is designed to help caregivers shift how they view their child's big behavior—no longer seeing it as an intentional choice to behave badly but an indicator that a massive amount of cortisol has just been released into their bloodstream. If caregivers can see the cues that a child's brain and body have been overwhelmed by cortisol, they can approach the child with compassionate responses aimed at meeting the child's underlying needs for co-regulation.

TREATMENT GOALS:

- Provide psychoeducation on the neurochemicals involved in the body's stress response system
- Shift the caregiver's paradigm around big behaviors to view them as cues for co-regulation

MATERIALS NEEDED:

- *Cortisol Cues* handout

DIRECTIONS:

1. Once the caregiver has been introduced to the previous neurochemical boxing match analogy (*Boxing with the Best of Them* [8.13]), explain that you will be discussing the specific ways that cortisol can serve as a cue that their child needs help. Sometimes, when we see big behaviors, like yelling or stomping, we think that a child is choosing to behave badly. But what if these behaviors are really clues that the cortisol has taken over? In this case, the reality is that the child may be drowning in massive amounts of stress hormones being released in their brain and body.
2. Ask the caregiver to identify some big behaviors their child exhibits that indicate their stress hormones may have taken over. This might include acting-out behaviors (e.g., hitting, biting, spitting, throwing things) or acting-in behaviors (e.g., withdrawing, self-injuring, dissociating, numbing out).
3. Offer the *Cortisol Cues* handout and instruct the caregiver to write each specific big behavior in the spaces between the ropes.
4. Explain that the next exercise will help them generate ideas about how to counter the cortisol.

Copyright © 2026 Paris Goodyear-Brown, *Big Behaviors in All Containers*. All rights reserved.

CORTISOL CUES HANDOUT

Between each rope, write one big behavior that your child exhibits. These are the cues that the stress hormone is in charge.

Copyright © 2026 Paris Goodyear-Brown, *Big Behaviors in All Containers*. All rights reserved.

8.15 COUNTERING CORTISOL

DESCRIPTION:

This intervention is designed to build on *Boxing with the Best of Them* (8.13) and *Cortisol Cues* (8.14). Once caregivers have identified the big behaviors that signal stress hormones have overtaken their child's brain and body, this exercise will help them identify specific strategies that offer oxytocin (the bonding chemical) and dopamine (the joy chemical). These strategies counter the cortisol by (1) meeting the underlying needs causing the dysregulation, (2) offering nurture, and (3) doing something fun.

TREATMENT GOALS:

- Provide psychoeducation on the neurochemicals involved in the body's stress response system
- Shift the caregiver's paradigm around big behaviors to view them as cues for co-regulation
- Identify oxytocin- and dopamine-boosting strategies to counter the child's dysregulation

MATERIALS NEEDED:

- *Countering Cortisol* handout

DIRECTIONS:

1. Once the caregiver has identified big behaviors that indicate their child is overwhelmed by stress hormones and no longer in their choosing mind, your role is to help them brainstorm specific strategies that counter the effects of cortisol with oxytocin (the bonding hormone) and dopamine (the joy chemical).
2. Explain that there are three main ways to co-regulate a child who is swamped by a cortisol response:
    a. Meeting the child's underlying needs (e.g., hydration, nourishment, rest)
    b. Offering nurture (e.g., giving a hug, snuggling to read a book)
    c. Doing something enjoyable together (e.g., riding bikes, going for a walk, preparing food together)
3. Discuss how these various activities promote the release of oxytocin and dopamine. For example, oxytocin can be released through nurturing touch, so offering a hug is one way to counter the cortisol. Similarly, swinging, rocking, or engaging in some other pleasurable rhythmic body movement can counter the cortisol through the release of oxytocin and dopamine. Sometimes, drinking a cold glass of water, eating a protein-rich snack, or taking a hot bath might counter the cortisol by meeting an underlying need. When an underlying need is met, oxytocin and dopamine are often released.

Copyright © 2026 Paris Goodyear-Brown, *Big Behaviors in All Containers*. All rights reserved.

4. Work with the caregiver to brainstorm some specific strategies they think might work for their child. Offer the *Countering Cortisol* handout and instruct the caregiver to write these strategies between the ropes of the boxing ring.

Copyright © 2026 Paris Goodyear-Brown, *Big Behaviors in All Containers*. All rights reserved.

COUNTERING CORTISOL HANDOUT

Between each rope, write one action you can take to offer nurture, fun, or need meeting to counter the stress hormone.

Copyright © 2026 Paris Goodyear-Brown, *Big Behaviors in All Containers*. All rights reserved.

8.16 THE SHOULD PILE

DESCRIPTION:

Caregivers often hold themselves to an impossible set of standards when it comes to their parenting or teaching abilities. Their standards are often characterized by should statements like *I should not feel frustrated with my child*, *I should never lose my temper*, and *I should be more compassionate to my child*. TraumaPlay therapists believe that these statements engender shame. When a caregiver is overwhelmed by a child's big behavior and responds by acting out with their own big behaviors, the "shoulds" are triggered and engender shame. Shame interferes with their ability to make a shift (either a paradigm shift or a shift of internal arousal state), so these shoulds need to be countered with more compassionate self-talk. Helping caregivers name their shoulds is the first step in teaching them to set imperfect (but good-enough) standards for their own caregiving abilities.

TREATMENT GOALS:

- Identify any unrealistic standards to which the caregiver holds themselves
- Offer alternatives for more compassionate and realistic self-talk

MATERIALS NEEDED:

- *The Should Pile* handout

DIRECTIONS:

1. Explain that caregivers often have a set of shoulds that guide their caregiving, like *I should never get angry with my child*, *My child should never scream at me*, and *My partner should always back me up*. If any of these shoulds are not met, it can cause shame and lead caregivers to turn their attention inward as they wrestle with their own sense of goodness as caregivers. During these times, caregivers can be so focused on themselves that they don't attend to the needs of the child in front of them.
2. Offer *The Should Pile* handout and invite the caregiver to write down all the shoulds they can think of that guide their caregiving:
    a. Shoulds for themselves
    b. Shoulds for their parenting or teaching partners
    c. Shoulds for the children in their care
3. Explain that identifying these beliefs is the first step to coming up with more compassionate and realistic self-statements that can help them stay present and engaged with their child, even during moments when they feel like they are failing.
4. Repeat one of the shoulds out loud. Then ask the caregiver to think of someone else they love (e.g., their parenting partner, a good friend who is also a mother) and invite

Copyright © 2026 Paris Goodyear-Brown, *Big Behaviors in All Containers*. All rights reserved.

them to say out loud what they would say to their loved one if that person was feeling shame because of this should. More than likely, the caregiver will extend compassion to the loved one, which normalizes the impossibility of grown-ups remaining regulated at all times or the impossibility of perfect parenting.

5. In subsequent sessions, you can revisit the should pile and help the caregiver craft compassionate self-talk to combat the should. For example, if the caregiver's should is *I should never get angry with my child*, the self-talk might be *All parents get angry with their kids sometimes. I am learning how to communicate my anger without hurting my child and while holding whatever boundary is needed.*

Copyright © 2026 Paris Goodyear-Brown, *Big Behaviors in All Containers*. All rights reserved.

THE SHOULD PILE HANDOUT

Write down as many shoulds as you can in two minutes. Don't censor yourself!

THE SHOULD PILE

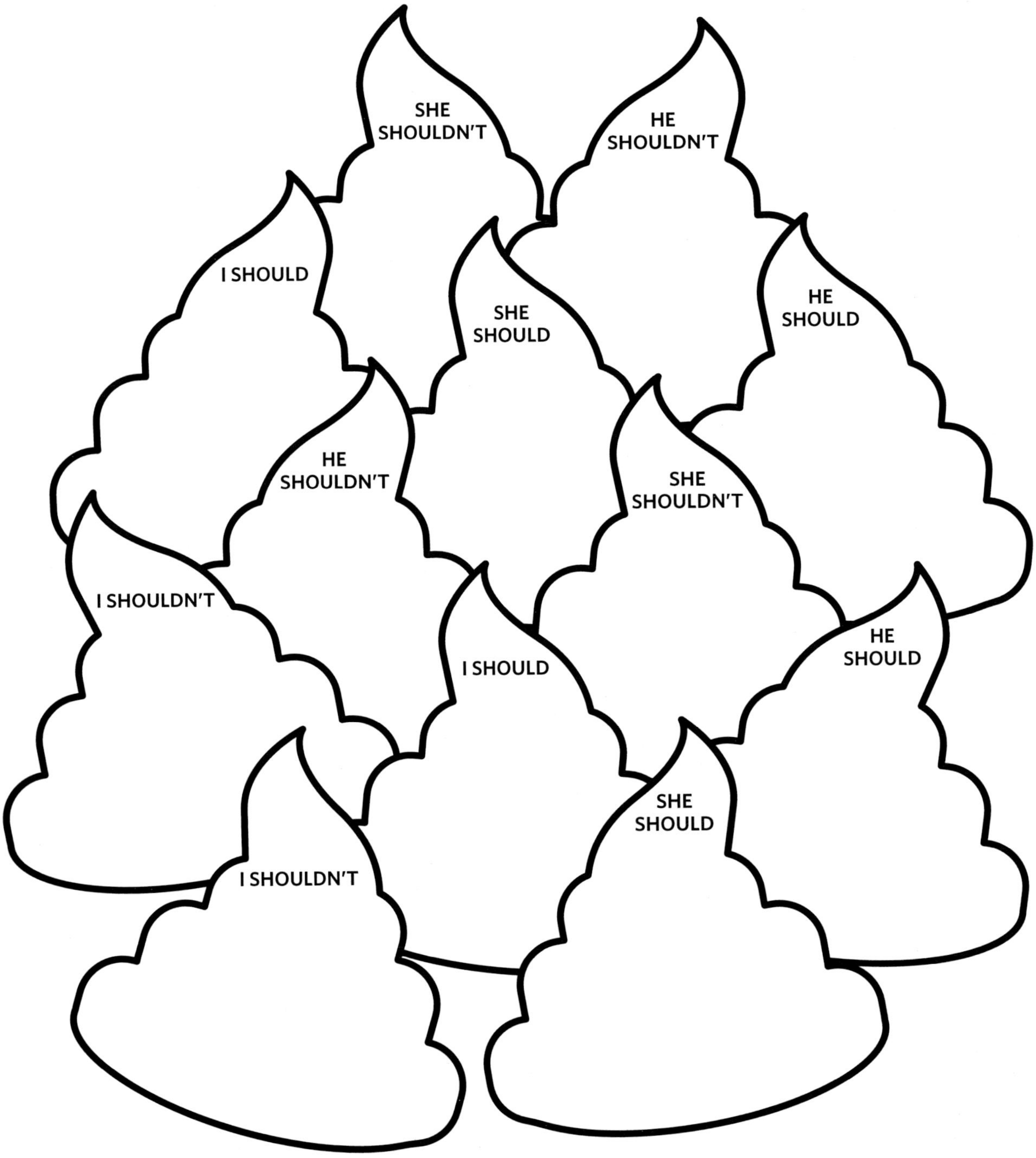

 Copyright © 2026 Paris Goodyear-Brown, *Big Behaviors in All Containers*. All rights reserved.

nine

When Parts of the Parent Trigger Parts of the Child, and Vice Versa

Play therapy lends itself to an exploration of the parts of both caregivers and children. One way to think about parts is through the lens of internal family systems (IFS), which was created by Richard Schwartz. In particular, Schwartz maintains that we all have various protector parts (known as *managers* and *firefighters*), victim parts (known as *exiles*), and a core seat of consciousness (known as the *Self*, which is a kind and compassionate energy who allows us to welcome and explore all the parts within us; Schwartz & Sweezy, 2019). Schwartz's (2021) book *No Bad Parts* amplifies the message at the heart of TraumaPlay, which is that we should assume all parts have positive intentions. As a result, it benefits us to welcome all our parts, to invite conversations between parts, to understand and have compassion for all our parts, and to work toward making each part feel like it has a place and a way to be useful.

TraumaPlay approaches parts work within the context of the TraumaPlay components. For example, clinicians might explore *adaptive and maladaptive coping parts* while working on the second TraumaPlay component (assessment and augmentation of coping). Or they might explore *negative and positive self-talk parts* while working within the sixth component of TraumaPlay (addressing the thought life). Similarly, as clinicians explore aspects of posttraumatic play through play-based gradual exposure, victim parts and perpetrator or instigator parts may emerge.

Parts work in TraumaPlay is child led when working with children and caregiver led when working with caregivers. Clients may identify parts using sand tray miniatures, visual art depictions, puppets, clay creations, avatars from the digital world, objects or forces in the natural world, and more. It is important that you come with no preconceived ideas about what kinds of parts will show up or how you should categorize them. Rather, you should allow the client to name the part and become curious about the ages of the parts, how long they have existed, how they came into being, what they need to feel safe, and why they do what they do. By using play therapy methods, you can also mitigate how you approach parts who feel scared, shamed, silenced, and isolated.

Importantly, when a child has survived trauma, many of their parts will engage in big behaviors, and the caregiver's parts may experience these behaviors as threats, leading to interruptions in the healing work of the child and grown-up alike. For this reason, it is valuable to do parts work with the child *and* caregiver. Since parts work can be very vulnerable, you must establish deep therapeutic rapport prior to diving into this work. The prompts in this chapter offer a variety of creative ways for you to explore and name parts, introduce parts to each other, and facilitate conversation between parts.

9.1 PROTECTOR PARTS

DESCRIPTION:

It is common for caregivers to become negatively activated and dysregulated when their child is engaging in big behaviors. In this intervention, the caregiver's negative activation is reframed in terms of protector parts who emerged in the caregiver's own childhood. For example, as a child, the parent may not have been allowed to make mistakes, so they now react in a way that shames their own child when the child makes a mistake. While this behavior might look cruel or punitive from an outsider's perspective, the parent's protective part wants to keep both itself and the child safe from the terrible consequences of making a mistake. The hurt, vulnerable parts of the parent are tenderized and triggered by the vulnerable parts of their child. When these parts continue to take over in the present day, it can lead the caregiver to engage in a variety of defensive strategies (e.g., screaming, withholding attention) that cause disconnection when the child actually needs the co-regulating, connected presence of their grown-up. To help both the caregiver and child heal, these protector parts will need to be reassured by the caregiver's Safest Self—who is bigger, stronger, wiser, and kinder—that they don't need to view the child as a threat.

TREATMENT GOALS:

- Provide psychoeducation about parts and how they relate to the caregiver's negative activation
- Explore the caregiver's protector parts
- Identify Safest Self parts who can remain connected to the child even when a protector part is active

MATERIALS NEEDED:

- Sand tray
- Sand tray miniatures

DIRECTIONS:

1. Explain how protector parts arise and what their perceived role is in the internal system:

   "When your child is having a big behavior, a part of the child is activated. You might call this the 'screaming part,' the 'whining part,' or the 'ignoring part.' For teenagers, you might label these parts as the 'sarcastic part' or the 'rolling-eyes part.' These parts of your child trigger parts of yourself who were originally created to protect you in some way. For example, if your parent smacked you across the face whenever you cried as a child, you may have developed a protective part to keep you from crying. That same part now takes over when your child screams, trying to keep you

Copyright © 2026 Paris Goodyear-Brown, *Big Behaviors in All Containers*. All rights reserved.

both safe. This part believes it is protecting you from danger when your child acts out, so it tells you to defend yourself by responding with your own big behaviors, like yelling, demanding, withholding affection, or shutting down. The problem is that these protector parts aren't super helpful because your child needs you to be a co-regulating, connected presence when they are dysregulated."

2. Invite the caregiver to choose a miniature to represent their child when the child is engaging in a big behavior that activates the caregiver. Instruct them to place this miniature in the sand tray.
3. Ask the caregiver to choose miniatures that represent each of their protector parts who get activated when the child is engaging in a big behavior. For example, the caregiver might choose a figure who is covering their eyes, a gigantic monster raging near the first symbol, or a flattened blob of modeling clay that represents their intense exhaustion in the face of this behavior. Instruct the caregiver to place these miniatures in whatever positions seem right in relation to the miniature they chose for the child.
4. Observe the sand tray together with the caregiver.
5. Have the caregiver take the perspective of the miniature representing the child's big behaviored part. Ask the caregiver, "Can you choose another miniature to show the more vulnerable part of the child who is buried underneath this big behavior? It might be a scared part, a tired part, or a frustrated part."
6. Invite the caregiver to place this vulnerable child part in the tray.
7. Encourage the caregiver to sit with the felt sense of this symbol and become curious about which part of themselves they want to show up when this vulnerable part of the child is present. Instruct them to choose a miniature for this part and place it in the tray.
8. This newly identified part can become a powerful symbol for the caregiver that they visualize and embody in moments when the child is buried underneath big behaviors.

Copyright © 2026 Paris Goodyear-Brown, *Big Behaviors in All Containers*. All rights reserved.

9.2 EMPATHIC PERSPECTIVES*

DESCRIPTION:

Oftentimes, caregivers have not learned the art of self-regulation because throughout their own childhoods, they had few to no positive experiences of co-regulation with their own parents. As a result, they may become stuck in their own activation when confronted with the dysregulation of their own child, leading to feelings of shame and failure. This intervention offers a change in perspective for the caregiver, giving them the space to reconnect with their child and develop, in a parallel process, empathy for themselves and the child in their care. This intervention builds on the previous one by creating safe environments for the parts of the parent who get activated in response to their child's big behaviors.

TREATMENT GOALS:

- Increase the caregiver's empathy for themselves and their child
- Increase co-regulation and self-regulation skills
- Enhance safety and trust between the caregiver and child

MATERIALS NEEDED:

- Paper
- Variety of colorful art materials (e.g., crayons, markers, colored pencils, paints)

DIRECTIONS:

1. Invite the caregiver to draw a symbol that best represents their child during their big behavior. For example, their child may have the pattern of crying out loudly in frustration whenever they feel unable to accomplish a task (like tying their shoes).
2. Then invite the caregiver to draw a symbol that best represents themselves during their child's big behavior. For example, when the child cries out in frustration, the parent may feel autonomically overwhelmed, and a protective part takes over who withdraws and hides. The parent might draw an ice cube to represent their sense of being frozen during these moments. Or the parent might draw a little child with their knees pulled into their chest to show how young and vulnerable they feel in these moments.
3. Next, direct the caregiver to create a symbol that best represents what they need in these moments. Offer the following questions to facilitate this exploration:
    a. What does it feel like to be the caregiver of your child during this interaction?
    b. What do you need in order to feel safe/connected/regulated?
    c. What would help you meet this need?

* Created by Dayna Sykes, LPC-S, MHSP, RPT-S.

Copyright © 2026 Paris Goodyear-Brown, *Big Behaviors in All Containers*. All rights reserved.

4. Finally, direct the caregiver to create a symbol that best represents what the child needs in these moments. Offer the following questions to facilitate this exploration:
    a. How might it feel to be your child during this interaction?
    b. What do you think your child needs to feel safe, connected, and regulated in this moment?
    c. How can you help provide for their needs?

VARIATION:

If the caregiver's partner also struggles with negative activation in response to their child's big behaviors, you may have each caregiver choose a symbol to represent the partner and engage them in the same sequence of exploration (first inviting them to create a symbol that represents their partner during the child's big behavior, followed by a symbol that represents what their partner may need in those moments).

Copyright © 2026 Paris Goodyear-Brown, *Big Behaviors in All Containers*. All rights reserved.

9.3 COMPASSIONATE SPACE*

DESCRIPTION:

Caregivers often show up in treatment with their own difficult childhood experiences, which only exacerbates their feelings of shame when they struggle to be a Safe Boss for their child. This intervention, which builds on the previous two, helps the caregiver hold compassion for themselves and connect to a Safe Boss experience of their own to build their confidence in their ability to connect with and welcome their child during moments of big emotions.

TREATMENT GOALS:

- Help the caregiver develop self-compassion to strengthen the connection between the caregiver and child
- Concretize the experience of self-compassion through expressive arts materials

MATERIALS NEEDED:

- Sand tray
- Sand tray miniatures
- Paper
- Variety of colorful art materials (e.g., crayons, markers, colored pencils, paints)

DIRECTIONS:

1. Invite the caregiver to share a story about a difficult parenting moment (e.g., an incident in which their child did not want to take a bath). Have them choose miniatures and create a sand tray to show elements of the story. If the parent seems to enjoy the symbolic work, you might invite them to choose a symbol to represent the child's panic and another symbol to represent their own felt sense in response.
2. Building on previous Safe Boss exercises, ask the parent whether they felt like they were able to be a Safe Boss for the child during the difficult parenting moment. If they were able to, celebrate with them. Most likely, though, there will be elements of their own reactions to the child's distress that were unlike a Safe Boss.
3. Explain that being a Safe Boss includes being able to be clear and kind when giving directions, setting limits, co-regulating kids through hard moments, and holding boundaries.
4. Explain that being a Safe Boss begins with feeling safe within themselves. Ask the caregiver, "Are there any items you could add or remove from the sand tray to feel safer within yourself during the difficult parenting moment?" The caregiver might create new boundaries between the symbols in their sand tray (e.g., using miniature fences or

* Created by Dayna Sykes, LPC-S, MHSP, RPT-S.

Copyright © 2026 Paris Goodyear-Brown, *Big Behaviors in All Containers*. All rights reserved.

blocks) or add symbols that represent comforting mantras, additional Safe Bosses, or specific self-regulation strategies they might use in the hard moment.

5. Invite the caregiver to also look at the physical distance between the figures in the tray.
6. If all of these layers of added safety for the caregiver shift their ability to respond differently to the child during the incident, encourage them to choose a symbol to represent this Safest Self and replace the first self-symbol with this one.
7. Whenever you are working with a sand tray or visual art that may shift over the course of session (such as when additions or changes are made), it is helpful to take pictures of each shift along the way. This helps you document the shifts and offers visual reminders to the caregiver that can become integrated into their learning around how to show up as a Safe Boss.

Copyright © 2026 Paris Goodyear-Brown, *Big Behaviors in All Containers*. All rights reserved.

9.4 FIVE AND DIVE

DESCRIPTION:

If you have equipped a caregiver with self-regulation tools but they continue to experience intense negative activation when their child demonstrates a big behavior, deeper therapeutic work may be needed. In these instances, you may need to trace the roots of their negative activation back to their own family-of-origin dynamics. This might involve assessing the cultural influences, belief systems, and attachment patterns that they have carried into their own caregiving patterns as adults. To do so, this intervention takes one question from the Adult Attachment Interview (George et al., 1985), which asks the caregiver to reflect on five adjectives that describe their relationship with their primary caregiver in childhood. TraumaPlay therapists call this *reflective attachment work*, and it is only possible once you have established strong therapeutic trust with the client.

TREATMENT GOALS:

- Identify family-of-origin issues that may contribute to the caregiver's own dysregulated responses to their child
- Explore relationship patterns between the caregiver and their primary attachment figure in early childhood

MATERIALS NEEDED:

- Round sand tray
- Sand tray miniatures
- Writing utensil
- *Five and Dive* handout
- Modeling clay

DIRECTIONS:

1. Explain that all caregivers become negatively activated with their children at some point. However, when self-regulation techniques (like deep breathing, mindfulness, distancing techniques) aren't working to quell this activation, it is often an indicator that family-of-origin dynamics are at play. Validate that it can be painful to look back at the way we were raised, but this reflective attachment work can open up new wells of compassion that help us make important connections to our current caregiving.
2. Ask the caregiver this key question from the Adult Attachment Interview: "When you think about your relationship with your primary caregiver in early childhood, ages 5 to 12, can you list five adjectives to describe that relationship?"
3. Instruct the caregiver to make a written list of these adjectives on the *Five and Dive* handout. If they have trouble coming up with five words, give them permission to write down whatever adjectives come to mind (either positive or negative). Some people feel that it is dishonoring or disrespectful to name anything negative in their relationship

Copyright © 2026 Paris Goodyear-Brown, *Big Behaviors in All Containers*. All rights reserved.

with their caregiver. Work with this hesitation gently while normalizing that all children have parts who enjoyed the way they were parented, as well as other parts who found it difficult.

4. Once the list of five adjectives is complete, offer the caregiver the circular sand tray and invite them to choose a sand tray miniature that symbolizes each adjective. For example, if the parent chose *loving* as one of their descriptors, they might choose a miniature heart or an adult figure holding a little one lovingly. If they chose *conflictual*, they might choose a lightning bolt, a sword, or an angry-looking figure.
5. Reassure the caregiver that there are no right or wrong ways to choose figures. If they can't find the symbol they need in your collection, invite them to create it out of modeling clay. Allow them to arrange the symbols in whatever way seems best to them.
6. If a sand tray and miniatures are not available, you can have the caregiver draw these five symbols on the *Five and Dive* handout as an alternative.
7. Invite the caregiver to share a story that illustrates how each of these five descriptors apply to their primary attachment figure. Here, you are "diving" into the caregiver's family of origin by giving your attention to each descriptor and asking the caregiver to share an example. For instance, you might say, "The first word you chose was *loving*. Can you tell me a story that exemplifies this loving aspect of your relationship with your parent?"
8. This strengthens your clinical position as a Storykeeper for the caregiver's family of origin so that you can gently help make any important connections between the caregiver's relationship with a primary caregiver from their childhood with difficult relationship dynamics they have with the child in their care currently.

Copyright © 2026 Paris Goodyear-Brown, *Big Behaviors in All Containers*. All rights reserved.

FIVE AND DIVE HANDOUT

List five adjectives to describe your relationship with your primary caregiver in early childhood (ages 5–12).

ADJECTIVES

1. ______________________________
2. ______________________________
3. ______________________________
4. ______________________________
5. ______________________________

In the circle below, draw one symbol to represent each descriptor.

Copyright © 2026 Paris Goodyear-Brown, *Big Behaviors in All Containers*. All rights reserved.

9.5 PARTS WORK AND PAPER CROWNS*

DESCRIPTION:

This intervention offers a creative way for traumatized children to explore the different parts of themselves. When children have experienced significant trauma, particularly trauma that is interpersonal in nature, they may have developed victim self-states, perpetrator parts, protector parts, or any number of other parts who reflect cognitive distortions, somatic experiences, or memory fragments. In this exercise, the child will have an opportunity to fold and cut paper to resemble a row of houses, much like a paper-doll chain. They'll draw parts of themselves whom they allow others to see on the front-facing side of each house, and parts of themselves whom they keep hidden or have difficulty acknowledging on the inward-facing side of each house. This can be a way to catalog parts and facilitate treatment planning for parts integration work.

TREATMENT GOALS:

- Identify parts of the child whom they share with others
- Identify parts of the child who may have emerged as a response to trauma

MATERIALS NEEDED:

- Paper
- Scissors
- Tape, glue, or staples
- Coloring utensils (e.g., crayons, markers)
- Stickers
- *Parts Work House Chain* handout

DIRECTIONS:

1. Invite the child to fold a piece of paper in half.

* Adapted from Paula Archambault, LMSW, RPT-S.

Copyright © 2026 Paris Goodyear-Brown, *Big Behaviors in All Containers*. All rights reserved.

2. Then have them fold each side in half again so the edges meet at the fold. Crease well.

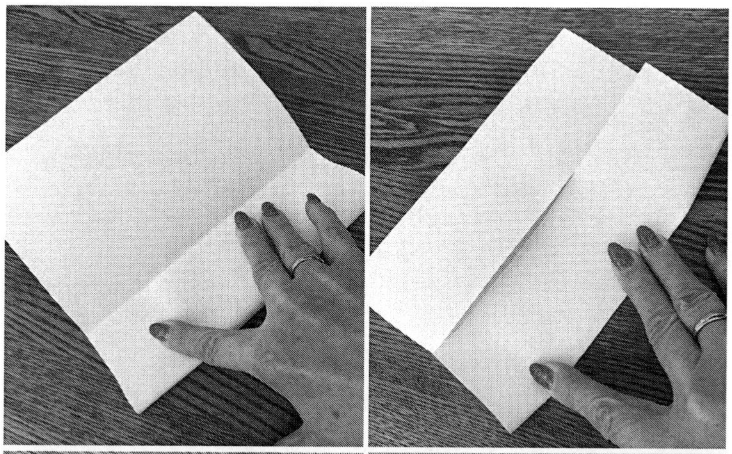

3. Have the child fold the paper in half again in the opposite direction. Clip the folded corners at a 45-degree angle to create two folded house shapes.

4. Open the folds and explain that each of these parts of the chain is like a little house where different parts of themselves live.
5. Help the client identify thoughts, feelings, or experiences that they try to keep hidden:

   "We all have feelings that we don't want other people to see. We all have thoughts that make us feel bad about ourselves. We try to keep others from seeing these too.

   "Name one feeling you don't want other people to see. Draw a symbol to represent this feeling part on the inside of the chain. Does this part have a name? Does it have an age?

   "Name one thought you don't want other people to see. Draw a symbol to represent this thought part on the inside of the chain. Does this part have a name? Does it have an age?

   "Name one story about a past experience that you don't want other people to know. Draw a symbol to represent this secret story part on the inside of the chain. Does this part have a name? Does it have an age?"
6. Once you have identified these various parts, invite the child to draw the parts of themselves they show to others in each of the outward-facing houses in the chain.

Copyright © 2026 Paris Goodyear-Brown, *Big Behaviors in All Containers*. All rights reserved.

7. Then invite them to draw the parts of themselves whom they are uncomfortable showing others (or whom they're perhaps even uncomfortable acknowledging themselves) in each of the inward-facing houses.

8. Tape, glue, or staple the ends together to create a crown.

9. Record these parts on the *Parts Work House Chain* handout for your own records, as the crown may be misplaced or go home with the child.

 Copyright © 2026 Paris Goodyear-Brown, *Big Behaviors in All Containers*. All rights reserved.

PARTS WORK HOUSE CHAIN HANDOUT

Draw the parts of yourself whom you show to others in each doorway. Write the name of the part above each doorway.

Draw the parts of yourself whom you hide from others or don't really like on the reverse side of each house. We tend to hide these parts from others. Write the name of the part above each doorway and the primary feeling you experience when other people see this part of you.

Copyright © 2026 Paris Goodyear-Brown, *Big Behaviors in All Containers*. All rights reserved.

9.6 THE aPARTment COMPLEX

DESCRIPTION:

This intervention offers an additional way for children and their caregivers to become curious about their parts, including the parts of them who feel safe and the parts of them who have been traumatized and use big behaviors to cope with their lack of felt safety. This work should be done in separate sessions (individually with the therapist and child, then the therapist and caregiver) because this work can be very tenderizing. Moreover, there are likely to be parts of the parent who formed in response to traumatic experiences that would not be appropriate to share with the minor child. In this intervention, the metaphor of an apartment is used to explain how parts may all live together in close proximity, but they may not know one another and may have very different lives. This exercise is normally combined with the following *My Parts Playground* (9.7).

TREATMENT GOALS:

- Become curious about the parts who existed before the trauma
- Identify the parts who may have emerged in response to the trauma
- Identify the coping strategies or needs of these various parts

MATERIALS NEEDED:

- *The aPARTment Complex* handout
- Coloring utensils (e.g., crayons, markers)

DIRECTIONS:

1. Introduce the concept of parts to the client:

   "Did you know that we are all made up of parts? That's right! For example, I have a part of me who loves to be social. I also have a part who loves to be alone and quiet. I have parts who want to protect other people, and I have angry parts who, when triggered, want to smash things.

   "We all have some parts who have existed from the time we're born, while other parts develop through our lives. For example, a hardworking part might emerge when we succeed at something, while an angry or sad part may develop when something hard has happened. Today, we are going to create an aPARTment complex for you and your parts. Each part will have its own space."

2. Offer *The aPARTment Complex* handout to the child or caregiver and invite them to begin labeling each apartment with a part of themselves. They might decide to label the parts who feel safest (or the parts they have had since early childhood) on the bottom floor of the apartment building. Conversely, they may want to put these at the top of the

Copyright © 2026 Paris Goodyear-Brown, *Big Behaviors in All Containers*. All rights reserved.

complex because these parts feel safest farther away from the ground level. There is no right or wrong way for clients to categorize their parts.

3. Once they're done labeling each part, invite the client to draw each part on the balcony of each apartment.
4. Help the client identify what each of their parts needs:

   "Now that you've identified your parts, let's ask them what they need. Some parts might like to sit out on their balconies and talk to their neighbors, so they might need a rocking chair. Others might like to sit outside in the sun but not want to talk to others. Those parts might need a lounge chair to sunbathe in as well as some vines to provide privacy between them and their neighbor parts. Still other parts might feel like they need to stay inside with the curtains drawn. All these parts are welcome in the aPARTment complex. Think about what each of your parts needs. For example, if you have a really active and athletic part, you might draw a bicycle or a basketball on the balcony next to this part."

5. Take the client through all of the parts they have identified and ask what they need.
6. You can titrate this exercise in small doses, adding just one aPARTment weekly for clients who need a different pace, or complete the whole exercise in one session.

Copyright © 2026 Paris Goodyear-Brown, *Big Behaviors in All Containers*. All rights reserved.

THE aPARTment COMPLEX HANDOUT

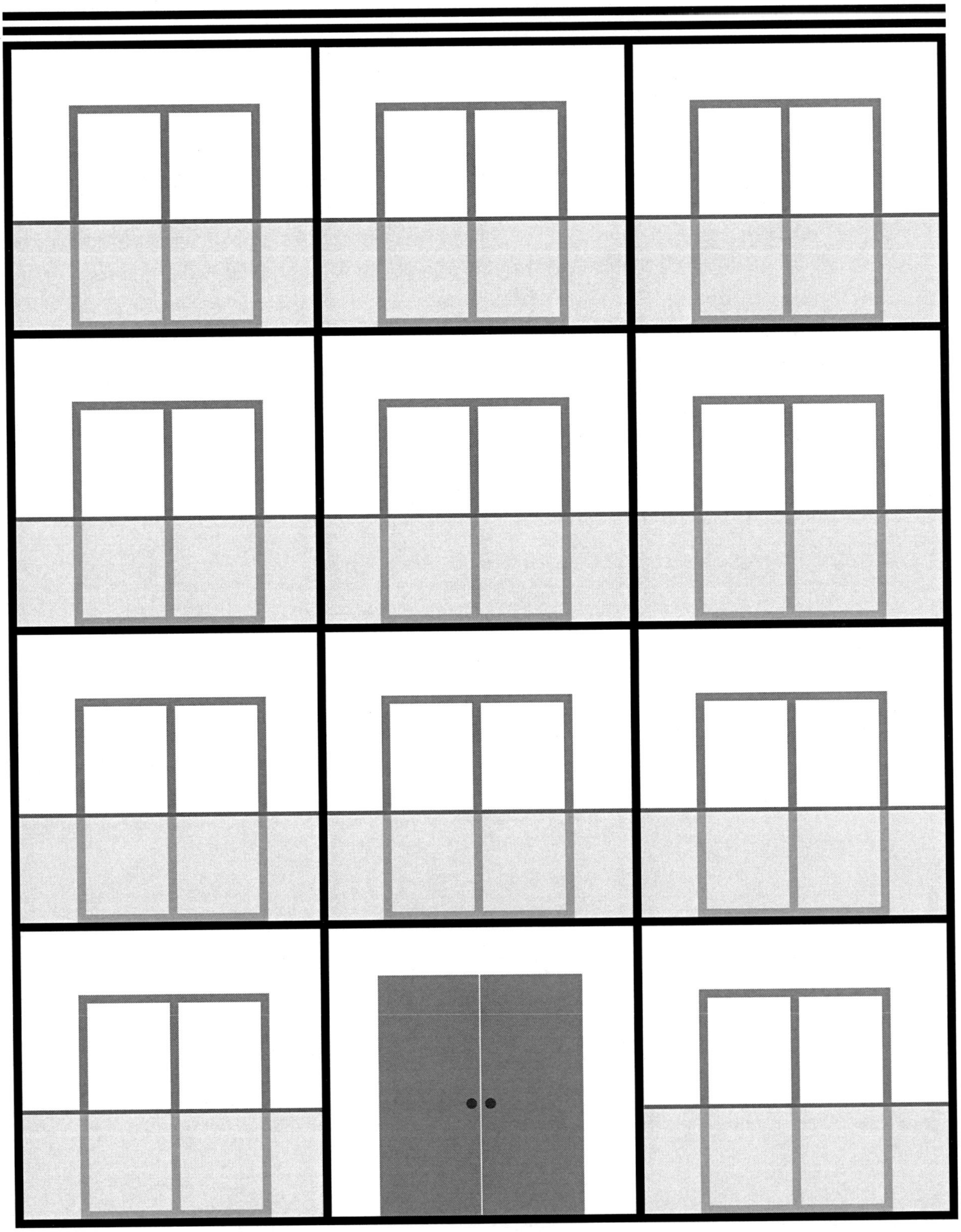

Copyright © 2026 Paris Goodyear-Brown, *Big Behaviors in All Containers*. All rights reserved.

9.7 MY PARTS PLAYGROUND

DESCRIPTION:

Once clients have identified their parts in *The aPARTment Complex* intervention (9.6), this exercise offers a safe space on the playground for parts to meet with one another and spend time getting to know one another. It also provides an opportunity for them to get to know their core Self. The overarching work of integrating parts in trauma recovery involves introducing various feeling parts, somatic parts, thought-life parts, or relational parts to each other. Since this book is geared toward both caregivers and their children, you can offer a variation of this intervention by offering a community courtyard to the caregiver in lieu of a playground.

TREATMENT GOALS:

- Offer a safe and organized projective space for the client's parts to begin to meet
- Identify and get to know the client's core Self
- Dramatize parts who need to have conversations with one another

MATERIALS NEEDED:

- *Parts Playground* handout (if working with a child)
- *Community Courtyard* handout (if working with an adult)
- Sand tray
- Sand tray miniatures, particularly playground pieces, humans, and animals

DIRECTIONS:

1. Provide a transition from the previous *The aPARTment Complex* intervention (9.6):

   "You have been working hard at naming your parts. If we look back at your past work, let's imagine that the apartment complex has a really fun playground right in the middle of it. Some parts come out to play on the playground every day. Other parts are afraid that nobody will play with them and stay inside."

2. Introduce the idea of the Self:

   "In addition to these parts, you also have something known as your core Self, with a capital *S*. This Self represents all the qualities you were born with that represent who you truly are on the inside. What qualities do you think represent your Self?"

Copyright © 2026 Paris Goodyear-Brown, *Big Behaviors in All Containers*. All rights reserved.

3. Once the client has identified the qualities that characterize their Self, decide together on how you will speak about it:
   a. Some children prefer to call it their "Big Boy [or Big Girl] Self," while others like to call it their "Safest Self," "Most Mature Self," or "Most Grown-Up Self." Some might even call their Self the "Youest You."*
   b. If you are working with the caregiver, especially those familiar with IFS, they may choose to call this their "Core Self."
4. Then ask where this Self is occupying space on the playground. Invite the client to draw their Self on the *Parts Playground* handout, or alternately, they might prefer to do this work in the sand tray, in which case you would invite them to place the figure on a playground they have created in the sand. If you are doing this intervention with the caregiver, you can offer them the *Community Courtyard* handout as an alternate meeting place for all their parts.
5. Become curious about each part the client previously identified in *The aPARTment Complex*, with a view toward where each one is on the playground in relationship to their Self. If some parts are hesitant to come out to the playground, ask what they might need to come out:

   "There may be parts who feel afraid to come out of their aPARTment at all. All parts are welcome on the playground, so what could we do to make sure these parts feel safe coming out? Sometimes, a part needs to have some sunglasses so they don't feel like they are looking directly into the eyes of their Self. Other parts might need a hoodie or a ball cap. What do your parts need to come and play? There are no right or wrong answers."
6. The client might also decide to make a banner on the playground that displays the message that all parts are welcome. Or they might decide to add a megaphone to the playground that can trumpet this message to all the parts in the complex.

* Thanks to Stefani Misiph for this.

Copyright © 2026 Paris Goodyear-Brown, *Big Behaviors in All Containers*. All rights reserved.

PARTS PLAYGROUND HANDOUT

Place your parts where they would feel safe on the playground.

Copyright © 2026 Paris Goodyear-Brown, *Big Behaviors in All Containers*. All rights reserved.

COMMUNITY COURTYARD HANDOUT

Place your parts where they would feel most comfortable in the courtyard.

Copyright © 2026 Paris Goodyear-Brown, *Big Behaviors in All Containers*. All rights reserved.

9.8 MEGAPHONES TO MAKE A POINT

DESCRIPTION:

Once the child or caregiver has identified the parts of themselves who need to be welcomed (and they've designed a safe space in which the parts can meet), it is time to welcome the parts. Some parts may come right out, take places of prominence, and try to take over. Other parts, particularly those who tend to hide or may feel ostracized, will benefit from an amplified message of welcome. This exercise can be used to offer a general message of welcome to all parts or to identify and welcome specific parts.

TREATMENT GOALS:

- Invite all parts to come to the safe space designated as the meeting spot
- Identify specific parts who may need an amplified message of safety or welcome
- Communicate specific safety messages or invitations to specific parts

MATERIALS NEEDED:

- Construction paper
- Tape
- Coloring utensils (e.g., crayons, markers)
- *Megaphones for Specific Parts* handout

DIRECTIONS:

1. Explain to the client that once they have designed a safe meeting space for all their parts (i.e., the playground or community courtyard), some parts may be thrilled to be invited and come right out. In fact, these parts might try to take over, dominate the conversation, or even close the gates and not let other parts join. In these cases, it will be important for the client's Self to offer a message of safety and welcome to all parts.
2. Offer the client a piece of construction paper and invite them to write down messages of welcome to all the parts in their system. These might be messages like "You are welcome here!" "I can't wait to get to know you!" or "Don't be afraid, I want to know you." It might even be something like "Hello! Come on in and make yourself comfortable!" or "I would like to play with you. Do you want to play with me?"
3. When they're done writing these messages, ask them to make a megaphone out of the paper by pulling together the top sides of the paper into a cone shape and taping it together.
4. Invite the client to use the megaphone and proclaim, "All parts are welcome here!" in a loud voice.

Copyright © 2026 Paris Goodyear-Brown, *Big Behaviors in All Containers*. All rights reserved.

5. Become curious with the client about the parts of themselves who might still want to hide or hang back, who might need a more specific message of welcome or invitation in order to come into the shared meeting space.
6. Offer the client the *Megaphones for Specific Parts* handout.
7. Invite the client to identify each part who might need a personalized message and have them write it on one of the megaphones. These messages can also be proclaimed out loud using the three-dimensional megaphone they already created in session.

 Copyright © 2026 Paris Goodyear-Brown, *Big Behaviors in All Containers*. All rights reserved.

MEGAPHONE FOR SPECIFIC PARTS HANDOUT

Write a personalized message for each part who has trouble trusting.

Copyright © 2026 Paris Goodyear-Brown, *Big Behaviors in All Containers*. All rights reserved.

ten

Storykeeping: Threading the Needle Backward

The stories we are told are the stories we become . . . until we learn a new story. This is the maxim that I embrace when working with traumatized children and their families, especially if dysregulation is the norm for either the caregiver or child. Parents, teachers, and siblings narrate the actions of the child in their care through their own worldview, which is informed by all the stories they were told about themselves too. Words like *selfish*, *aggressive*, *stupid*, *impulsive*, and *limited* all have the power to shape this story. This is why it is critical to understand the lens through which the caregiver views the world and, more specifically, how the caregiver holds the child's story in their own mind.

TraumaPlay defines *storykeeping* as the process of taking the big behavior we see in front of us and threading the needle backward, all the way to its earliest origins—to the earliest unmet needs of the child. Much can be explained when we understand that interpersonal trauma (e.g., sexual abuse, physical abuse, domestic violence, incarceration of a parent, mental health issues of a parent, drug abuse by a parent) all have one thing in common: They rob the child of an attuned, responsive caregiver. When this becomes the story understood by the Storykeeper, the caregiver can shift their posture from one in which their arms are lifted defensively against the child to one in which their arms are outstretched to provide aid to the little one who is in distress.

The storykeeping process is meant to create a coherent narrative of the hard things that have happened while leaching the emotional toxicity out of them so the child and their caregiver can name the trauma without becoming activated in the present moment. To that end, TraumaPlay titrates telling the story through three separate posttraumatic play processes: the continuum of disclosure, experiential mastery play, and trauma narrative (Goodyear-Brown, 2009, 2024). This chapter offers interventions that support this trauma narrative work, especially for children who are mired in avoidance symptoms and need more structure to approach the story of what happened. You will need to discern when caregivers are strong-enough containers to be involved in narrative sessions with the child at the start of this phase of treatment versus when caregivers will need more growth and preparation (Goodyear-Brown, 2021).

Sometimes, the caregiver will have valuable pieces of the story that help create coherence, especially when trauma was experienced prelinguistically. For example, a child who was exposed to methamphetamines in utero and born addicted to meth may benefit from their caregiver offering a developmentally sensitive account of those early days in the NICU. In many cases, there is a need to make sense of the metaphorical shrapnel (e.g., smells, sounds, visual images, tactile sensations) that may be splintered and unconsciously stored in the child's brain and body as a result of this trauma. This shrapnel can trigger trauma responses whenever these sensory experiences are reencountered in the present day. In this chapter, you'll find several interventions to help integrate this sensory content and create a more coherent story of what happened.

10.1 THREADING THE NEEDLE

DESCRIPTION:

One way that TraumaPlay defines *storykeeping* is the process of looking at a child's current big behavior and threading the needle all the way back to the child's earliest experiences. Adults who care for traumatized children can often feel exhausted and disgusted (both with the child and with themselves) by the time they come into treatment. When clinicians use the intake session to trace the origins of the big behavior backward and tell the story of the early in utero injuries, grief, loneliness, abuse, or neglect, they help the caregiver reopen their compassion well. Many caregivers, especially those who foster or adopt children from hard situations, have plenty of compassion for the child when they first arrive. However, the sheer exhaustion of having to manage big behaviors day in and day out may have dried up their well of compassion. It may be entirely closed up by the time the family enters treatment. Reflecting on the child's earliest experiences during the biopsychosocial-cultural assessment can help this well reopen.

TREATMENT GOALS:

- Connect the child's earliest experiences to their current big behavior
- Conduct a biopsychosocial-cultural assessment of the child's history

MATERIALS NEEDED:

- *Threading the Needle* handout

DIRECTIONS:

1. Normalize how difficult it can be to deal with big behaviors day in and day out and how this can deplete the caregiver's resources and make it hard for them to keep their well of compassion open.
2. Explain to the caregiver that becoming a Storykeeper for their child is one of the most important ways to build trust, maintain compassion, and stay grounded in the midst of a big behavior. Let them know that you will be asking them questions today in order to trace the origins of these behaviors all the way back to their child's earliest experiences.
3. Introduce the *Threading the Needle* handout to the caregiver, as visual aids can help them orient to the kinds of curiosity you will have about the child's early life.
4. Here are some questions related to early childhood development that you will want to ask:
    a. Was there any additional stress for you during the pregnancy?
    b. How was the delivery?
    c. Was any medical intervention necessary, or did your child spend time in the NICU?

Copyright © 2026 Paris Goodyear-Brown, *Big Behaviors in All Containers*. All rights reserved.

d. As an infant, would you consider your baby to have been easygoing, slow to warm up, difficult to soothe, or kind of colicky?

e. When did walking, talking, and potty training happen? Were they within normal developmental parameters?

5. Continue your biopsychosocial-cultural interview by asking about traumatic events, early attachment relationships, family psychiatric history, substance use, school involvement, and academic needs.
6. Whenever possible, work to capture epigenetic information relevant to disenfranchised cultural contexts. For example, ask questions that examine how dynamics of oppression (e.g., racism, sexism, ableism, poverty) may have shaped the child's experiences, both now and in utero. If a birth parent lived in poverty, it is unlikely that there was plentiful access to nourishing foods during the child's development. Does the child evidence any food insecurity now? If so, asking these reflective questions can help build the connections between the child's current thoughts, feelings, and behaviors and where they came from.

Copyright © 2026 Paris Goodyear-Brown, *Big Behaviors in All Containers*. All rights reserved.

THREADING THE NEEDLE HANDOUT

Following the threads of big behaviors back to the child's earliest experiences

Big behaviors

____

____

____

____

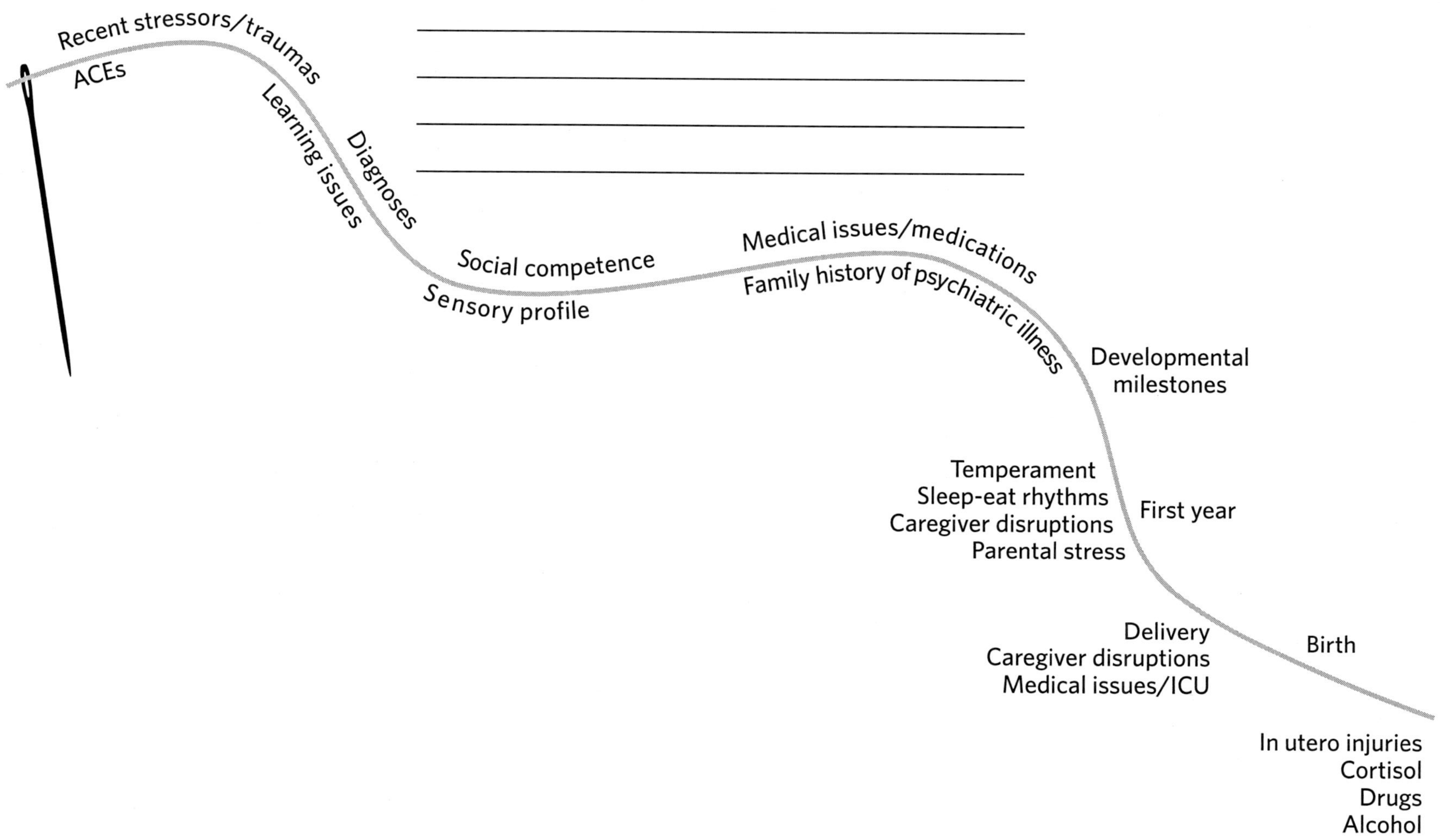

Copyright © 2026 Paris Goodyear-Brown, *Big Behaviors in All Containers*. All rights reserved.

10.2 BRING IT IN THE ROOM

DESCRIPTION:

This intervention is meant to encourage the caregiver to name the hard thing that happened to their child. Far too often, children experience traumatic events that the grown-ups then work diligently to avoid naming. The problem is that when a child experiences a vacuum of silence around their trauma—but they feel the tension, stress, grief, or fear in the room—they make up a story to explain it. Sometimes, that story is worse than what actually happened. Caregivers sometimes say that they are protecting the child from more pain, but it is often that they are protecting themselves from the suffering of the child. It seems counterintuitive to many caregivers, but naming the trauma elevates the grown-up as both a Safe Boss and Storykeeper who can hold the hard story and relieve the child of the autonomic confusion that occurs when they have a felt sense that something terrible has happened, but none of the grown-ups will talk about it with them.

TREATMENT GOALS:

- Provide psychoeducation on the importance of naming the hard thing that happened
- Amplify the caregiver's role as a Safe Boss and Storykeeper

MATERIALS NEEDED:

- Sand tray
- Sand tray miniatures (including various elephants)
- *Bring It in the Room* handout

DIRECTIONS:

1. Explain to the caregiver that when a child has experienced trauma but the grown-ups around them avoid talking about it, it prevents the child from processing the thoughts, feelings, sensory experiences, and relational ruptures that may have occurred during or after the trauma. By naming, in a matter-of-fact tone, the hard thing that happened, it lets the child know that the caregiver is a Storykeeper who is strong enough to hold the hard story. It also elevates the caregiver's role as a Safe Boss. To stay connected to their child, the caregiver will want to strengthen their role of Safe Boss and Storykeeper before graduating from trauma treatment.
2. Invite the caregiver to choose a miniature from the sand tray collection to represent themselves and a miniature to represent their child.
3. Ask the caregiver to place the two figures in the sand tray with the physical distance between them that feels reflective of their closeness in real life (physically, psychologically, or emotionally).

Copyright © 2026 Paris Goodyear-Brown, *Big Behaviors in All Containers*. All rights reserved.

4. Invite the caregiver to verbally name the traumas that happened to the child, as well as any secrets or taboos that the caregiver has not shared with the child about their story. For example, a child might be in foster care because their birth mother is no longer in the home. The foster parent may have left out salient details about the mother's whereabouts (e.g., jail, rehab) or been vague about her expected return. Another common example occurs among children who have been adopted (and who know that they are adopted) but who don't know any details about their birth story or birth parents.
5. Offer the sand tray and various miniature elephants to the caregiver. (You might have elephants made out of different materials, painted different colors, and so on).
6. Ask the caregiver to choose an elephant to represent each of the pieces of the story that they feel uncomfortable naming in front of the child. Reassure them that you will not be blurting out these details or insisting that they tell all the details immediately. Rather, you will be working to craft a developmentally sensitive narrative of events with the caregiver, giving the simplest but most honest story that is clinically appropriate.
7. Ask the caregiver to insert the elephant(s) between the child and caregiver in the sand tray and talk about how the elephant in the room makes it difficult for the child and caregiver to remain deeply connected.
8. Using the *Bring It in the Room* handout, have the caregiver write the simplest story of what happened, which might name the kind of trauma, such as sexual abuse, suicide, or cancer.

Copyright © 2026 Paris Goodyear-Brown, *Big Behaviors in All Containers*. All rights reserved.

BRING IT IN THE ROOM HANDOUT

Write down one of the uncomfortable pieces of information you avoid talking about with your child. If it is a big thing, write it in one of the larger elephants; if it feels like a small thing to you, use a smaller elephant.

Copyright © 2026 Paris Goodyear-Brown, *Big Behaviors in All Containers*. All rights reserved.

10.3 SCARY STORIES VS. NURTURING NARRATIONS

DESCRIPTION:

There are times when a child and caregiver will work their way through treatment, going through all of the necessary components of TraumaPlay, but the trauma symptoms do not resolve. This seems to occur most frequently with adoptive parents who want to keep their child's traumatic past alive or be seen as the rescuer who saved the child from a vilified mother. In these cases, it may be useful to ask to see the "life book" or "memory book" the family keeps in relation to the adoption. A scary story about the child's birth parent may exist within this book that may need to be tweaked to become a nurturing narration. We know it is healthiest for adopted children to be able to assign positive intentionality to their birth parent whenever possible. Since the child is the direct genetic offspring of their birth parent, they will always benefit from a sense of having been cared about, thought about, and even loved by them.

TREATMENT GOALS:

- Identify trauma content that may have been presented in a developmentally insensitive way
- Design a new narrative that assigns positive intentionality to the child's birth parent

MATERIALS NEEDED:

- The adopted child's life book
- *Scary Stories vs. Nurturing Narrations* handout

DIRECTIONS:

1. Ask the caregiver to bring in the life book they have created surrounding their child's adoption. Look for any content in this book that might vilify the birth parent, highlight themes of abandonment, or insinuate a lack of care. Sometimes, the scary story will be blaringly clear, while other times you may need to look for any implied or unspoken scary stories. For example, when caregivers haven't told their child important parts of their own history, it will result in the child filling in the gaps with scary stories.
2. Use the *Scary Stories vs. Nurturing Narrations* handout to identify any scary stories the child may currently be rehearsing and help the caregiver craft an alternative narrative that might be more connecting, contextualized, or compassionate. For example:
   a. Scary story: "Your birth mother abandoned you, leaving you on the side of the river in the cold, dark night. When someone finally found you, you were hungry and cold and dehydrated. They took you to the hospital and weren't sure whether you would live."

Copyright © 2026 Paris Goodyear-Brown, *Big Behaviors in All Containers*. All rights reserved.

b. Alternate nurturing narrative: "Your birth mom loved you so much, and she wanted a better life for you than she thought she could provide. So, she took you to the river, where she knew people came to get water every day and would find you."

3. Have the caregiver write the scary story on the tombstone with zombie arms creeping over the back. In some cases, the child might have made up the scariest version of the story (e.g., "She threw me out with the garbage"), in which case this story is written on the tombstone. Then invite them to write an alternate nurturing narration on the loving memorial. When they're done, ask them to title each story on the bottom of the monuments.

Copyright © 2026 Paris Goodyear-Brown, *Big Behaviors in All Containers*. All rights reserved.

SCARY STORIES VS. NURTURING NARRATIONS HANDOUT

Scary Story

Write the scary story here.

Nurturing Narration

Write an alternate nurturing narration here.

Copyright © 2026 Paris Goodyear-Brown, *Big Behaviors in All Containers*. All rights reserved.

10.4 TAPE IT, PAINT IT, INTEGRATE IT*

DESCRIPTION:

Children who have experienced trauma may have learned to avoid and compartmentalize their experiences as a way to cope. When these traumatic experiences have not been integrated, they may manifest as big behaviors in the home because unprocessed grief, shame, or anger often manifest as extreme behaviors like sudden spikes of aggression or sudden shutdown or dissociation. In order to reduce these behaviors, it is important to uncover and integrate specific events from the child's past, always moving at the child's pace, in order to create a more coherent trauma narrative. To do so, this intervention offers a structured way to playfully support children who present with parts of themselves who have been consciously or unconsciously covered up.

TREATMENT GOALS:

- Mitigate avoidant behaviors to reprocess trauma
- Identify, uncover, and integrate traumatic parts of the self
- Create a trauma hierarchy for reprocessing

MATERIALS NEEDED:

- Large canvas or canvas board
- Masking tape in different colors
- Paintbrushes
- Paint
- Pencil

DIRECTIONS:

1. This intervention can only be done at a point in therapy when the child has been able to name previously hidden, denied, or sublimated traumatic events, as well as any coping behaviors that were necessary at the time of the trauma but may now be getting in the child's way.
2. Write down each previously identified trauma and put each one in a separate envelope. Number each envelope in the order in which the child would like to work on them, as this allows you to create a hierarchy for trauma processing.
3. Explain that today, the child will have an opportunity to create a painting of the hard things they put in their envelopes.

* Created by Lindy Swimm, MAE, LCSW.

Copyright © 2026 Paris Goodyear-Brown, *Big Behaviors in All Containers*. All rights reserved.

4. To begin, work with the child to make a color-coded key for each envelope—for example, envelope 1 might be red, envelope 2 might be blue, and so on. Allow the child to choose the colors.
5. Then invite the child to take the hard thing out of envelope 1 and write that hard thing on their canvas. Instruct them to immediately cover up the hard thing with a piece of masking tape.
6. Invite the child to continue doing this with subsequent envelopes in numerical order, allowing them to decide how many events they would like to work with today. The child can continue to choose what trauma material to put on the canvas until all of the targets have been written down. This may take one or many sessions.
7. After the child covers each hard thing with a piece of masking tape, make sure to number the masking tape so it matches the number on the envelope it came out of.
8. Once all targets are on the canvas, ask the child to paint the rest of the canvas over the tape.
9. During subsequent sessions, gradually pull off each piece of tape to uncover what's underneath. The unveiling of each should be done after the work around thoughts, feelings, and negative beliefs associated with the initial trauma target have been integrated. If you are trained in EMDR, you can use bilateral stimulation to further install the beauty that this uncovered section of the painting adds to the overall artistry.
10. If you'd like, it can be helpful to offer the child a playful body movement break after each trauma tape is removed from the canvas.
11. Once you're done removing all the coverings from the canvas, the child can choose to paint over the uncovered trauma parts or leave them exposed.

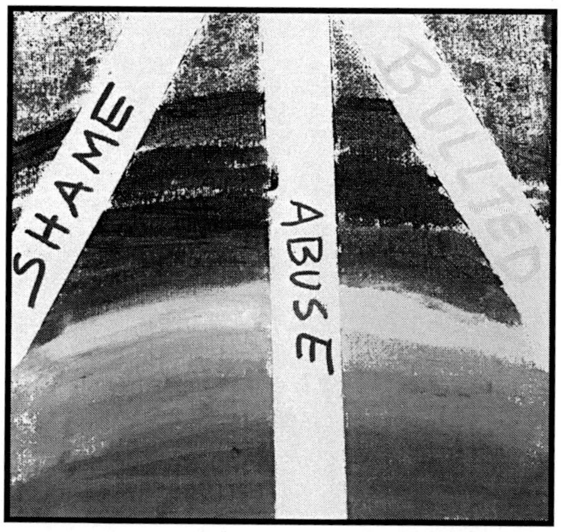

Copyright © 2026 Paris Goodyear-Brown, *Big Behaviors in All Containers*. All rights reserved.

10.5 FROM HOLE TO WHOLE: TRAUMA NARRATIVE DOLLS*

DESCRIPTION:

Traumatized children often feel like a part of them is missing, that they are broken in some way or left with a hole where nurturing care might have been. This exercise encourages the child to care for themselves while allowing them to better understand and integrate the hard thing that happened. It invites the child to explore the various thoughts, emotions, somatic experiences, and relational ruptures associated with the trauma in a safe and imaginative environment.

TREATMENT GOALS:

- Create a physical representation that the trauma story is a part of the child forever, but the painful wounds will heal

MATERIALS NEEDED:

- Several plastic dolls
- Drilling tool
- Half-inch-wide satin ribbon
- Gel pens
- *Trauma Narrative Ribbon* handout
- Scissors
- Heart-shaped buttons
- Super glue or hot glue

DIRECTIONS:

1. Prior to the session, make sure to drill a hole into the left-hand side of the chest (i.e., the heart area) for each doll.
2. Invite the child to choose a doll they would like to work with today.
3. Explain that when something really hard happens to us, we can feel like it leaves a hole in our heart. Sometimes, telling the story of what happened (especially to a trusted Storykeeper) can help fill the hole and jump-start the healing process.
4. Invite the client to write the story of what happened on a long piece of satin ribbon. They can write the story themselves using a gel pen, or they can tell the story out loud as you write it on the ribbon for them.
5. If you don't have ribbon available, or if the child wants to keep a copy of the story for themselves, offer the *Trauma Narrative Ribbon* handout to write the story on. Then cut the ribbon from the handout.

---

* Created by Paula Archambault, LMSW, RPT-S.

Copyright © 2026 Paris Goodyear-Brown, *Big Behaviors in All Containers*. All rights reserved.

6. Invite the child to fill the hole in the doll's heart with their satin or paper ribbon.
7. Talk about the people and experiences that have helped them begin to heal from the trauma. Explain that you will be affixing something to the doll to represent the healing that has started.
8. Allow the child to choose a heart-shaped button and glue this onto the doll to cover the wound.

VARIATION:

Some children are uncomfortable with leaving the ribbon inside the doll and prefer to pull it out before placing the heart button over the hole. If so, you can place the ribbon inside the doll and have the child read the narrative as you pull it from the doll. Then cover the hole with the heart button and secure it with glue.

Copyright © 2026 Paris Goodyear-Brown, *Big Behaviors in All Containers*. All rights reserved.

TRAUMA NARRATIVE RIBBON HANDOUT

Write the story of what happened on the ribbon below.

Copyright © 2026 Paris Goodyear-Brown, *Big Behaviors in All Containers*. All rights reserved.

10.6 ROSE-COLORED GLASSES*

DESCRIPTION:

In TraumaPlay, the goal is never to help the child forget about the trauma or make the trauma narrative have a happy ending. Rather, it's to leach the toxicity out of the trauma story so the child can name it and integrate it into the rest of their life narrative without it causing activation in the present moment. Once this has been accomplished, we begin working with the last goal of the TraumaPlay model: making positive meaning of the posttrauma self. In this activity, the child is encouraged to don whimsical rose-colored glasses and immerse themselves in a world where their trauma is transformed, exploring the transformative power of perspective through creative play and reflection.

TREATMENT GOALS:

- Reflect on the child's therapeutic work
- Mark the achievement of treatment goals
- Identify positive meanings the child made from the healing process after trauma

MATERIALS NEEDED:

- Reversible frog/prince plush toy (or a frog puppet and a prince puppet)
- Rose-colored glasses
- Miniature red flags
- *Rose-Colored Glasses* handout
- Premade cardboard glasses and pink cellophane (optional)

DIRECTIONS:

1. Begin by inviting the child to look at the red flags with their naked eye.
2. Then invite them to put on the rose-colored glasses, which are intended to filter the red color out of the flags. You might consider quoting *BoJack Horseman*: "When you look at the world through rose-colored glasses, all the red flags just look like flags."
3. Explain that trauma treatment is meant to help strip the color out of traumatic events so that the child can look back on these events without becoming overwhelmed by their thoughts, feelings, and body sensations in the present moment.
4. Using the frog puppet, explain that when trauma occurs, it can make us feel different, voiceless, or ugly.
5. Put the rose-colored glasses on the frog and explain that as the child processes their trauma, they can come back into their true self. Then invite the client to turn the frog

* Created by Paula Archambault, LMSW, RPT-S.

Copyright © 2026 Paris Goodyear-Brown, *Big Behaviors in All Containers*. All rights reserved.

inside out to reveal a prince. (If you do not have a reversible plush toy, you can just bring out the prince puppet to replace the frog one.)

6. Ask the child to identify any triggers they used to experience as a result of the trauma. For example, a child might have moved into a freeze response prior to treatment whenever they heard a loud noise. Now they can play outside and trust their brain and body to know which noises need their true attention.
7. Offer the *Rose-Colored Glasses* handout. On the right lens, ask the child to identify the smells, tastes, sounds, people, places, and so forth that used to trigger them but that they have since worked through. On the left lens, invite the child to write truths they have learned about themselves that have allowed them to counter these (e.g., "I can tell my body that I am safe. I can soothe myself through loud noises. I am lovable. I am a survivor.").
8. If desired, you can purchase premade cardboard glasses and pink cellophane to create a three-dimensional set of rose-colored glasses unique to the client that they can take home with them as part of graduation from treatment.

Copyright © 2026 Paris Goodyear-Brown, *Big Behaviors in All Containers*. All rights reserved.

ROSE-COLORED GLASSES HANDOUT

Write truths about your survivor self in this lens.

Write trauma triggers you unpaired in this lens.

Copyright © 2026 Paris Goodyear-Brown, *Big Behaviors in All Containers*. All rights reserved.

10.7 NARRATIVE DOMINOES

DESCRIPTION:

Traumatized children frequently carry false responsibility for the hard thing that happened. They may believe that some action of their own caused it. They may also believe that if they had just acted differently, they could have kept the terrible thing from happening. I created this intervention after working with a young boy whose father had had a heart attack in his study and died instantly. My client, who had been watching TV with his brother, went into his dad's study to ask for a snack and called 911 after being unable to awaken his father. The dispatcher instructed my client on how to do CPR until the ambulance arrived. This child continued to believe that if he had just been stronger, or if he had just acted more quickly, he could have saved his father. He clung to this belief until we co-created this intervention, which uses the metaphor of a domino effect to illustrate that when something hard happens, there is often nothing we can do to change the outcome of the situation.

TREATMENT GOALS:

- Counter the false responsibility the child may feel regarding a traumatic event
- Identify the specific moments involved in the trauma

MATERIALS NEEDED:

- Dominoes
- Sticky notes
- Writing utensil
- Camera phone or digital video recorder

DIRECTIONS:

1. Take the child, step-by-step, through the traumatic event, asking questions like "What happened first? Then what happened? What happened next?"
2. Give very little feedback until the child has given you as many specifics as possible. Write each moment on a separate sticky note as the child names them.
3. Next, invite the child to set up a domino that represents the first thing they saw or did during the trauma. For example, in the situation I mentioned earlier, my client first went to his father's office to ask for a snack. So, you would write "Went to Dad's office to ask for a snack" on a sticky note.
4. Invite the child to set one domino in place for this part of the story while you place the sticky note just next to it.
5. Repeat this for each part of the story, being sure that the dominoes are spaced at equal intervals where they will hit each other when the first domino falls over.

Copyright © 2026 Paris Goodyear-Brown, *Big Behaviors in All Containers*. All rights reserved.

6. Invite the client to notice all the steps in sequence.
7. Set up a slow-motion video recording of all the dominoes and invite the client to tap the first domino and watch what happens. All the dominoes fall down. There is nothing that could have changed the outcome. While this is a painful truth, it also allows the child to let go of the false responsibility they carry.
8. Once all the dominoes have fallen, invite the client to watch the slow-motion video of the dominoes falling. This can combat the child's false sense of responsibility that they could or should have done something to keep the trauma from occurring. The slow-motion version amplifies the sound of each domino knocking down the next domino and gives the child a visceral sense of the inevitability of the steps of the trauma happening exactly as they did.

Copyright © 2026 Paris Goodyear-Brown, *Big Behaviors in All Containers*. All rights reserved.

10.8 AT ARM'S LENGTH*

DESCRIPTION:

Rupture and repair are a normal part of the life within a family. However, many times either the caregiver or child is mired in so much shame that they are unable to make repairs after they have acted in a way that hurt the other person. Although ruptures can result in emotional, psychological, and perhaps even physical distance between a caregiver and child, there are steps that can be taken for repair. This activity provides a safe way for the caregiver and child to reflect on past conflicts, recognize their emotions, and work toward mutual understanding and connection.

TREATMENT GOALS:

- Identify conflicts that have triggered a rupture between the caregiver and child
- Remember moments of connection and joy between the caregiver and child
- Identify small reparative steps that each person can take toward reconnection

MATERIALS NEEDED:

- *At Arm's Length* handout
- Scissors
- Tape, glue, or staples
- Coloring utensils (e.g., crayons, markers)

DIRECTIONS:

1. Ask the caregiver and child to identify a recent conflict they experienced that has caused tension in their relationship.
2. Offer the caregiver and child the *At Arm's Length* handout. On each section of the forearm, invite them to list the actions or behaviors that felt upsetting to them during the conflict. For example, this might include "rolled their eyes" or "slammed the door." Ask them to identify how these actions made them feel in their bodies (e.g., tense, anxious).
3. Next, on each palm area, invite the caregiver and child to recall one or two positive memories they have had with each other. These should include moments of joy, delight, or gratitude. For example, this might include "The time we went driving in the Jeep with the doors off singing at the top of our lungs" or "When you read to me at night."
4. Finally, on each finger, invite the dyad to write a small action they can each take to reconnect and move forward. For example, "I'll keep my tone calm," "I'll listen

---

* Created by Dora Henderson, LMHC, RPT-S, TraumaPlay supervisor, EMDR consultant.

Copyright © 2026 Paris Goodyear-Brown, *Big Behaviors in All Containers*. All rights reserved.

attentively," "I'll try not to react with frustration," and "I'll apologize if I hurt them." These actions symbolize reaching out with empathy and understanding.

5. Cut out the two forearms on the handout and give the caregiver and child their respective cutout. Starting from the wrist end of the arm, invite them to fold the forearm into an accordion. This symbolizes setting aside past misunderstandings and focusing on what can be addressed in the present.
6. Once this is complete, have the dyad take turns holding up their traced hands and gently touching fingers. As each "connection" point is touched, invite them to share ideas for moving past the conflict and nurturing mutual support.

Copyright © 2026 Paris Goodyear-Brown, *Big Behaviors in All Containers*. All rights reserved.

AT ARM'S LENGTH HANDOUT

On the forearms, write down what upset you. On the palms, write down happy memories you've had together. On the fingers, write down small ways to repair your relationship. Fold accordion style and see how much closer you are to each other!

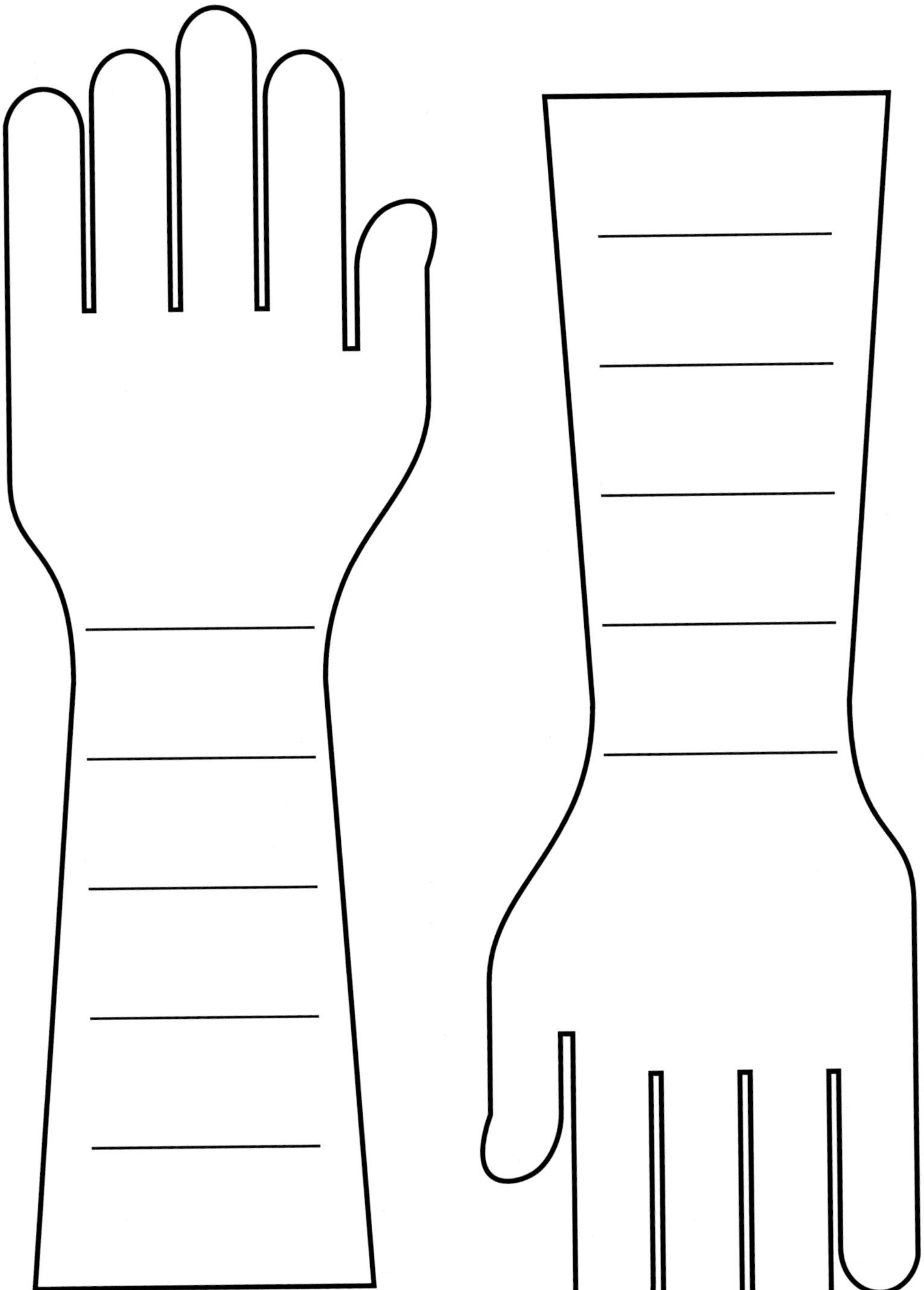

Copyright © 2026 Paris Goodyear-Brown, *Big Behaviors in All Containers*. All rights reserved.

10.9 MONSTER EARS

DESCRIPTION:

Many children have "witnessed" domestic violence from under their covers, behind closed doors, or under a table. These children encode multiple sounds related to the trauma: raised voices, shattered glass, a caregiver crying, a door slamming. It is human nature to try and make sense of these sounds, to create a story about what happened that supports the narrative. However, the story the child creates may be worse than what actually happened. This intervention provides an opportunity to build a more coherent and accurate narrative about the situation. For many children, it can be relieving for their distortions to be corrected to the truth.

TREATMENT GOALS:

- Identify auditory memories related to the traumatic event
- Correct any faulty visual memories associated with the auditory memories
- Desensitize the child to the auditory trauma reminders

MATERIALS NEEDED:

- Variety of novelty costume ears (e.g., oversized ears, fairy ears, elf ears, hairy ears)
- Writing utensil
- *Ears That Hear* handout

DIRECTIONS:

1. Validate the child's experience in witnessing interpersonal violence in their home:

   > "One of the things I know about you is that there has been violence in your family. When kids live with one caregiver who is hurting another, they often have to hide when things become scary. You have probably heard sounds from under your covers or around the corner that scared you."

2. If you have specific examples that you are already aware of, give a specific instance to the child.
3. Invite the child to explore the different pairs of ears and ask them to choose a pair for themselves and a pair for you.
4. Once you have both donned your ears (and looked in the mirror at how silly they might look), encourage the child to imagine that these ears amplify the sounds related to the scary thing that happened. Explain that these auditory memories might feel like shrapnel in their brain and may be out of order.

Copyright © 2026 Paris Goodyear-Brown, *Big Behaviors in All Containers*. All rights reserved.

5. Offer the *Ears That Hear* handout and ask the child to say out loud the sounds they heard during the scary thing that happened. While they are verbalizing the sounds, write the sounds down on the handout or ask them to do so.
6. Explain that when we hear things but can't see them, we often create a story of what that sound means, a story of what happened. Ask the child, "What is the story you made up about what happened when you heard these sounds?"
7. If what the child narrates is worse than what actually happened, correct to the truth. For example, imagine the child lists four sounds: the door slamming, Dad yelling, glass shattering, and Mom crying. When you ask for the story, the child explains that they think Dad was angry because Mom forgot to buy beer for him, so he took the pickle jar and threw it at her face, cutting her face all up. Perhaps what really happened is that Dad threw the pickle jar at the wall, and it shattered (which is still not okay), but Mom did not get hurt.
8. After the distortions are corrected, ask whether the client can generate statements that are true and make them feel better. For example, "Mom's face is okay" or "She is safe right now."
9. If clinically appropriate, it might be helpful to consider enlisting the help of the caregiver in renarrating the story to provide a more coherent shared narrative for the dyad, especially if the dyad is physically safer now from the threat of interpersonal violence. In this case, the caregiver can help the child come up with compassionate self-talk statements, like *We are getting safer together.*

Copyright © 2026 Paris Goodyear-Brown, *Big Behaviors in All Containers*. All rights reserved.

EARS THAT HEAR HANDOUT

In the ears, list the sounds you heard during the scary thing that happened.

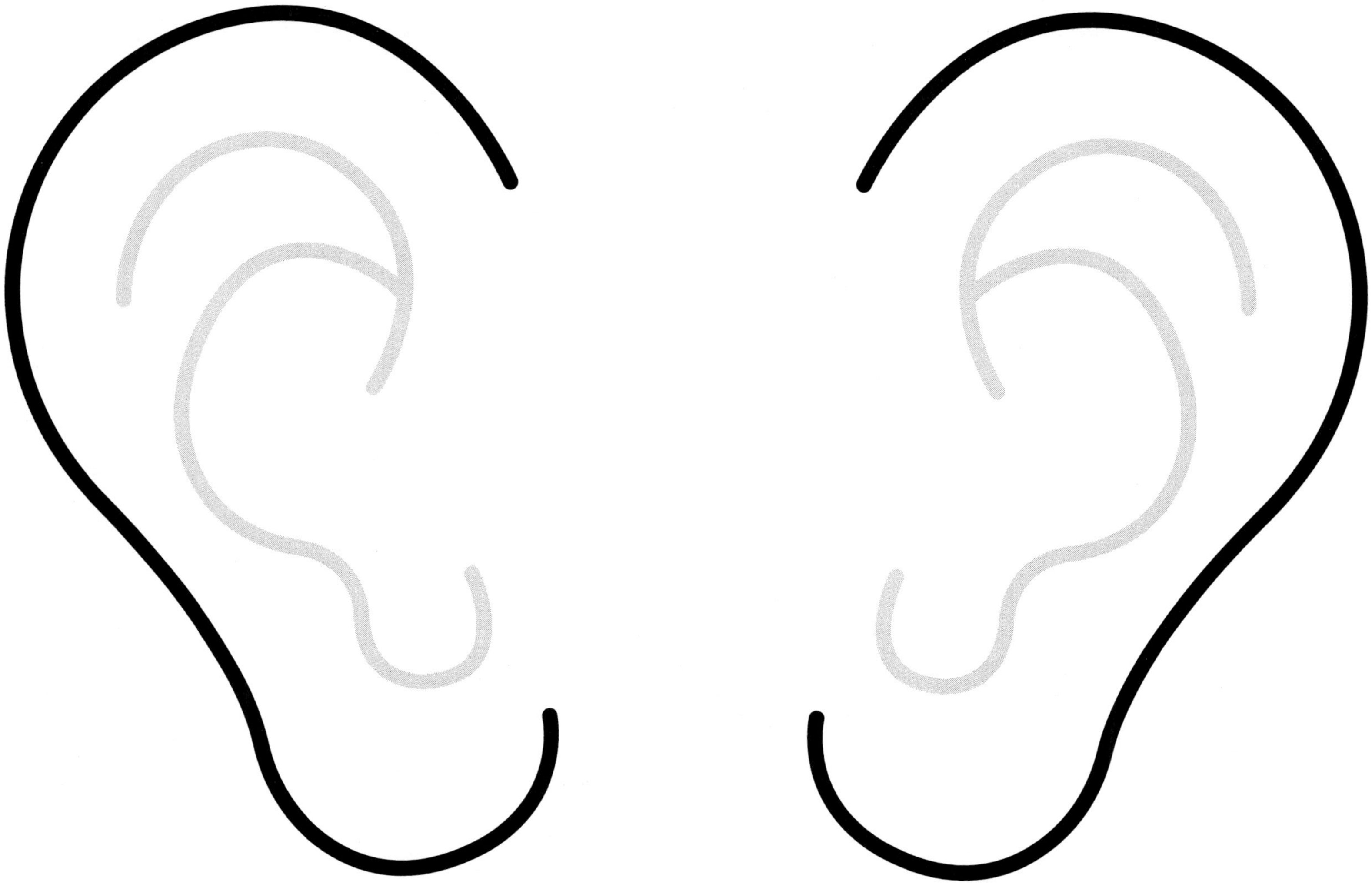

Copyright © 2026 Paris Goodyear-Brown, *Big Behaviors in All Containers*. All rights reserved.

10.10 PUTTING THE PIECES TOGETHER

DESCRIPTION:

When a child and caregiver have been involved in the same traumatic event, they may have similar sense memories, in which case it can be normalizing and connecting for them to name the smells, sounds, and so on that they shared. In other cases, a caregiver may not have been present during the child's trauma, in which case the child may be unconsciously protecting the caregiver from knowing the upsetting sensory details of their experience. The child may believe that their co-regulator will become too overwhelmed if they hear these details. However, it can strengthen the caregiver's role as a Storykeeper if they can hold the hard story in its entirety. This intervention offers a playful way for dyads to explore and integrate the sensory aspects of the trauma.

TREATMENT GOALS:

- Identify sense memories related to trauma
- Increase coherence in the trauma narrative by integrating sensory details
- Strengthen the caregiver's role as a Storykeeper

MATERIALS NEEDED:

- Large wooden face puzzle with facial pieces that can be removed
- Brown paper bag
- Writing utensil

DIRECTIONS:

1. Explain to the caregiver and child that when someone has experienced trauma, not only do they have a verbal memory of what happened but also sensory memories related to the experience:

    "When something scary happens, our brains and bodies hold on to the details of what we heard, saw, smelled, tasted, and touched at the time, without us even trying to remember them. For example, if someone was in a bad car accident, they might remember the smell of the burning rubber as the driver was trying to brake, the sound of the tires screeching, or the sound of the crunching metal. These sensory experiences can be sort of like shrapnel, stored in various parts of our memory. When we hear tires screeching again, our whole body might tense and think the car accident is happening all over again. When we combine the story of what happened with the sense memories related to the story, it's like we are taking a big magnet and pulling all the shrapnel back together."

 Copyright © 2026 Paris Goodyear-Brown, *Big Behaviors in All Containers*. All rights reserved.

2. Introduce the dyad to the face puzzle and invite them to take out the eyes, ears, nose, and mouth.
3. On the brown paper bag, write "What did you see? Hear? Smell? Taste? Touch?"
4. Then invite them to put all the face puzzle pieces into the brown paper bag and shake it up.
5. If the traumatic event was shared, instruct the caregiver and child to take turns fishing out a face puzzle piece. If they pick up the eye, they talk about one thing they saw during the scary thing that happened. If they pick up the nose, they talk about one thing they smelled during the scary thing that happened. In this way, the empty places in the face puzzle are filled, much like the gaps in the trauma story are filled by integrating the sense memories into the narrative.
6. If the child was alone in the trauma, make sure that you've done prework to equip the caregiver to hear the child's sensory experiences without being further traumatized themselves. Normally, titrated doses of the child's experience will have been shared with the caregiver in collateral consultation sessions, and you will have helped them integrate this content before the child shares it in this context.

Copyright © 2026 Paris Goodyear-Brown, *Big Behaviors in All Containers*. All rights reserved.

10.11 SEE NO EVIL, HEAR NO EVIL, SPEAK NO EVIL

DESCRIPTION:

This intervention offers another way for the caregiver and child to explore and integrate the sensory experiences of trauma. It can be especially powerful for dyads in which the caregiver has struggled with addiction. After a caregiver has maintained sobriety for a period of time, it can increase trust in the system for the child to have permission to name one thing they wish they hadn't seen during the parent's active addiction, one thing they wish they hadn't heard, and one thing they wish they hadn't had to say.

TREATMENT GOALS:

- Increase coherence in trauma narrative work by integrating sensory details
- Strengthen the caregiver's role as Storykeeper for the child

MATERIALS NEEDED:

- Sand tray
- Sand tray miniatures of three monkeys, elephants, or other animals depicting the "see no evil, hear no evil, speak no evil" postures
- Writing utensil
- *The Three Threats* handout

DIRECTIONS:

1. Explain that when a child has experienced something scary, especially when it involves their caregiver, they may experience sensory memories that come back over and over again to bother them. These memories may be related to things they wish they hadn't had to see, hear, or say at the time.
2. Present the animal miniatures to the child and point out that one animal is covering its eyes, the other is covering its ears, and the third is covering its mouth—much like the child wishes there were things they didn't have to see, hear, and say during the scary thing that happened.
3. Instruct the child to place each of the animals in the sand tray.
4. Offer the child *The Three Threats* handout and ask them, "What's one thing you wish you hadn't had to see during the scary thing that happened?" The child may decide to say it out loud or write it down. Conversely, they might want to draw a picture of it and slip it underneath the sand beneath the animal miniature that has covered its eyes.
5. Repeat this process with the questions "What's one thing you wish you hadn't had to hear during the scary thing that happened?" and "What's one thing you wish you hadn't had to say during the scary thing that happened?" Sometimes, children will

Copyright © 2026 Paris Goodyear-Brown, *Big Behaviors in All Containers*. All rights reserved.

respond to these question with statements like "I wish I hadn't had to tell my mom to wake up and take me to school" or "I wish I hadn't had to get in between my mom and dad and yell, 'Stop fighting!'"

6. If the caregiver is grounded and available, it can support their Storykeeper role to have them involved in this session. You may need to do prework with the caregiver to offer titrated doses of the sensory story prior to putting caregiver and child together. Especially for caregivers who have struggled with addiction, it is important for them to acknowledge that when they were high or passed out, their child may have experienced something that the caregiver doesn't remember, but this doesn't make it any less true for the child and will need verbal validation from the caregiver.

Copyright © 2026 Paris Goodyear-Brown, *Big Behaviors in All Containers*. All rights reserved.

THE THREE THREATS HANDOUT

What do you wish you
hadn't had to see?

What do you wish you
hadn't had to hear?

What do you wish you
hadn't had to say?

Copyright © 2026 Paris Goodyear-Brown, *Big Behaviors in All Containers*. All rights reserved.

References

All templates and handouts are available for download at www.pesipubs.com/BBAC

Baumgarten, B. (2015). *Beautiful hands* (K. Otoshi, Illus.). Blue Dot Press.

Booth, P. B., & Jernberg, A. M. (2009). *Theraplay: Helping parents and children build better relationships through attachment-based play* (3rd ed.). Jossey-Bass.

Chapman, G., & Campbell, R. (2016). *The 5 love languages of children: The secret to loving children effectively.* Northfield Publishing.

Colandro, L. (2014). *There was an old lady who swallowed a fly!* (J. Lee, Illus.). Scholastic.

Coyne, J., Powell, B., Hoffman, K., & Cooper, G. (2019). The circle of security. In C. H. Zeanah Jr. (Ed.), *Handbook of infant mental health* (4th ed., pp. 501–513). Guilford Press.

George, C., Main, M., & Kaplan, N. (1985). *Adult Attachment Interview (AAI)* [Database record]. APA PsycTests. https://doi.org/10.1037/t02879-000

Gil, E. (2014). *Play in family therapy.* Guilford Press.

Goodyear-Brown, P. (2009). *Play therapy with traumatized children: A prescriptive approach.* Wiley.

Goodyear-Brown, P. (2010). *The worry wars: Anxiety workbooks for kids and their helpful adults!*

Goodyear-Brown, P. (2016). *A safe circle for Little U* (E. Gott, Illus.). Self-published.

Goodyear-Brown, P. (2021). *Parents as partners in child therapy: A clinician's guide.* Guilford Press.

Goodyear-Brown, P. (2022). *Big behaviors in small containers: 131 trauma-informed play therapy interventions for disorders of dysregulation.* PESI Publishing.

Goodyear-Brown, P. (2024). Treatment planning in TraumaPlay: Storykeeping for the family system. In L. L. Wonders & M. Affee (Eds.), *The play-based and expressive therapies treatment planner: A guide to working with children and adolescents* (pp. 169–180). Routledge.

Goodyear-Brown, P., & Kenney-Noziska, S. (2024). The genius of the disembodied self: Coping with child sexual abuse. In P. Goodyear-Brown & L. Yasenik (Eds.), *Polyvagal power in the playroom: A guide for play therapists* (pp. 42–58). Routledge.

Martin, B., Jr. (2011). *Brown bear, brown bear, what do you see?* (E. Carle, Illus.). Henry Holt and Company.

Penn, A. (2007). *The kissing hand* (R. Harper, Illus.). Tanglewood.

Porges, S. W. (2011). *The polyvagal theory: Neurophysiological foundations of emotions, attachment, communication, and self-regulation.* W. W. Norton & Company.

Porges, S. W., & Dana, D. (Eds.). (2018). *Clinical applications of the polyvagal theory: The emergence of polyvagal-informed therapies.* W. W. Norton & Company.

Purvis, K. B., Cross, D. R., Dansereau, D. F., & Parris, S. R. (2013). Trust-Based Relational Intervention (TBRI): A systemic approach to complex developmental trauma. *Child & Youth Services, 34*(4), 360–386. https://doi.org/10.1080/0145935X.2013.859906

Schwartz, R. (2021). *No bad parts: Healing trauma & restoring wholeness with the Internal Family Systems model.* Sounds True.

Schwartz, R. C., & Sweezy, M. (2019). *Internal family systems therapy.* Guilford Press.

Stein, D. E. (2012). *Pouch!* (D. E. Stein, Illus.). Nancy Paulsen Books.

Taback, S. (2002). *This is the house that Jack built* (S. Taback, Illus.). G. P. Putnam's Sons.

Vygotsky, L. S. (1978). *Mind in society: The development of higher psychological processes.* Harvard University Press.

Wood, A. (2005). *The napping house* (D. Wood, Illus.). Harcourt.

About the Author

Paris Goodyear-Brown, LCSW, RPT-S, is an EMDR-approved consultant, the creator of TraumaPlay, the executive director at the TraumaPlay Institute, the clinical director of Nurture House, an adjunct instructor of psychiatric mental health at Vanderbilt University, and a TED Talk speaker. As a master clinician and thought leader in the fields of child trauma and play therapy, she has received the Association for Play Therapy's (APT) Award for Play Therapy Promotion and Education and has served as the executive director of the Lipscomb Play Therapy and Expressive Arts Center.

She is the president-elect of the Tennessee Association for Play Therapy (TNAPT) and has written over 20 chapters and articles and 13 books, including *Play Therapy with Traumatized Children, Trauma and Play Therapy, Parents as Partners in Child Therapy, Big Behaviors in Small Containers*, and her newest edited volume, *Polyvagal Power in the Playroom*. Paris delights in serving traumatized children at Nurture House and finds great joy in equipping child trauma therapists all over the world to deepen their roles as Safe Boss, Nurturer, and Storykeeper through training, supervision, and certification in TraumaPlay.

For more information on booking speaking engagements, visit www.parisgoodyearbrown.com. For more information on TraumaPlay training, supervision, and certification, visit www.traumaplayinstitute.com.

For examples of how you might set up therapeutic spaces that enhance the healing recovery of traumatized children and their families, visit www.nurturehouse.org.